AF262757

Wayne Thiebaud

American Still Life

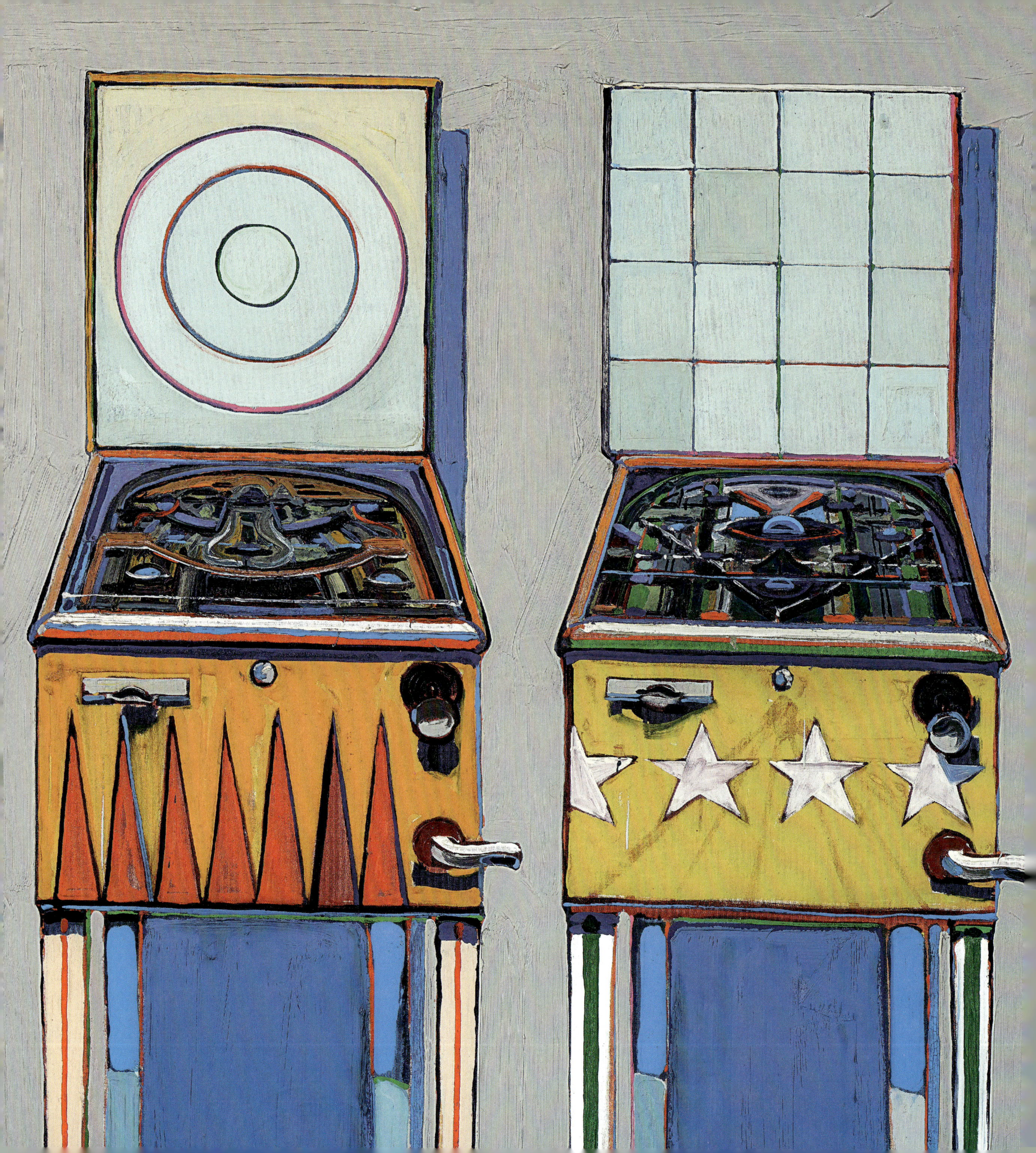

Wayne Thiebaud
American Still Life

Karen Serres and Barnaby Wright

with contributions from
Lucy Bradnock, Chloe Nahum,
Richard Shiff and Rachel Teagle

The Courtauld

in association with
Paul Holberton Publishing

First published to accompany the exhibition

Wayne Thiebaud
American Still Life

The Courtauld Gallery, London
10 October 2025–18 January 2026

The Courtauld Gallery is supported by
Research England.

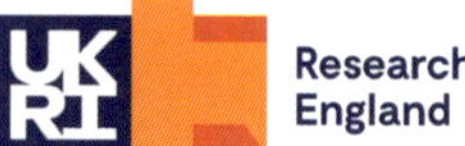

The exhibition is presented in the Denise Coates
Exhibition Galleries and in the Gilbert and Ildiko
Butler Drawings Gallery.

The programme of displays in the Drawings Gallery
is made possible with the support of:

James Bartos
The International Music and Art Foundation

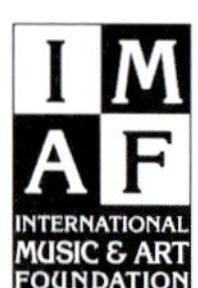

Karen Serres is Senior Curator of Paintings at the
Courtauld Gallery, London.

Barnaby Wright is Daniel Katz Curator of
20th-Century Art and Deputy Head of the Courtauld
Gallery, London.

Lucy Bradnock is Reader in Modern and
Contemporary Art and Dean for Research at the
Courtauld Institute of Art, London.

Chloe Nahum is Bridget Riley Art Foundation
Curatorial Fellow at the Courtauld Gallery, London.

Richard Shiff is Effie Marie Cain Regents Chair in Art,
University of Texas at Austin.

Rachel Teagle is Founding Director of the Jan Shrem
and Maria Manetti Shrem Museum of Art, University
of California, Davis.

ISBN 978-1-913645-89-2

British Library Catalogue in Publishing Data

A CIP record of this publication is available from the
British Library

Produced by Paul Holberton Publishing
paulholberton.com

Designed by Laura Parker

Printed by 4-Flying Srl trading as e-Graphic, Verona,
Italy

Front cover: detail of cat. 18
Back cover: detail of cat. 17
Frontispiece: detail of cat. 9

Contents

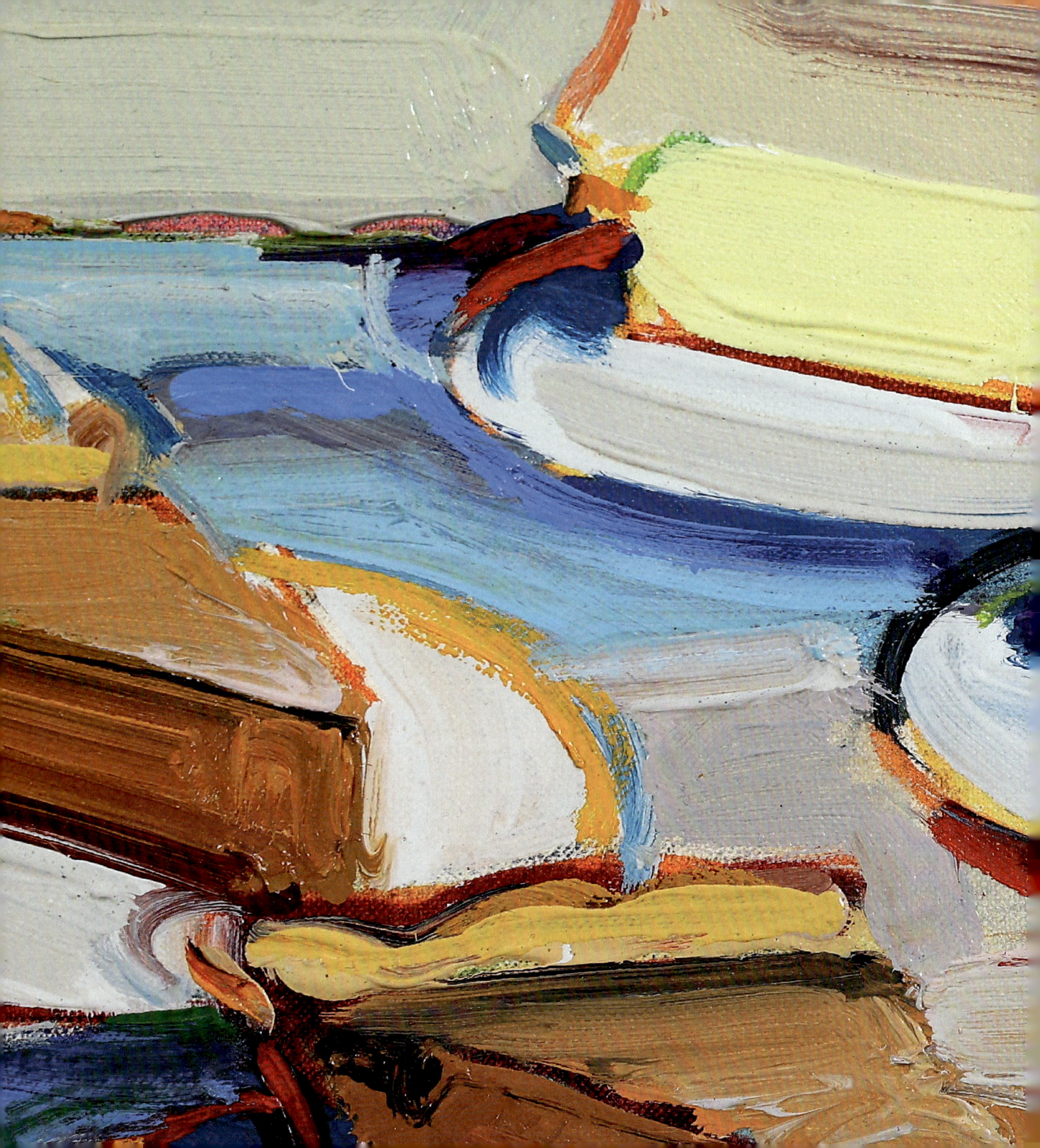

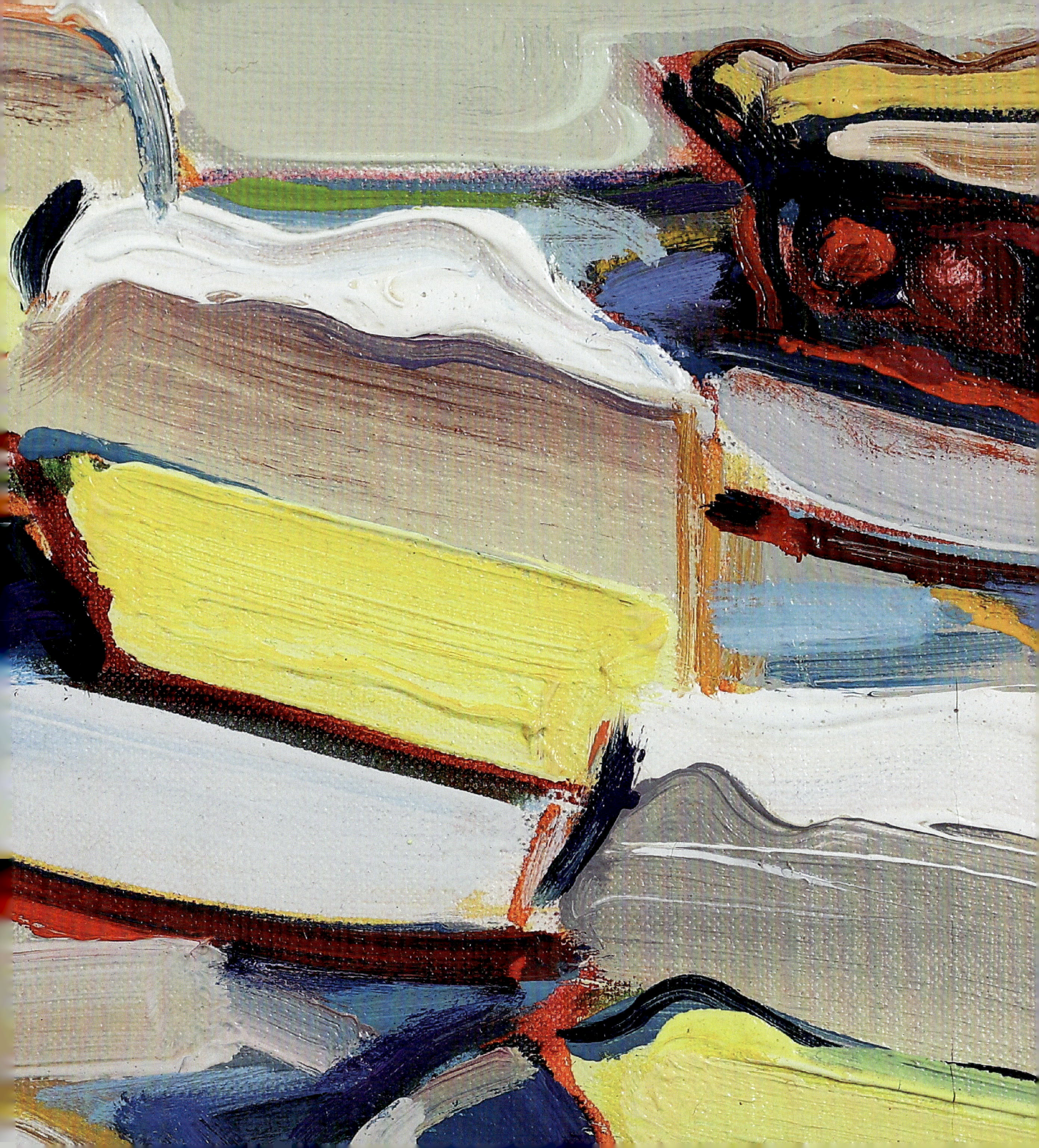

Exhibition Supporters

Title Supporter

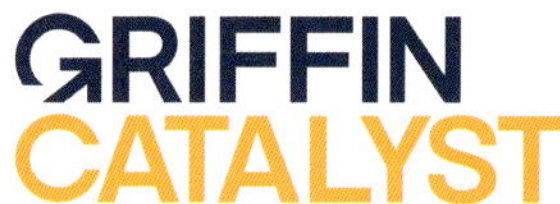

Supported by
Kenneth C. Griffin

With additional support from
Helen Lee-Warren and David Warren
The Aldama Foundation

This publication has been supported by
The Wayne Thiebaud Foundation

Daniel Katz Curator of 20th-Century Art
The post of the exhibition's co-curator, Dr Barnaby Wright, is funded by
Daniel Katz. The Courtauld would like to thank him warmly for his continued
support of this position.

Bridget Riley Art Foundation Curatorial Fellow
We would like to thank the Bridget Riley Art Foundation (BRAF) for their
generous support of this fellowship. The fellowship is currently held by
Dr Chloe Nahum, who has contributed to this exhibition and publication.

The Government Indemnity Scheme
This exhibition has been made possible by the provision of Government
Indemnity. The Courtauld would like to thank HM Government for providing
Government Indemnity and the Department for Culture, Media and Sport,
and Arts Council England for arranging the indemnity.

Detail of cat. 23

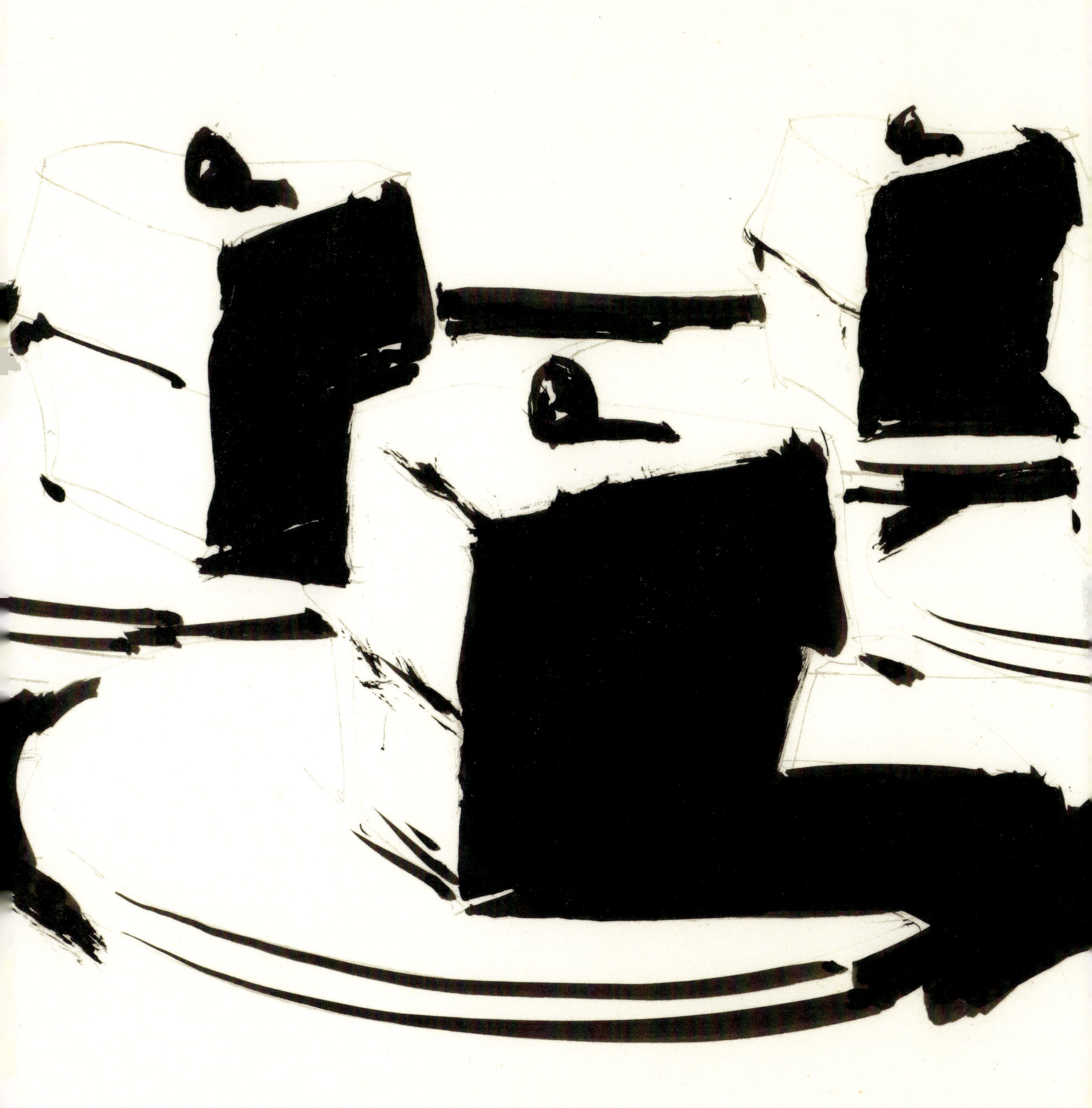

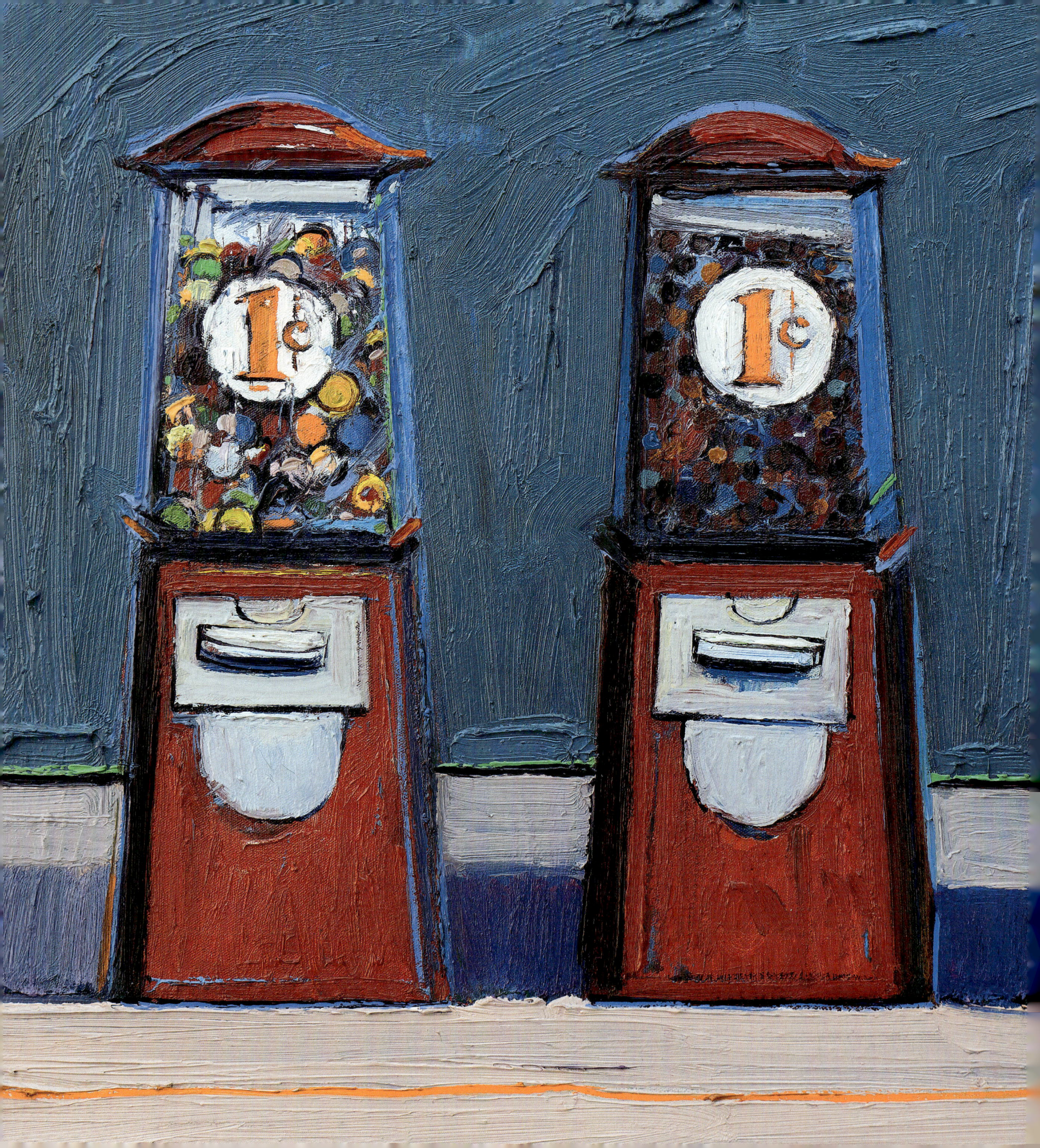

Director's Preface

Mark Hallett

Märit Rausing Director,
The Courtauld Institute of Art

In an artist's statement published in 1962, Wayne Thiebaud noted that 'Each era produces its own still life.' In the same text, he wrote that his own still-life paintings were taken from 'window displays, store counters, supermarket shelves, and mass-produced items from manufacturing concerns in America'. Finding inspiration in these everyday sites and subjects, Thiebaud produced a highly original kind of still-life painting. It was one that saw him turning his back on the indoor settings – the domestic interior, the artist's studio – that were traditionally associated with the genre, and engaging instead with the outdoor, consumer-driven spaces of the contemporary urban environment – the store, the shop, the diner, the arcade. And it was one that saw him focusing on subjects that had hitherto been largely ignored in the sphere of fine art. The things he painted included the brightly coloured dispensers of pleasure and distraction that were part of the new, youth-fixated landscape of entertainment that emerged in post-war America: pinball machines, jackpot machines, gumball machines, penny machines, even yo-yos. Thiebaud also focused on the processed foods – hamburgers, hot dogs, cakes, pies and sweets – being sold to millions of his contemporaries. He offered a remarkable pictorial meditation on these kinds of foodstuffs: on their distinctive visual character, on the patterns they made when arranged for sale, on the glass receptacles in which they found themselves being displayed, and, most subtly of all, on the kinds of light – often as manufactured as the goods themselves – in which they were bathed on the shop or diner countertop, as they waited to be purchased.

Dwelling with great sensitivity on such subjects and translating their aesthetics and associations into the language of advanced painting, Thiebaud captured something quintessential about modern American culture. In equal measure, however, his work makes an unforgettable contribution to the long tradition of the still life. This tradition, famously, includes the work of an earlier artist mentioned by Thiebaud in his 1962 statement, Paul Cézanne. Given Cézanne's centrality to the Courtauld's collection, it feels especially fitting for us to find Thiebaud name-checking his great French forebear. Our wonderful new exhibition, *Wayne Thiebaud. American Still Life*, allows us to appreciate both the power and richness of his paintings in their own right and the dialogue they offer with the works of artists such as Cézanne and Édouard Manet (another favourite of Thiebaud's), hanging nearby.

For conceiving and curating this beautiful, eye-catching exhibition, I would like to offer my heartfelt thanks to my colleagues Karen Serres and Barnaby Wright. I would also like to thank the Wayne Thiebaud Foundation and, especially, Matt and Maria Bult (members of the artist's family) for their great support from the outset. The Foundation has also very generously sponsored this catalogue. I would further like to thank our title supporter, Griffin Catalyst, and Kenneth C. Griffin himself, for once again exemplifying the very best in philanthropy. Finally, I would like to mark my appreciation for our other exhibition supporters, Helen Lee-Warren and David Warren – long-standing friends of The Courtauld – and The Aldama Foundation. In today's financially challenging environment, the generosity of such enlightened individuals and foundations is becoming ever more important. We salute them.

Foreword

Ernst Vegelin van Claerbergen

Head of the Courtauld Gallery

Wayne Thiebaud. American Still Life is the first museum exhibition in the UK dedicated to the work of Wayne Thiebaud, one of the greatest artists of post-war America. The exhibition focuses on the early 1960s, when Thiebaud made his name with his beguiling and lusciously painted depictions of creme pies, deli counters and the pleasurable ephemera of American consumer culture. Thiebaud recast the long tradition of still-life painting for the modern age, and in an emphatically American idiom. In his captivating paintings, drawings and prints, he directs our attention to objects that were so familiar and ubiquitous as to be almost invisible, elevating this prosaic subject matter for serious scrutiny and contemplation, as well as for visual delight. The apparent simplicity of his works belies both the brilliance of their making and the range of meanings that they invite. Thiebaud's gumball machines, food counters, penny slots and pinballs allow us to reflect on America's cultural hegemony during the post-war years, at the start of a period of profound social, political and economic change.

Alongside the main exhibition in the Denise Coates Galleries, we are very pleased to show *Wayne Thiebaud. Delights* in the Gilbert and Ildiko Butler Drawings Gallery. Arranged around the artist's eponymous 1965 portfolio of seventeen prints, it offers further insight into his favoured still-life subjects and allows us to appreciate Thiebaud as a draughtsman and printmaker.

The Courtauld has long been interested in Wayne Thiebaud, and we were delighted when Linda Karshan's promised gift of *Cake Slices*, a drawing from 1963, presented the immediate spur for this exhibition. Certainly, Thiebaud's work feels at home in a museum that traces painterly traditions in art and includes works he very much admired, such as Édouard Manet's *A Bar at the Folies-Bergère*, with its countertop array of modern still lifes. Thiebaud's role as a committed teacher at the University of California, Davis, also resonates in the academic context of the Courtauld Institute of Art.

We are deeply grateful to the Wayne Thiebaud Foundation for their support throughout this project; the friendship of Matt and Maria Bult has been absolutely essential to us. Equally, we are most grateful to the museums and private owners who shared our ambition to present this first UK exhibition at the very highest level of quality. I want to thank them for supporting this project so generously with genuinely exceptional loans, including many of Thiebaud's most celebrated works. Special thanks are also due to Eleanor Acquavella Dejoux and the Acquavella Galleries for their invaluable assistance.

I would like to record my gratitude to Rachel Teagle, Founding Director of the Jan Shrem and Maria Manetti Shrem Museum of Art at the University of California, Davis, which Thiebaud helped establish. Rachel was instrumental in getting our project off the ground and has also contributed an essay to this catalogue. The catalogue is further enriched with illuminating contributions by Lucy Bradnock and Richard Shiff, and I am very grateful to them both. Warm thanks are also due to Amy Graves, registrar for the exhibition, and Chloe Nahum, for her curatorial contribution. Finally, I want to thank my colleagues Karen Serres and Barnaby Wright for their expertise and care in curating this exhibition. With *Wayne Thiebaud. American Still Life*, they have created an exhibition that will introduce a completely new audience to this wonderful artist, and they could not have done so in a more beautiful and thought-provoking way.

Detail of cat. 27

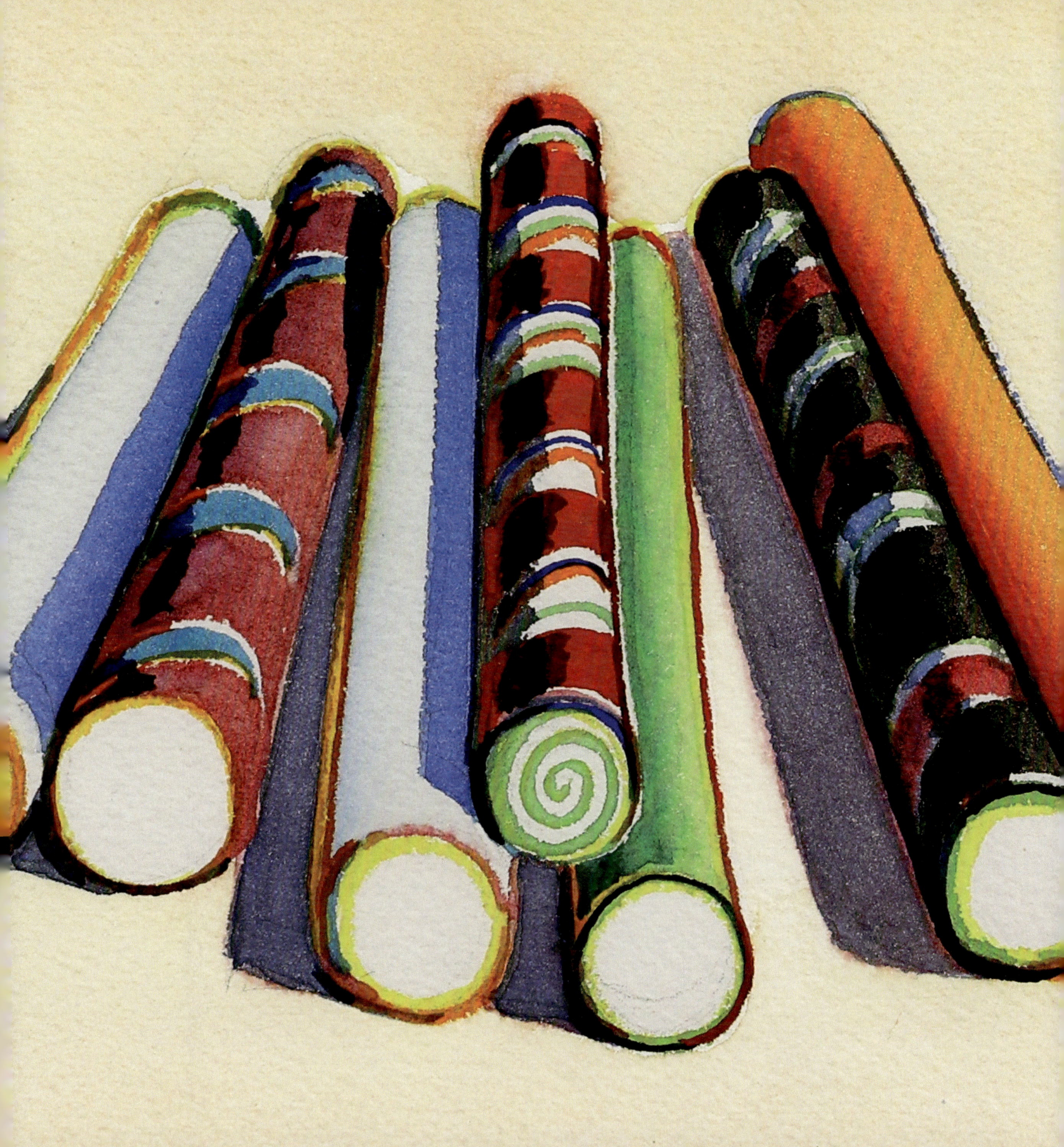

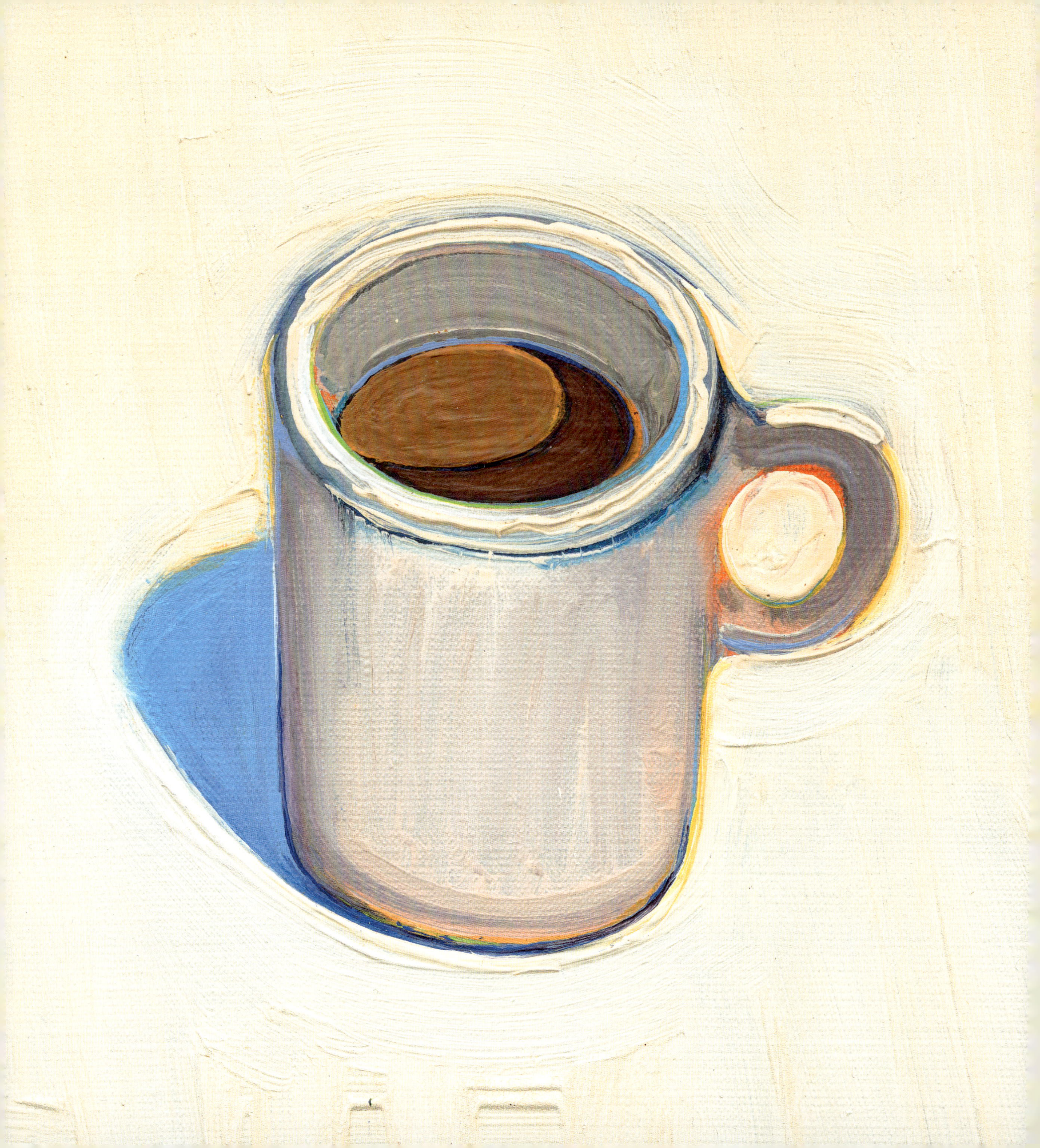

Acknowledgements

It is a pleasure to express The Courtauld's gratitude to the many individuals and institutions that have made this exhibition and publication possible. First and foremost is the Wayne Thiebaud Foundation and, most especially, Matt and Maria Bult, who were incredibly generous and supportive from the very outset of the project.

Our warm thanks also go to Rachel Teagle, Founding Director of the Jan Shrem and Maria Manetti Shrem Museum of Art, University of California, Davis, who has been a close partner in this exhibition.

The project has benefited from generous loans from numerous public institutions. We would like to thank the Anderson Collection at Stanford University, Palo Alto (Jason Linetzky and Jean MacDougall); Buffalo AKG Art Museum (Janne Siren, Cathleen Chaffee, Holly Hughes and Laura Brill); Crocker Art Museum, Sacramento (Agustín Arteaga, Lial Jones, Scott Shields, Francesca Wilmott and Erin Aitali); Fine Arts Museum of San Francisco (Thomas Campbell, Timothy Burgard and Julian Drake); Jan Shrem and Maria Manetti Shrem Museum of Art, University of California, Davis (Rachel Teagle and Haley Di Pressi); The Menil Collection, Houston (Rebecca Rabinow, Michelle White, Paul R. Davis and Susan Slepka Anderson); National Gallery of Art, Washington, D.C. (Kaywin Feldman, Harry Cooper, Margaret Doyle, Elizabeth Walmsley and Rebecca Myles); San Diego Museum of Art (Roxana Velásquez, Anita Feldman, Aldo Cervantes and Kaitlyn Sturgis-Jensen); Smithsonian American Art Museum, Washington, D.C. (Jane Carpenter-Rock, Randall Griffey, Melissa Ho, Laura Augustin Fox, Anne Hyland and Jennifer Schneider) and Whitney Museum of American Art, New York (Scott Rothkopf, Mary Creed, Barbi Spieler and Amy Black).

Equally important to this exhibition are the loans of major works from private collections. We would like to thank most sincerely Bill and Donna Acquavella, John Berggruen, The Bransten Family Collection, The Kondos Collection and those individuals who wish to remain anonymous.

We are hugely grateful to the many people who shared information and advice throughout the various stages of the exhibition's development. We thank especially Eleanor Acquavella Dejoux and the staff of the Acquavella Galleries in New York, who were very supportive from the start and facilitated major loans; Sasha Baguskas from Crown Point Press, San Francisco, who answered a number of important research questions; Timothy Burgard, who generously shared his expertise; Scott Shields, whose knowledge of Thiebaud and his work was invaluable; and Jennifer Wagelie, who made crucial introductions for us at the very outset of the project and has been supportive throughout. Our thanks to the staff at the Archives of American Art, Smithsonian Institution, Washington, D.C. for their help with archival research.

At The Courtauld, numerous colleagues have contributed to the project. We would like to thank in particular Amy Graves and Chloe Nahum, who have been central to the exhibition. Special thanks to Graeme Barraclough, Kate Edmondson, Tanya Millard, Abi Pole and Matthew Thompson. Karin Kyburz was incredibly helpful in researching and sourcing images for this publication. We are also grateful to Rob Baker (and his Marketing and Communications team), Caitlin Brooker, Leyla Bumbra, Fergus Carmichael, Aimee Clark, Savash Djemal, Ketty Gottardo, Helen Higgins (and her colleagues in the Learning Department), Hannah Kauffman, Camilla Knight, Beattrys John, Gerlind May, Siân Morris, Charlotte Newton, Dervla O'Shea, Jon Ping (and his Commercial and Visitor Services team), Sarah-Lily Russ, Éleonore de Sibert (and her Advancement team), Rachel Sloan, Margot Sprague-Davies, Ashleigh Toll, Anthony Tyrrell (and his Estates and Facilities team) and Charlotte Yates.

Thank you very much to Belinda Moore for her work on the exhibition interpretation graphics; to Zerlina Hughes and her team at ZNA for lighting the exhibition; to Pippa Nissen and her team at Nissen Richards Studio for aspects of exhibition design; and to Erica Bolton, Daisy Taylor, Ashleigh Chow and the team at Bolton & Quinn. We would also like to thank Amberley Jamieson at DACS for her support.

For their work on the design and production of this publication, warm thanks are due to Paul Holberton, Laura Parker, Ilaria Bernocchi, Katherine Bogden Bayard, Kristen Wenger and the team at e-Graphic.

Detail of cat. 17

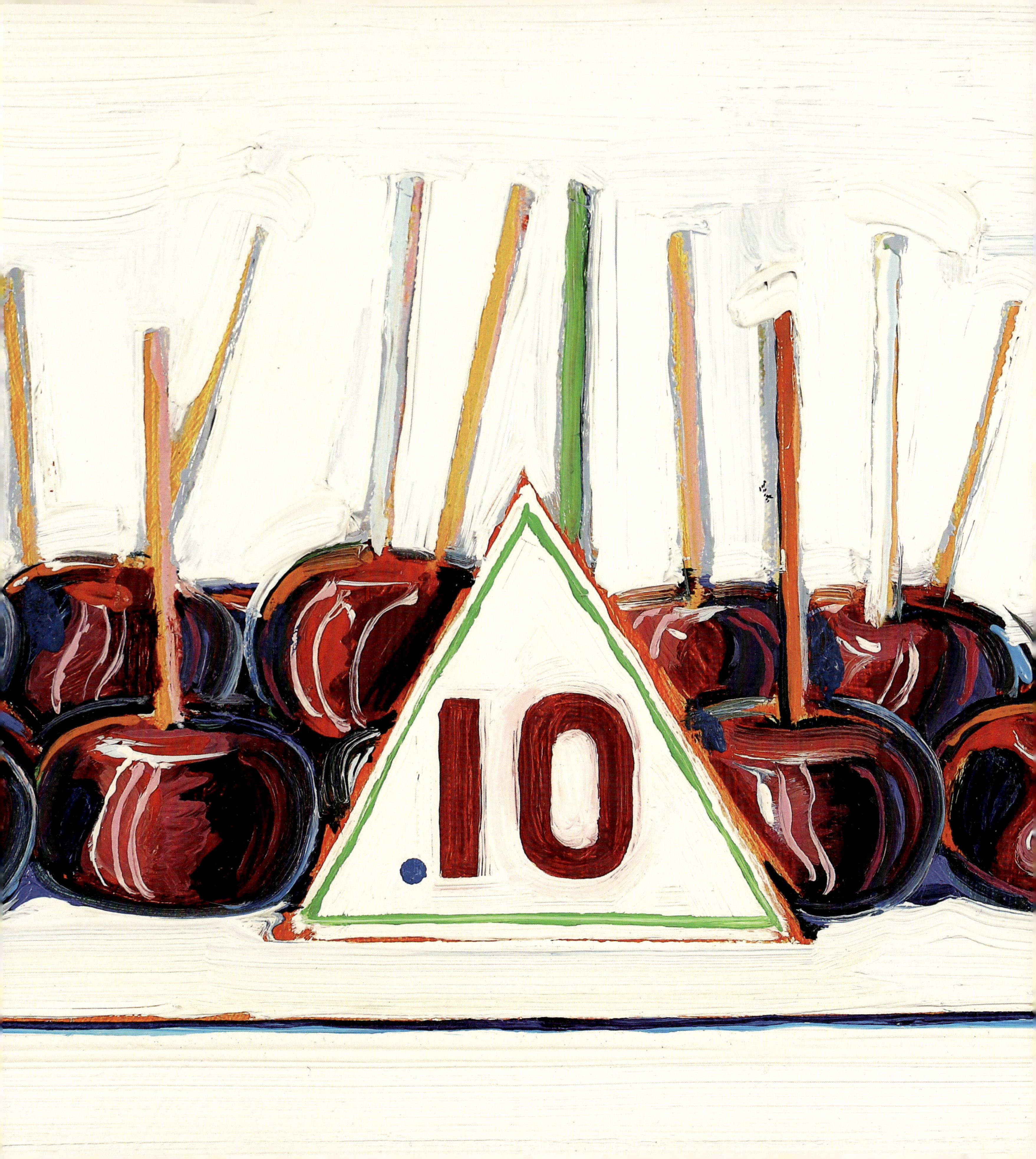
.10

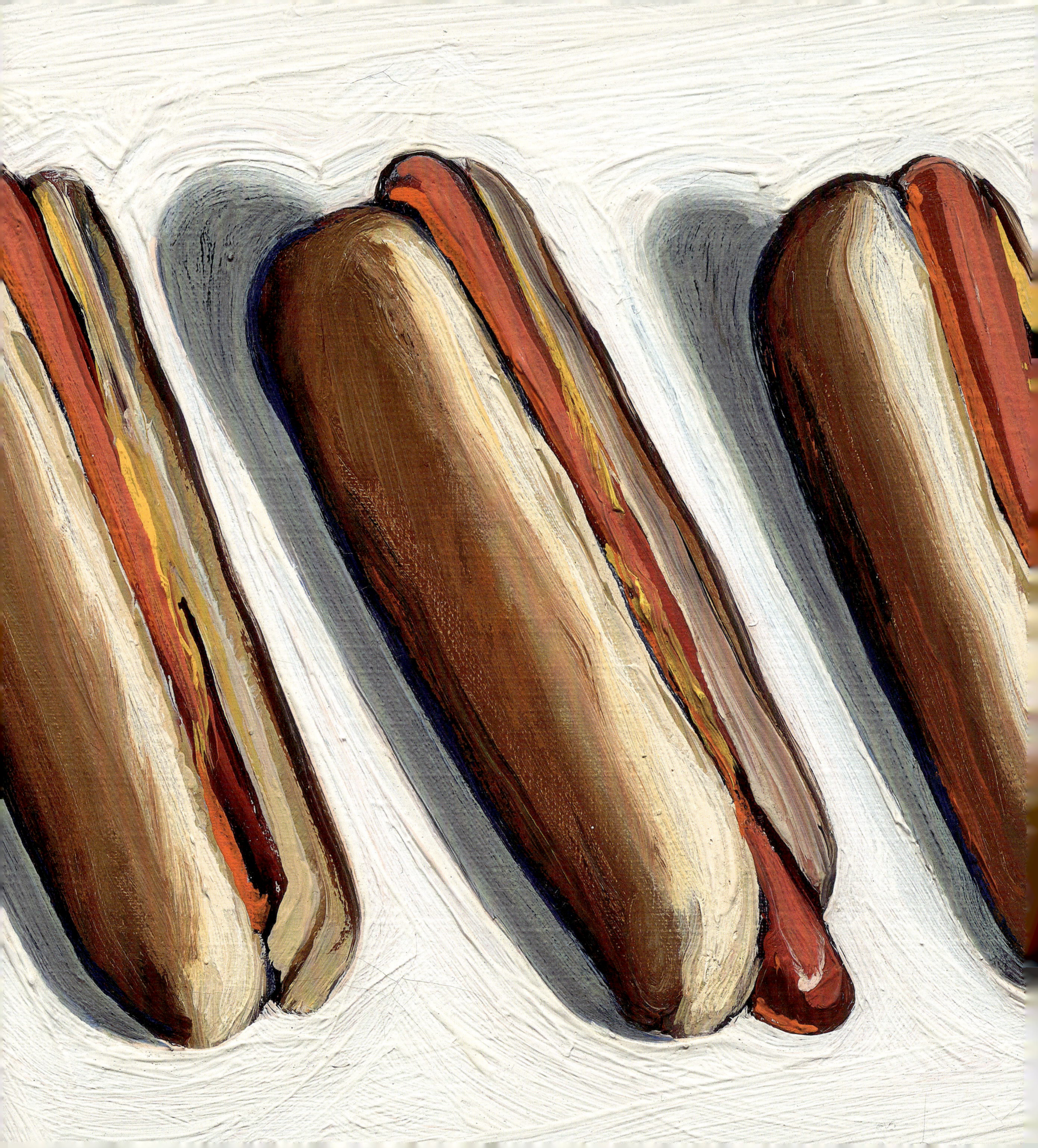

Wayne Thiebaud

American Still Life

Rachel Teagle

At an extraordinary moment in art history, Wayne Thiebaud (1920–2021) proposed a radical take on painting. It was the beginning of the 1960s and Pop Art had hit the United States with what critic Harold Rosenberg described as 'the force of an earthquake'.[1] Thiebaud was swept up in the momentum and, over the course of one spectacular year, he participated in two seminal exhibitions that would determine the future of the avant-garde in the United States. However, few people understood that Thiebaud was up to something completely different. While his contemporaries moved away from what they perceived to be the moribund nature of painting, Thiebaud luxuriated in the propensities of paint. Rather than being rooted in advertising graphics and methods of mass reproduction, or concerned with flat print-like surfaces, Thiebaud's work was painterly almost to the point of exaggeration and based upon close observation and memory of the consumable objects that fascinated him. Crucially, he considered these objects to be vital features of contemporary American life, best expressed by renewing the traditional genre of still life for the modern age. He saw his work as continuing the radical legacy of still-life paintings by Jean-Siméon Chardin (1699–1779), Paul Cézanne (1839–1906) and Édouard Manet (1832–1883) among others, and he took seriously the importance of commonplace objects that might otherwise be overlooked or considered merely kitsch. For him, lemon meringue pies and glossy cream cakes were the stuff of serious modern painting (fig. 1). The exhibition *Wayne Thiebaud. American Still Life* charts this extraordinary moment when Thiebaud's painterly project coalesced and he found his artistic voice, creating a highly original way of painting and drawing in order to express his vision of American consumer culture in the years of post-war expansion, optimism, dissent and change. His lushly painted, vibrantly coloured pictures of the everyday offerings of American diners, bakeries and stores captivate and draw the viewer deep into their world, generating a range of meanings that belie their direct and simple appearance.

As a young man, Thiebaud found a remarkable array of ways to put his artistic talents to work. While still in high school, he worked at Walt Disney Studios in the animation department as an 'in-betweener', filling in the sequential frames of cartoons. The Second World War cut short his college career and Thiebaud completed his army service as an artist in the First Motion Picture Unit of the Air Force and was a cartoonist for the base newspaper. When discharged, he had a young family to support, so he picked up any kind of art job he could get. Universal-International Studios hired him to design movie posters. When Ava Gardner's knees presented a 'problem', Thiebaud turned to the history of painting and found a solution in a figure by the Flemish artist Peter Paul Rubens (1577–1640).[2] He developed a lifelong habit of finding answers in the history of art. In 1946, he landed full-time work as an advertising art director at Rexall Drug Company, where he learned to lay out store window displays.[3] The experience of working at Rexall had a profound impact. During the post-war economic boom, Rexall pioneered the use of private label (or own-brand) marketing, sustained by national campaigns and, as a result, Thiebaud worked to develop in-store displays that

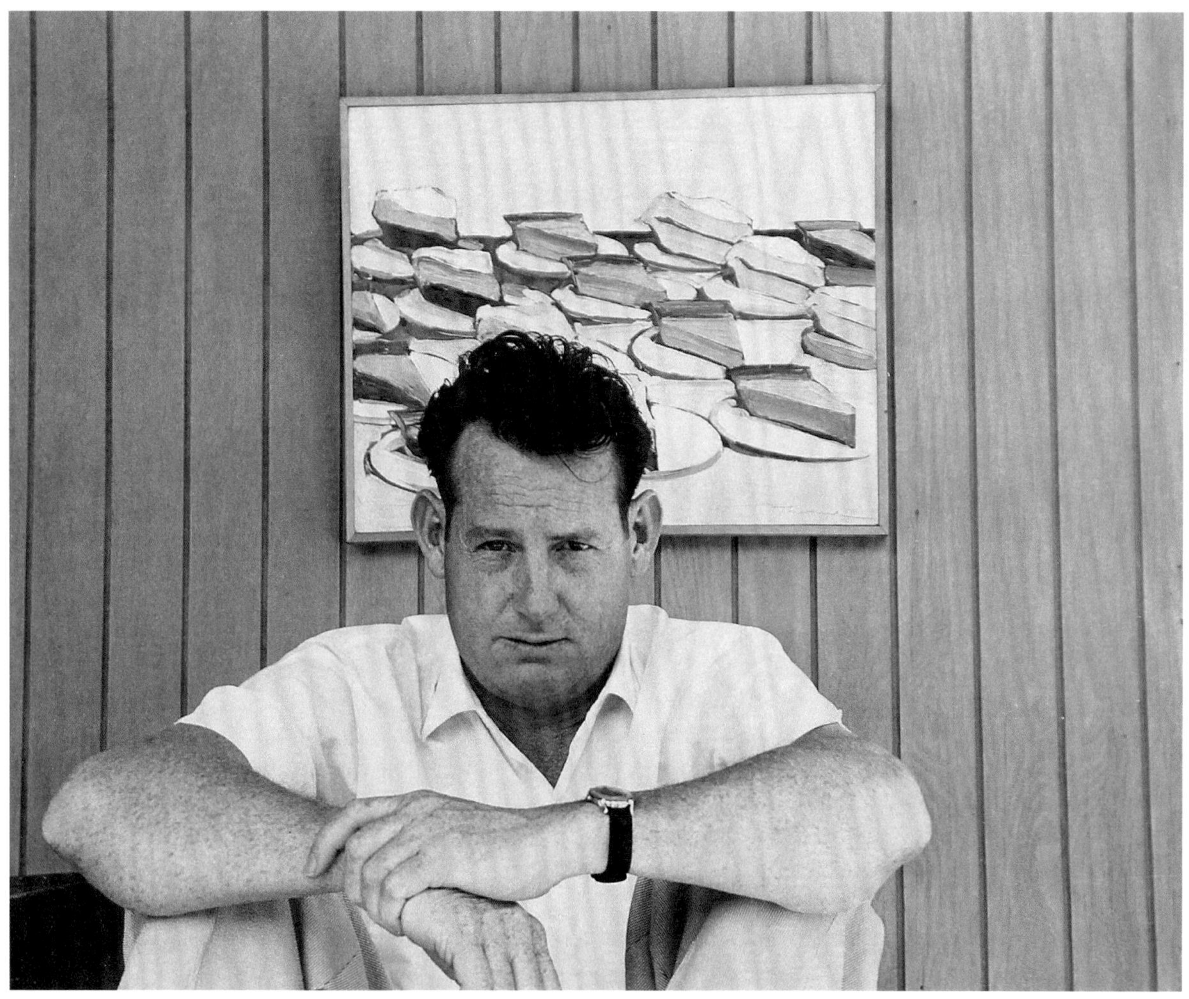

1 Wayne Thiebaud in his studio in Sacramento in 1961, with his painting *Pies* (Family collection of Harry W. and Mary Margaret Anderson). Photographer: Betty Jean Thiebaud. Collection of the Wayne Thiebaud Foundation

centred on depictions of products for sale. On the job, he learned a repertoire of visual strategies and developed a sense of what he would later call 'clearly identified objects'.[4] Lessons learned as a tradesman would prove to be valuable and later became the basis of Thiebaud's painting practice.

It took Thiebaud five years to muster the courage to leave commercial art and return to college. Teaching was the goal because he saw it as a means to dedicate himself to painting. In 1953, at the age of 31, he finally graduated. He taught at Sacramento City College, produced instructional art films, ran the annual art exhibition at the California State Fair and even won a national contest for a Dave Brubeck album cover he designed in 1958, all while painting seriously for the first time. Landscapes of California's Central Valley, river scenes and mountain vistas filled his canvases.

Thiebaud's wide-ranging expertise in the commercial arts sustained his young family and yet, the fine art of painting remained his personal measure of success. In 1956 he took a sabbatical from teaching and moved to New York with the express purpose of meeting his heroes. It is no coincidence that Thiebaud pursued Willem de Kooning (1904–1997), a painter who openly acknowledged his beginnings as a commercial artist. During a visit to his studio, de Kooning challenged Thiebaud with a simple question: 'Why are you painting anyway?' Stopped in his tracks, the young artist responded, 'Well, I love doing it.' De Kooning shot him down and set him straight: 'you have to find something you really know about and something you are really interested in'.[5] At a pivotal moment, Thiebaud took de Kooning's direction to heart. He began to paint the very stuff he worked with as an advertising art director – products on display.

Not long after his visit to de Kooning, Thiebaud began *Meat Counter* (cat. 2), a painting that would occupy his easel during a formative period in his development. He set his intentions in this early version of a scene that he would return to throughout his career. When picturing products for sale, lighting and its manifest effects were always his real interest. Look, for example, at the dark recesses of the case's interior. The black backdrop provides a stark contrast with a countertop so flooded with light that the slabs of meat cast deep shadows. Those cerulean shadows portend the future. With so many signifiers of light in place, *Meat Counter* should appear bright and yet, the overall effect is dark, as it is in *Pinball Machine,* also from 1956 (cat. 1). Throughout this composition, he applied silver highlights. The metallic pigment lends a shimmer to the canvas but not the sensation of light. His marks are not clear statements; instead, as Thiebaud's wife, Betty Jean (1929–2015), would later describe, 'these objects were submersed by Abstract Expressionism mannerisms'.[6] Thiebaud had found the ideas and elements that would sustain his practice but he had not yet distilled them into a special alchemy all his own.

Thiebaud later explained, 'at the end of 1959 or so I began to be interested in a formal approach to composition. I'd been painting gumball machines, windows, counters, and at that point began to rework paintings into much more clearly identified objects. I picked things like pies and cakes – things based upon simple shapes like triangles and circles – and tried to orchestrate them.'[7] Clarity is key to Thiebaud's achievement. He continued, 'Working from memory, I tried to arrange them in the same way that an art director arranges things.' Following his hero's advice, Thiebaud allowed skills he developed in commercial art to play out in his painting. More important still, he began to paint from memory, that is from his mind's eye. Releasing himself from the conventional boundaries of realism emboldened Thiebaud. This subtle shift set him on a path to create paintings that *feel* real as much as they look like realistic renderings of his subjects.

At this exact moment, the end of 1959, Thiebaud accepted a faculty position at the University of California, Davis. Throughout his life, he described himself as self-taught because he was never formally trained.[8] His degree was in arts education and he took his teaching seriously. He later reflected, 'Teaching requires a real clarity of thought and intention if you want your ideas to convey to students.'[9] In the process of training himself to

be an educator, he discovered teaching to be generative. 'The reason,
I suppose, I got so interested in teaching, is that it was really my education.'[10]
Thiebaud assumed the title of Professor with earnest conviction. As he had
hoped, teaching also afforded time in the studio. He seized the opportunity.
Looking back, he explained, 'During a two-and-a-half-year session, I
produced … approximately one hundred oil paintings which were eventually
exhibited widely'.[11] Suffice it to say, Thiebaud favoured understatement.

What follows is a story as remarkable today as it was when he lived it.
In the summer of 1961, Thiebaud packed up a few of his new paintings and
drove cross-country from his home in Northern California to the capital of
the art world, New York City. He loved to tell the story of knocking on doors,
exhausted, always rejected. In his recounting, the Allan Stone Gallery was his
last stop. Finally, he was well received at this new gallery, which had opened
just the year before. In December 1961, Stone (1932–2006) included two
emerging artists in a holiday group show: Thiebaud shared his premiere
with Andy Warhol (1928–1987), another up-and-comer who was getting his
first shot.

Back at home, Thiebaud had just opened his first solo exhibition in
San Francisco. Art Unlimited announced Thiebaud's November 1961 opening
with a photograph from the artist's studio (fig. 2). Ever the art director,
Thiebaud managed the shoot. In a series of photographs, he arranged his
paintings to feature the array of subjects now taking centre stage in his work:
cakes, slices of pie, gumball machines, cups of coffee, meat and cheese,
hot dogs and candy, too. In each photograph of the shoot, he stacked his
paintings two to three deep and filled the frame top to bottom, emphasising
an abundance of recent work. Everything about the photographs broadcasts
'straight from the studio, hot off the press, new'. Newer still was the very
idea to take modern American food seriously as the subject of high art.
In a photograph that includes the artist (fig. 3), two important paintings take
pride of place: *Cup of Coffee* (cat. 7) rests in Thiebaud's hand and *Five Hot Dogs*
(cat. 6), from the same year, resides at the centre of the composition, just
behind the artist's knee. From his choice of subject to how he laid down his
paint, Thiebaud established, with these deceptively simple paintings,
a trajectory that he would pursue for the rest of his career.

Both paintings share expansive white backgrounds that appear to
be empty. As with so much of Thiebaud's style, excitement builds from
the mundane. These heavily worked and seemingly undifferentiated
grounds would become a hallmark of the artist's mature work, essential to
their magic. Thiebaud readily acknowledged that he lifted these heavily
brushstroked grounds directly from painters he admired. Early on, critics
recognised Manet's *The Fifer* (1866, musée d'Orsay, Paris) as an important
precedent.[12] Applied in differing densities with wide, long and fast marks,
paint accumulated in ridges that cast shadows and formed valleys to catch
the light.[13] No longer reliant on metallic pigment, Thiebaud used his very
brushstrokes to create a lively play of light across the canvas.[14] The bravura
brushwork that underscores *Cup of Coffee* is so spirited that it is easy to
imagine it as a celebration – by borrowing from great painters who came

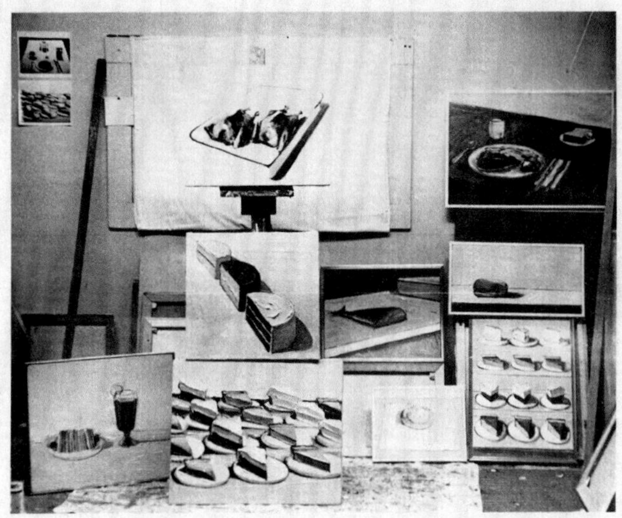

before, Thiebaud found his technique. He signed the painting by incising his name into the thick paint, a flourish that seems to say 'more than my name, these strokes are my signature'.

In formal terms, *Cup of Coffee* is nothing more than a study of circles. Circles within circles define the coffee's creamy surface with another echoed in its handle. In pursuit of clarity, Thiebaud started from simple forms. He often recounted the origin story of his iconic pies as an exercise in geometry: 'A piece of pie is a triangle on a saucer, which can take on various elliptical

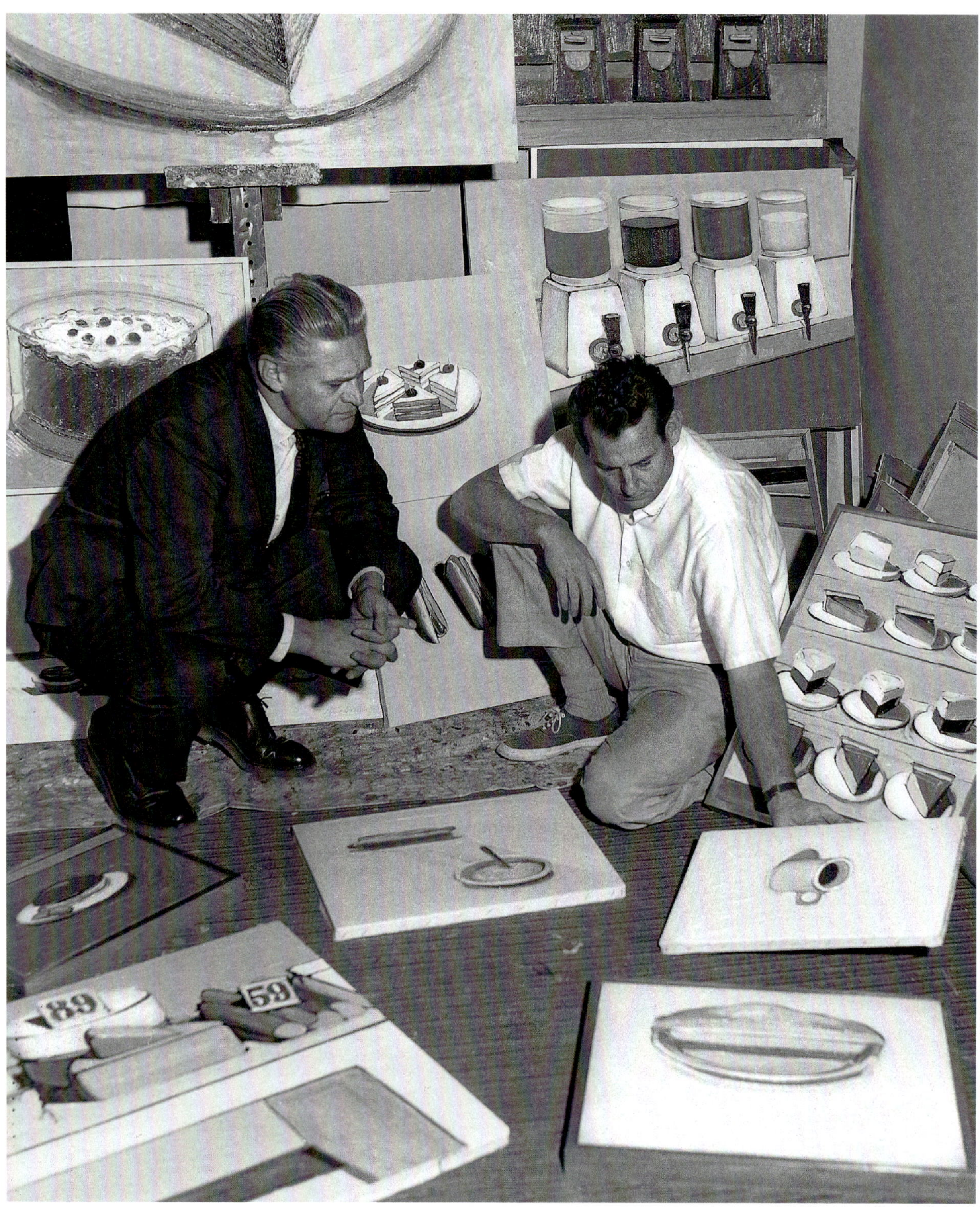

3 Wayne Thiebaud in his studio in Sacramento
with Professor Paul Beckmann, 1962.
Collection of the Wayne Thiebaud Foundation

shapes on two rectangles, the bottom plane and the top plane.'[15] Following Thiebaud himself, many critics understand the artist as working within Cézanne's famous dictum, 'Treat nature in terms of the cylinder, the sphere, the cone' and yet, the practice applies as much to the tactics of hand-drawn commercial design as to what Thiebaud liked to call painting's 'grand tradition'.[16] Instead of developing a singular gesture, Thiebaud found his mature style by sourcing techniques from every place he found a meaningful form of mark making. His signature became the effortless way he conflated high and low.

Thiebaud marched his simple geometric forms across his canvases, repetition becoming one of his most powerful tools. In each iteration he found some slight deviation to punctuate his straightforward approach. He nudged every bun in *Five Hot Dogs* up or down to create a pleasing syncopation, a little disruption to lend excitement. 'Tempo' is how Thiebaud described it, and music is an apt metaphor. However, the mechanics of the comic strip hit closer to home. Adept at all forms of painterly mark making, Thiebaud worked as much like a cartoonist as he did a classical painter. He would find common subjects, distill their essence and bestow character with variations to his deceptively simple lines. John Updike could have been writing about Thiebaud when he described Charles Schulz's *Peanuts*, which also took off in the mid-1950s, as 'setting new standards of minimalist subtlety and quiet daring'.[17] More recently, the essayist Adam Gopnik nicely summarised the artist's agility in making many trades his own: 'He absorbed the cartoonist's feeling for scribble, the crosshatched studiousness of the illustrator, the art director's formula for glamour, and let them inflect his virtuoso, traditional technique.'[18] Thiebaud deployed a panoply of what he liked to call 'cheap tricks' accumulated from working every art gig he could muster.[19]

His resplendent approach to colour was no different. In 1963, the painter and influential teacher Josef Albers (1888–1976) published *Interaction of Color*, a compendium of lectures refined over decades of delivery. 'In visual perception,' Albers explained, 'a color is almost never seen as it really is, as it physically is.'[20] Thiebaud activated Albers's theories on the relativity of colour – that is, how colours take on aspects of adjacent colours – by organising complementary colours into thin bands that define the edges of his objects. In 1971, Betty Jean Thiebaud made a film about her husband's work and her narration explained the effect succinctly: 'He begins a painting by drawing in color with the brush in lime green, yellow and orange. These lines of color leak through and are eventually restated, clarified, and become a transition between forms, giving a glow or 'halation' to the edges heightening the color.'[21] Thiebaud discovered that the smallest amount of complementary colours, adjacencies plotted with care, enlivens an entire canvas, giving the most commonplace of objects new life.

Betty Jean's film, *Wayne Thiebaud,* captured a visual inventory of the common objects that caught his attention. In style and tone, the film so thoroughly represents Thiebaud that it amounts to an artist's statement with her camera doing most of the talking. Long shots of food stalls and store windows take up as much footage as the artist at work (fig. 4). Thiebaud

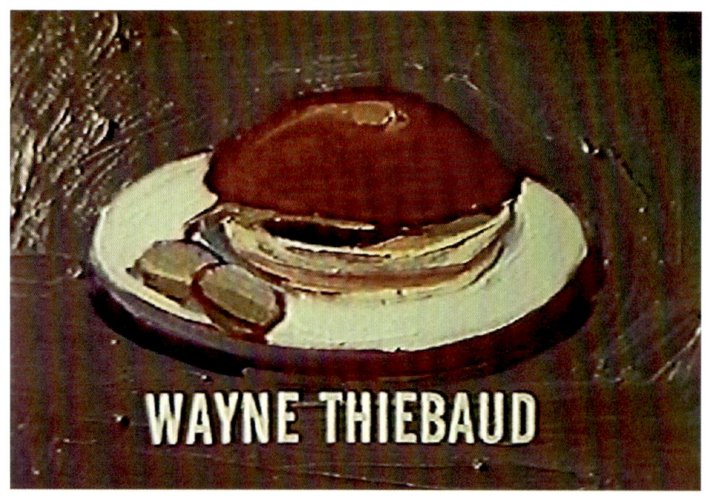

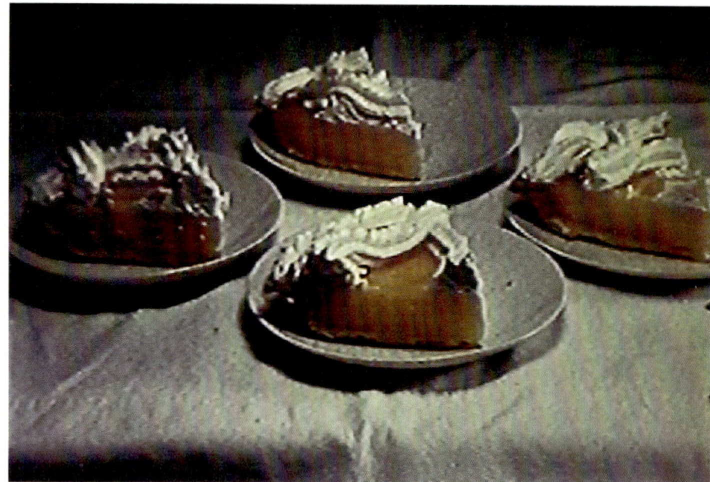
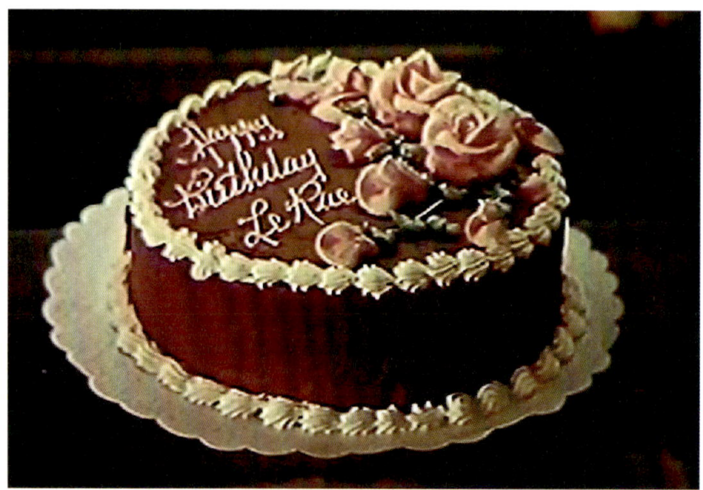
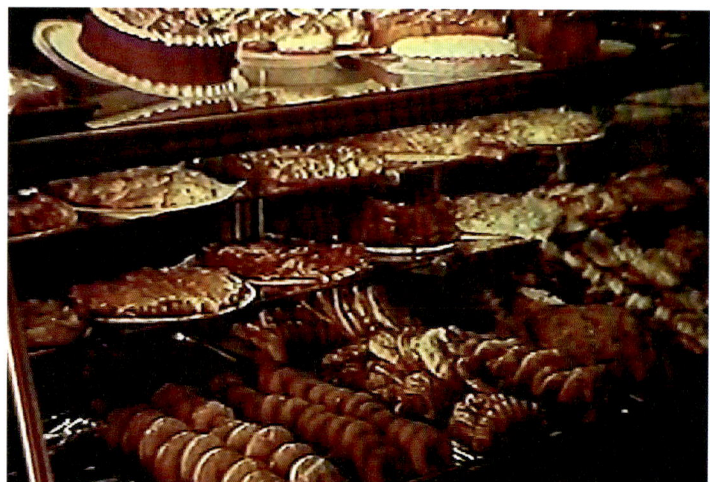
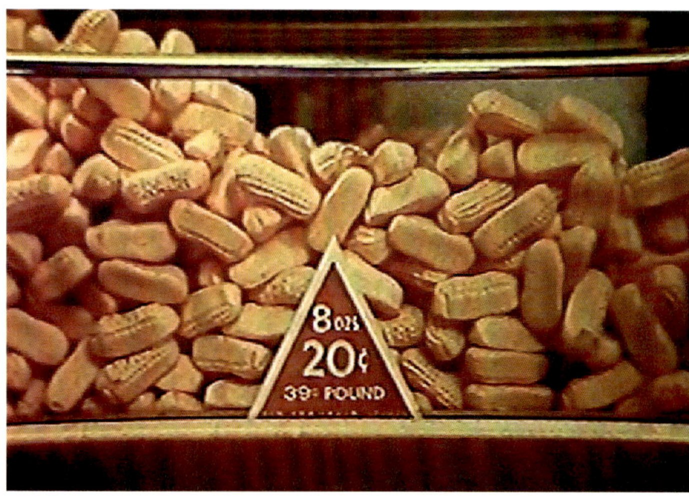

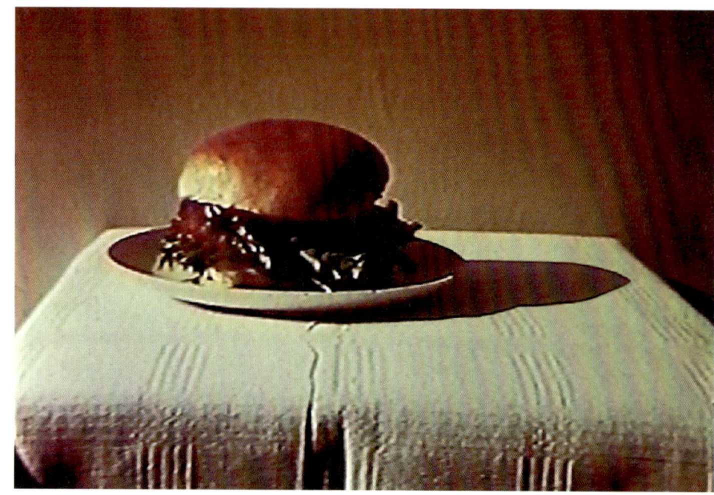

4 Stills from the film *Wayne Thiebaud* by Betty Jean
Thiebaud (1929–2015), 1971, running time: 20 minutes
16 seconds, Collection of the Wayne Thiebaud Foundation

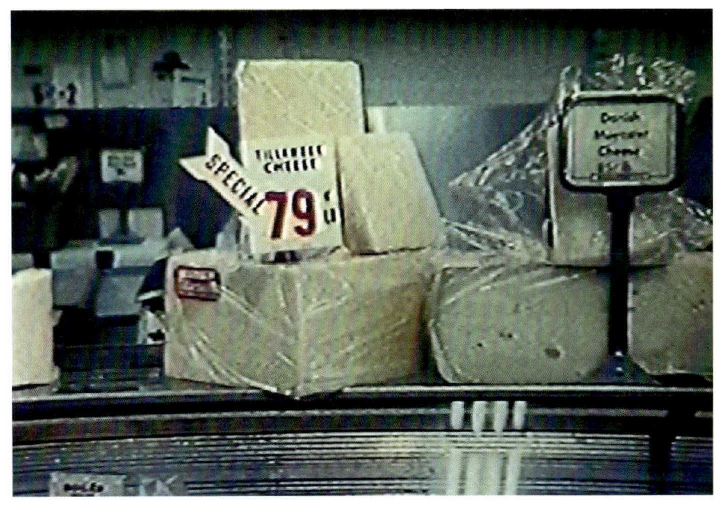
TILLAMOOK CHEESE
SPECIAL 79 ¢ LB
Danish
Muenster
Cheese

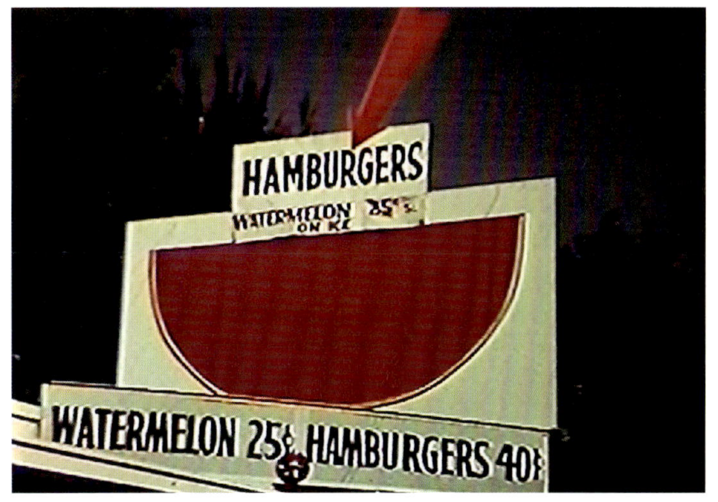
HAMBURGERS
WATERMELON 25¢
ON ICE
WATERMELON 25¢ HAMBURGERS 40¢

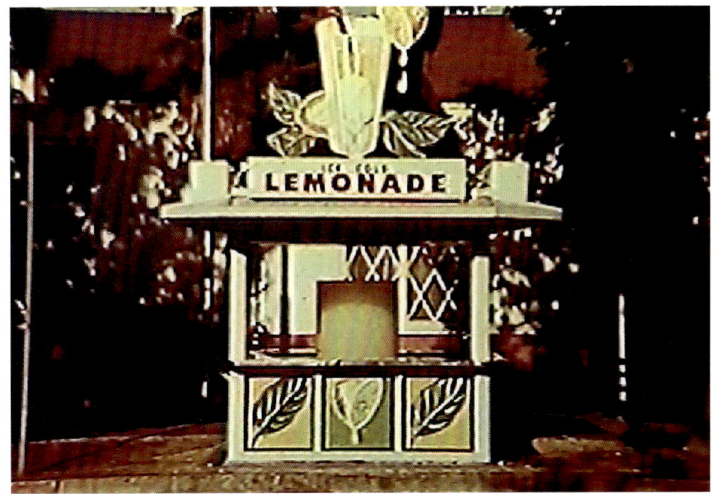
ICE COLD
LEMONADE

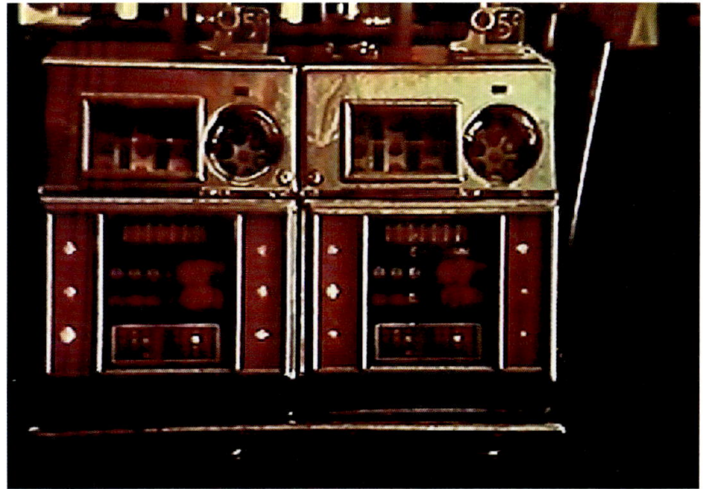

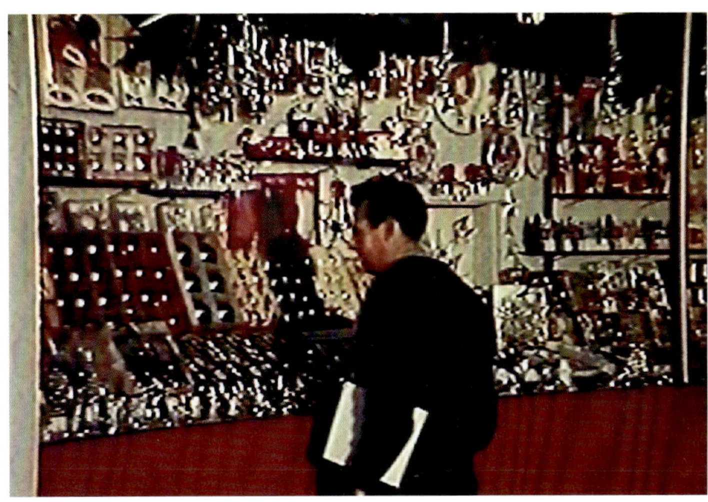

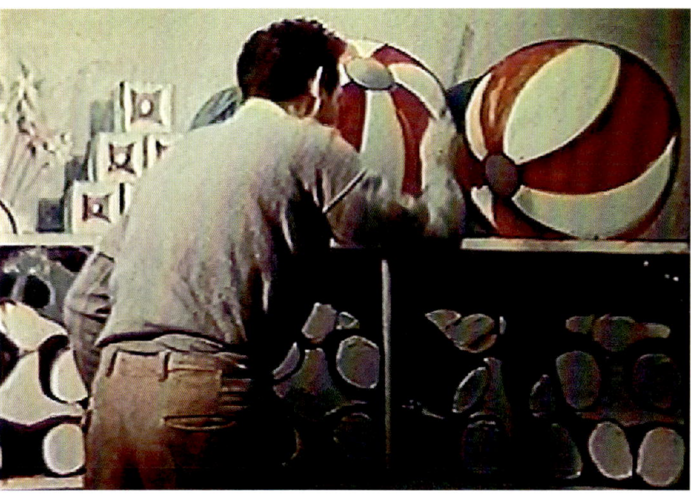

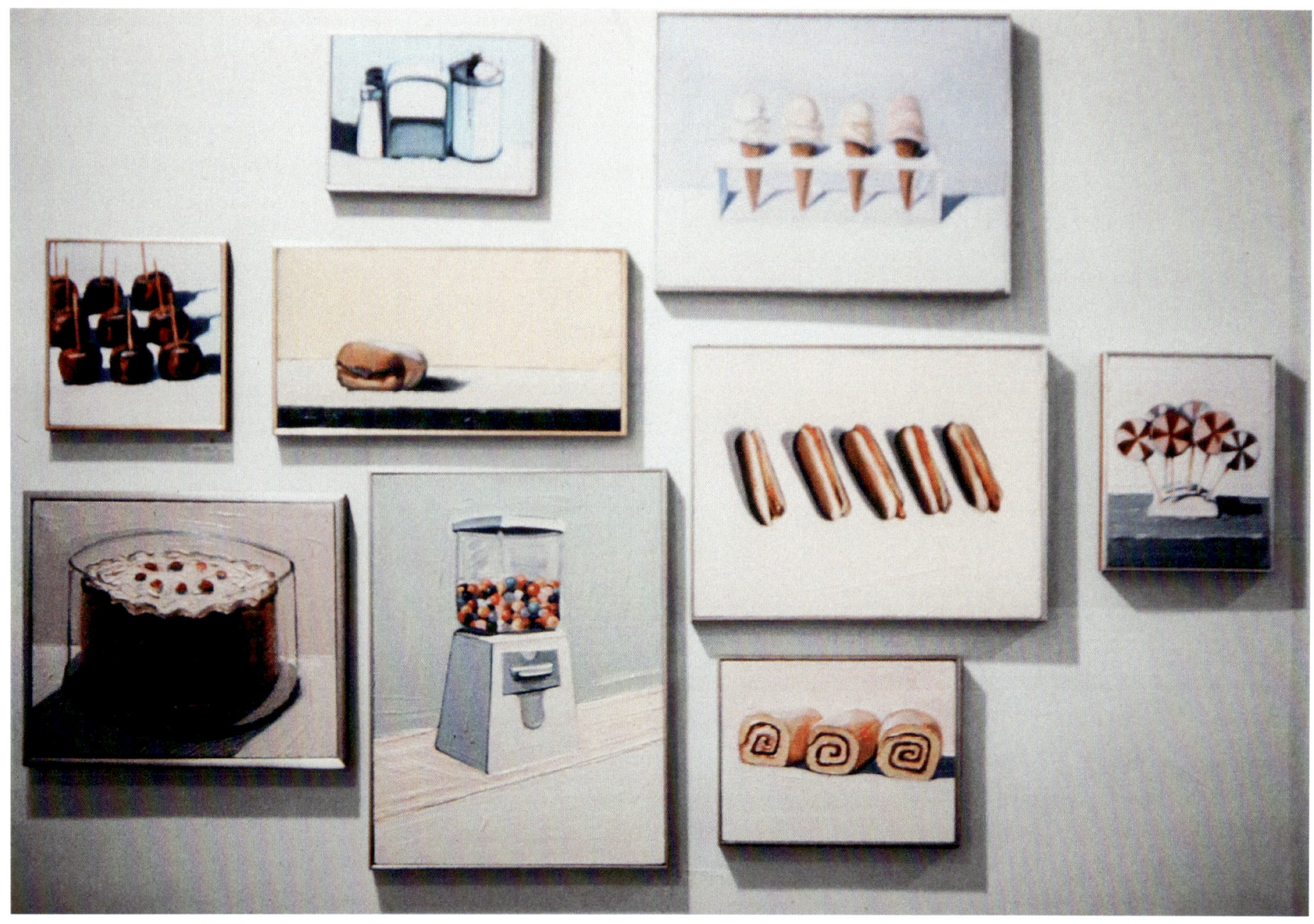

appears, his back to the camera, studying a pawn shop window. Clearly, the former ad man still nurtured an abiding interest in the tactics of display. Meanwhile, Betty Jean narrates a concise script as her camera lingers on brightly lit hamburgers, stacks of ice cream cones and cakes. 'Most of these images', she explains, 'are uniquely common to the American environment.'[22] In a film with so few words, Betty Jean's paradoxical phrasing was no mistake. 'Uniquely common' perfectly describes a slight, but important, shift in the objects that found their way onto Thiebaud's canvases at the start of the 1960s. Hot dogs, of course, are more than just simple cylindrical forms. Uniform in size, consistent in their colouring, they are industrialised food, fast food, American food. They are denizens of the modern American supermarket. Just a few years later and the meat counter already looked old fashioned.

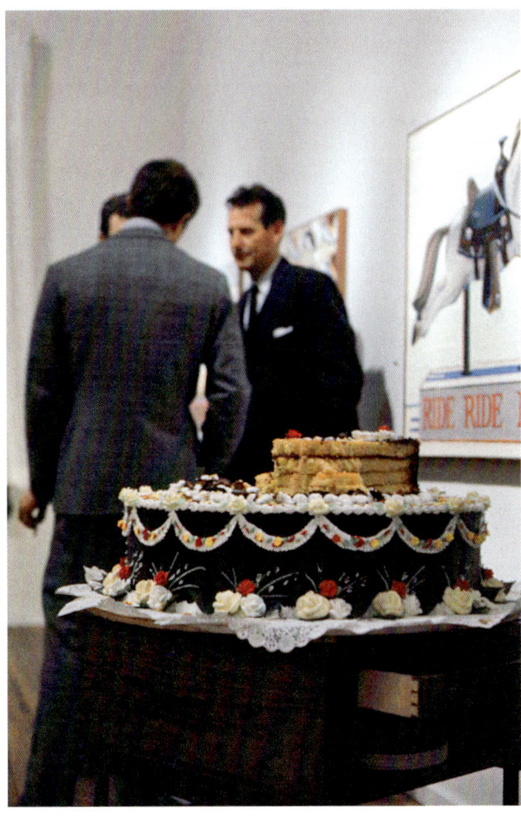

6 Wayne Thiebaud at the opening of *Wayne Thiebaud: Recent Paintings*, Allan Stone Gallery, New York, April 1962, Collection of the Wayne Thiebaud Foundation

In a 1969 interview, Thiebaud admitted, 'I chose a pie for a couple of reasons; because of its basic shape and because I had never seen a pie painted. I have seen a pie in some of Breugel's [sic] paintings, but never a piece of pie in a cafe. As I started painting these very simple triangles on platters, I got more and more intrigued with pies.'[23] Thiebaud's pies are of the modern variety, manufactured confections utterly unlike the confections of Pieter Bruegel the Elder (active 1550–69) or the brioches represented by Chardin. Likewise, *Cup of Coffee* takes as its subject a thick ceramic mug so ubiquitous as to be an icon of American diners. It is easy to take it further – Thiebaud's mug is a 'cup of joe' for the 'Average Joe'. The subjects that first brought Thiebaud fame were decidedly unpretentious and distinctly American.

They were also of the moment and somehow already out of date. 'Commonplace objects are constantly changing', Thiebaud explained as the interview went on. 'When I paint the ones I remember I am like Chardin tattling on what we were. The pies, for example, we now see are not going to be around forever …. The Breugel pies I mentioned earlier were vastly different from our pies, as will be pies in 1985.'[24] Thiebaud wrought the remarkable sense that his hot dogs and pies are truly present by giving them a wistful quality. They convey a deep awareness of the impermanence of things. Study his ice cream cones and you'll see that they are always already a little soft.

Thiebaud's opening at Art Unlimited in November 1961 garnered little attention, yielding not much more than a joke about a surprise sale that Thiebaud liked to tell: his mother was incredulous that a painting of five hot dogs sold immediately and for the high sum of $500. The punchline goes something like 'Would they have paid $800 for eight?'

Immediately following Art Unlimited, Allan Stone opened Thiebaud's now legendary New York City solo exhibition in April 1962 (fig. 5). To Thiebaud's delight, Stone festooned the gallery in lollipops and served up cake and pie on pedestals at the opening (fig. 6). The show immediately sold out. The Museum of Modern Art and the Wadsworth Atheneum purchased paintings. Major collectors followed suit, including the architect Philip Johnson, the publisher Harry Abrams and the critic Max Kozloff. Barnett Newman, still at the height of his painterly powers, attended the opening along with the critic Harold Rosenberg. The soon-to-be famous sculptor Donald Judd reviewed the show. Thiebaud's paintings were the talk of the town among the art world's cognoscenti.

Later that same year, Thiebaud was included in what would be credited as the first exhibition of Pop Art in the United States. *New Painting of Common Objects*, at the Pasadena Art Museum, featured an array of subjects that fit Betty Jean's description of objects 'uniquely common to the American environment'. Thiebaud's *Five Hot Dogs* fit right in with Warhol's *Campbell's Cream of Chicken* (fig. 20). *Actual Size* (fig. 7) by Ed Ruscha (born 1937) and *Roto Broil* (fig. 8) by Roy Lichtenstein (1923–1997) also featured distinctly American food products specific to the profusion of branded goods on offer in post-war America. Ruscha's painting depicts a can of Spam (represented life size) and

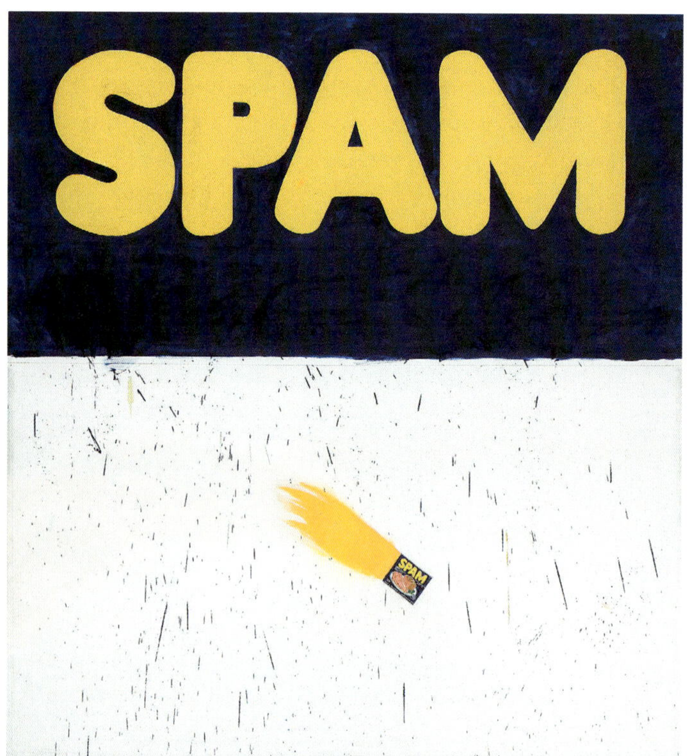

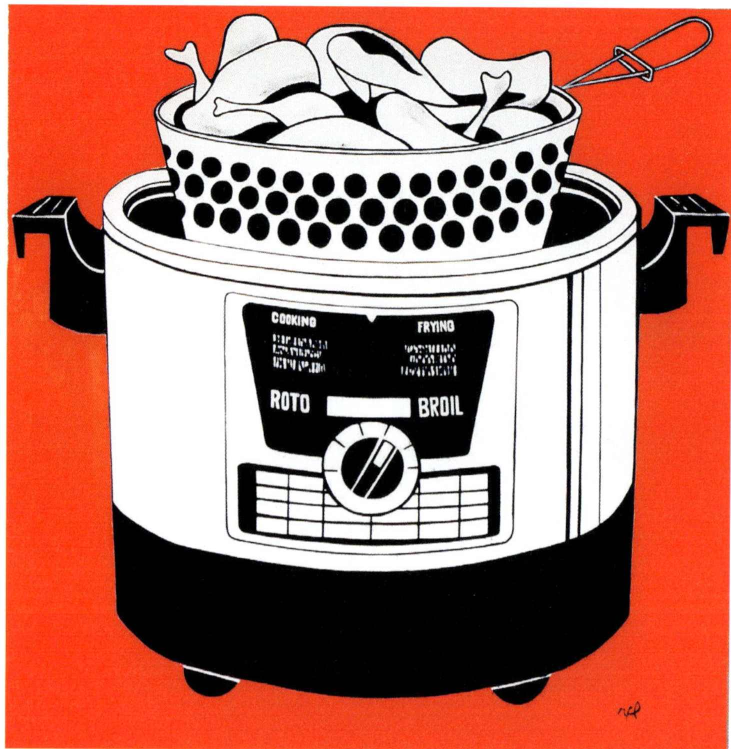

7 Edward Ruscha (born 1937), *Actual Size*, 1962, oil on canvas, 170.3 × 183 cm, Los Angeles County Museum of Art

8 Roy Lichtenstein (1923–1997), *Roto Broil*, 1961, oil and graphite pencil on canvas, 172 x 172 cm, Tehran Museum of Contemporary Art, Iran

Lichtenstein's, a common kitchen appliance. *Life Magazine* first reported on this new phenomenon of art inspired by the supermarket with a colour reproduction of Thiebaud's painting *Pies* (fig. 9; see also cat. 5) and an article that began, 'Cooking up new art is as easy as pie – or so it would seem from the latest variety served up by some U.S. painters.' The critic Calvin Tomkins identified the obvious cause: 'supermarket food is so American'.[25] With tongue in cheek, he questioned the capacity of 'the great conveyor belt of our largest industry' to deliver 'the world's highest standard of living'. In his review of *New Painting of Common Objects*, John Coplans, founder of *Artforum* magazine, set the tone for how Pop would be understood: 'Man, having engineered a society to an undreamed-of state of mass production, now labors solely in order to consume with the same ferocity as he produces.'[26] Consumerism was the message and painting its medium. Built on the logic of 'pile it high and sell it cheap', the supermarket, like Thiebaud, came of age during the Great Depression.[27] By the 1950s, traditional grocery stores, with clerks who pulled fresh cuts, were already a distant memory. In their place, self-serve supermarkets featured pre-packaged 'convenience' foods. Thiebaud's cupcakes, like Warhol's soup cans, were denizens of the mid-century American supermarket.

Thiebaud's rise in the early 1960s coincided with a tumultuous period in the history of art and of the United States. Often and not unproblematically

In cafeterias, billboards and comic strips,

artists find prosaic ingredients for provocative paintings

Something New Is Cooking

Cooking up new art is as easy as pie—or so it would seem from the latest variety served up by some U.S. painters. Inspired by commonplace, mass-produced aspects of everyday life, they are faithfully filling their canvases with everything from baked goods to billboard beauties and comic strips.

The creators of this provocatively prosaic brand of art have been lumped together under various labels: Commonists, Vulgarists or, ironically, the New American Dreamers. But each artist developed independently, oblivious of other contributors to the "movement." While painters around New York and New Jersey have focused on images from commercial art (*following pages*), Wayne Thiebaud in California has concentrated on cafeteria goodies. Assembly lines of pies and cakes march across his canvases. Glaringly illuminated, Thiebaud's desserts seem deserted, a lonely caloric crowd untouched by human hands. To the 42-year-old artist, his paintings are both "criticism and celebration." He is offended by the impersonal sameness that results from displaying things "in great gobs." But he is attracted by the "beauty of the fluffy pies," and also their taste. "I eat chocolate pies" he confesses, "and enjoy them—sometimes."

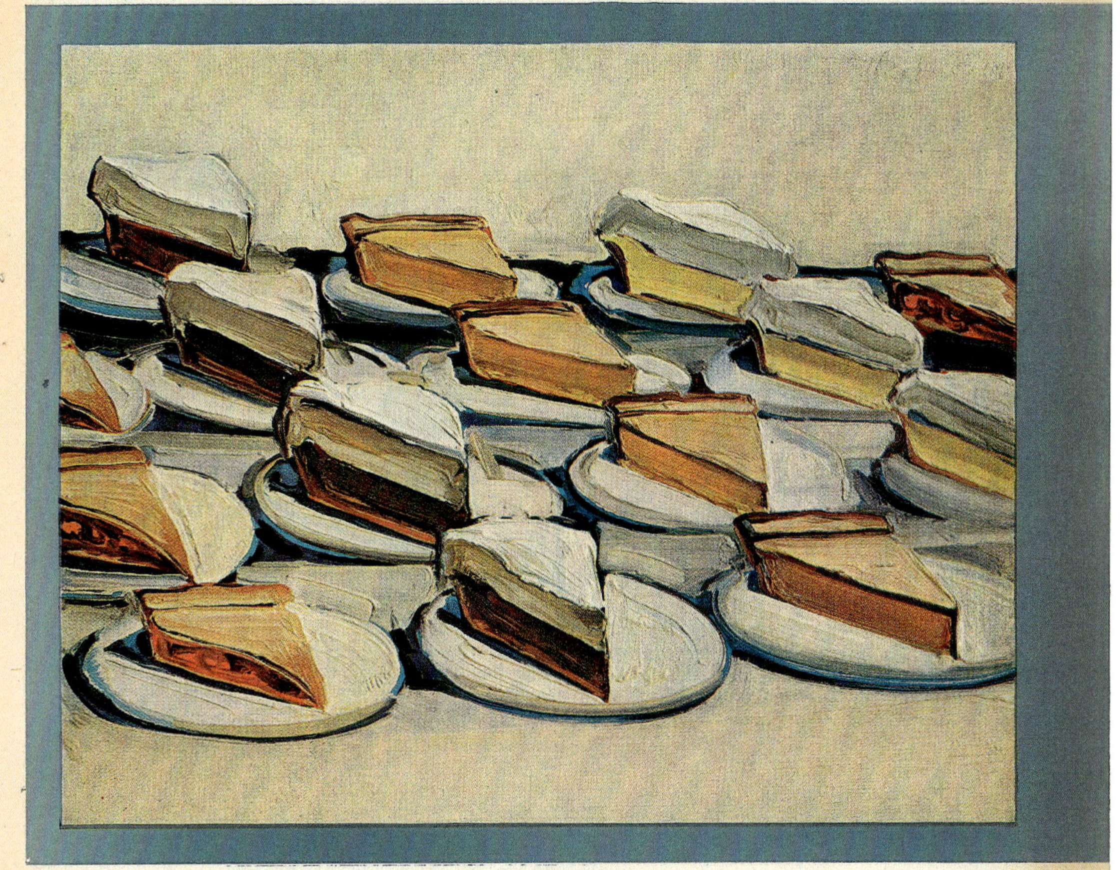

'PIES' BY WAYNE THIEBAUD

CONTINUED

9 'Something New Is Cooking', *Life Magazine*,
vol. 52, no. 24, 15 June 1962, p. 115

characterised as America's 'golden age', the 1950s had seen rapid economic growth, fuelling a booming consumer culture and a sense of optimism. However, the country would soon enter one of its decades of greatest upheaval, challenging the image it had constructed of itself. The crystallisation of Thiebaud's approach to painting occurred at the moment of transition between the Eisenhower and Kennedy eras. The deepening Cold War, epitomised by the Cuban Missile Crisis six months after Thiebaud's breakthrough exhibition in 1962, was the first of the decade's many shocks, which profoundly unsettled American culture and society. Thiebaud's own fashioning of quintessentially American subject matter aptly presented for scrutiny and contemplation a vision of Americana, rooted in its consumable objects, at a time when the country's very identity was being challenged and transformed.

Dissent was growing and times of crisis necessitated new forms of artistic expression. It was in this context that a new interest in realism, albeit one procured from popular and commercial sources, came to prominence in the art world. Pop's adoption of impersonal, manufactured objects was a statement about an uneasy abundance and the rampant consumerism that defined contemporary life in the United States. It was also a decisive rejection of Abstract Expressionism's more personal symbolism. A new generation of painters, Thiebaud foremost among them, rediscovered the outmoded genre of still-life painting as the perfect means to display the products of contemporary life for both delectation and disdain. Better yet, still life carried with it a zest of revolutionary zeal borrowed from the likes of Manet and Cézanne.

Coplans identified Pop's adoption of still life from the moment of its inception. 'Lichtenstein's painting of a hand holding a hairspray', he wrote in his review of *New Painting of Common Objects*, 'tells you nothing about a hairspray, any more than one of Cézanne's apples tells you about an apple, both are formal devices, but with an important difference. Cézanne's apple is mute, but Lichtenstein's hairspray carries a moral judgment.'[28] In the late nineteenth century, history painting, portraiture, just about any kind of painting, was understood to be a more important artistic endeavour than what was commonly dubbed the 'lowly' still life. Precisely because the genre was so overlooked, Cézanne found freedom in the depiction of common objects (see fig. 32), and apples were among his favourite. Still life's staged format served as a means of accessing the artificiality of painting itself. 'Cézanne's apple' served as shorthand for questions about the purpose of painting, how it operates and what it could achieve. Coplans finished his analogy with a critical assessment: Thiebaud, he wrote, 'lacks the guts and the total commitment of the others in this group'.[29]

Donald Judd's review of Thiebaud's debut at the Allan Stone Gallery more closely hewed to Thiebaud's intent: 'The main point', Judd wrote, 'is the existential nausea of innumerable things.'[30] During that heady summer of 1962, Thiebaud articulated his 'philosophic viewpoint' in the only artist's statement he would ever publish: 'Painting a row of cakes the way they are displayed on a lunch counter suggests some rather obvious notions about conformism, mechanized living, and mass produced culture.'[31] With the Cold

War insinuating itself even into an artist's statement, it was between the poles of 'totalitarian or utopian' that Thiebaud described his 'endless rows' in terms of 'a kind of lonely togetherness'. The melancholy of Thiebaud's lonely cupcakes is undeniably existential but not enough to satisfy his colleagues. Judd went on, 'The juiciness of the paint is a little gross; a little grossness, like a little scepticism is a little impossible.' However, instead of scepticism, Thiebaud's painterly pleasures prevailed. While his colleagues Ruscha, Warhol and Lichtenstein adopted still life as a means to dispense with modernism's assertion that painting should be about the nature of painting, Thiebaud doubled down. At a decisive moment, Thiebaud aligned himself with Cézanne and never looked back.

Like his predecessor, Thiebaud crafted his subjects with remarkably few brushstrokes. Just five, six or seven passes of his brush brought to life hot dogs so replete they feel more real than any faithful depiction. Painting from memory, he summoned your own. His is the tastiest hot dog you have ever eaten, the happiest birthday cake you have ever enjoyed. In a regression of influences so dense that they match Thiebaud's tendency to borrow from precedents, the critic Michael Kimmelman put it this way: 'What Proust wrote about Chardin's views of brown crockery and dead rabbits applies also to Mr. Thiebaud's hot dogs: "You have already experienced it subconsciously, this pleasure one gets from the sight of everyday scenes and inanimate objects, otherwise it would not have risen in your heart when Chardin summoned it in his ringing commanding accents."'[32] In his 1962 artist's statement, Thiebaud invoked 'the copper pots and clay pipes of Chardin' (see fig. 23) when he declared, 'Each era produces its own still life.'[33]

Thiebaud's affiliation with Pop Art launched his career and then plagued him for the rest of his life. His love of painting was received by critics as out-of-step or, worse yet, not very good Pop.[34] Misunderstood, but undeterred, Thiebaud committed himself to the craft of painting and dedicated his practice to common objects from his everyday life. As critics celebrated more conceptual approaches to making, as the very notion of art became ever more capacious and many pronounced painting dead, Thiebaud receded from the limelight. For the rest of his life, when you introduced Thiebaud as an artist, he always corrected you; he preferred to be known as a painter. The distinction mattered to him.

Thiebaud continued painting cakes, pies and hot dogs throughout his career, although other subjects crept onto his easel. The year after his New York debut, he turned to the human figure (see fig. 29). By the time of his first travelling exhibition in 1968, toys and tools – the painter's as well as the handyman's – had also found their way into his oeuvre. Women's cosmetics and men's haberdashery occupy complete bodies of work. His subjects kept pace with the times; as one example among many, his neckties got wider during the 1970s. By the 1980s, Thiebaud settled onto a new subject, the visual complication of San Francisco's vertiginous streets (see fig. 33). His commitment to still life, however, remained steadfast. He repeated the same subjects because each painting posed a new formal problem to be solved.

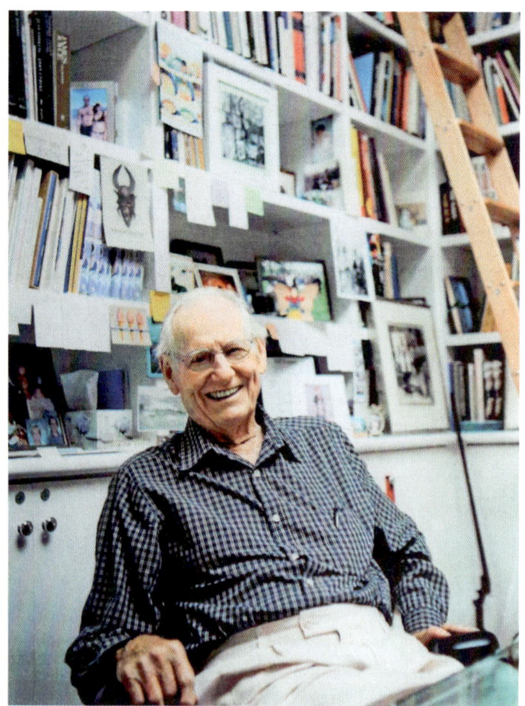

10 Wayne Thiebaud in his studio in Sacramento, 2010. Courtesy of the Wayne Thiebaud Foundation

Given his love of art history, it seems fitting that Thiebaud now shares the Courtauld's walls with the likes of Georges Seurat (1859–1891), Cézanne and, most of all, Manet's *A Bar at the Folies-Bergère* (fig. 28), the quintessential painting of modern life that he studied with love and enthusiasm throughout his long career.[35] While several of Manet's works found their way into Thiebaud's own, *A Bar at the Folies-Bergère* alone prompted at least a dozen finished paintings in addition to many direct studies. The placement of his work within view of a painting that Thiebaud considered a personal touchstone completes a cycle essential to his life's work. Looking back and assimilating the history of art always provided Thiebaud with a path forward. Now his own paintings offer the same to the next generation.[36]

From the start, Thiebaud carried the torch for painting's promise. Existing beyond the art world's latest fashion and hanging near the heroes from whom he borrowed so much, his achievement is now readily apparent. His quiet paintings portend a different future where every painter would admit that the best are open thieves. 'Steal, adapt, borrow. It doesn't matter where one takes things from. It's where one takes them to', is how the influential designer Jonathan Anderson recently restated an old adage to students at London's University for the Creative Arts.[37] Over the course of several decades, and at a time when it was woefully unpopular, Thiebaud delivered the same pronouncement to his students (fig. 10). Looking at his early work from the vantage of today, we can see him taking painting to a new place. Thiebaud was holding open a door, serving as a champion for painting and painters yet to come.

Notes

1 Harold Rosenberg, 'The Art Galleries. The Game of Illusion', *The New Yorker*, 24 November 1962, pp. 161–67, at p. 162.

2 Martin Kuz, 'Wayne Thiebaud (The First 90 Years)', *Sactown Magazine*, first appeared in the October–November 2010 issue, https://www.sactownmag.com/wayne-thiebaud-the-first-90-years/ (accessed 25 March 2025).

3 Thiebaud spoke often of his time working in commercial art and used many different descriptions of his roles. He often referred to himself as an 'ad man' and 'layout designer'. The title 'advertising art director' comes from the film *Wayne Thiebaud* by Betty Jean Thiebaud, 1971.

4 Strand 1983, pp. 188–89.

5 The de Kooning anecdote is documented in many sources, most notably in Larsen 2001. The quotes here are sourced from Thiebaud's last published interview: Kaufman 2023, p. 144.

6 Thiebaud film 1971, 3'45"–3'52".

7 Strand 1983, p. 188.

8 Betty Jean Thiebaud's narration explained, 'He longed to attend art school but could not afford to do so and therefore learned primarily from commercial and fine art associates': Thiebaud film 1971, 1'05"–1'14".

9 Interview with the author, August 2020.

10 Dervaux 2018a, p. 361.

11 Unpublished transcript of an application to a Guggenheim fellowship, 1966, Allan Stone Gallery records, 1960–2019, box 88, folder 60, Archives of American Art, Smithsonian Institution.

12 Jeff Perrone, 'Wayne Thiebaud from Phoenix to Des Moines', *Artforum*, vol. 15, no. 7, March 1977, p. 43.

13 I am indebted to Richard Shiff's observations in front of *Cup of Coffee* during the Thiebaud study day, 1–2 March 2018 at the Manetti Shrem Museum of Art, UC Davis, in conjunction with the exhibition *Wayne Thiebaud 1958–1968*.

14 At the request of the Museum of Modern Art, Wayne Thiebaud submitted an artist's statement, now archived in the Painting and Sculpture Object Files, dated 10 July 1962 (reproduced in Teagle 2018, pp. 149–50). The same statement was published in the San Francisco Chronicle on 15 July 1962. In it, he explained, 'uninterrupted single colored backgrounds are used, and this allows the brush marks to be seen more clearly and play their role. This background also suggests a kind of stainless steel, porcelain, enameled, plastic world that interests me now.'

15 Benson with Shearer 1969, p. 66.

16 Quoted in Robert Goldwater, *Primitivism in Modern Art*, New York: Vintage, 1967, p. 155.

17 John Updike, 'Sparky from St. Paul', *The New Yorker*, 22 October 2007, p. 164.

18 Adam Gopnik, 'The Art World. Window Gazing', *The New Yorker*, 29 April 1991, pp. 78–80, at p. 80.

19 Thiebaud often used the term 'cheap tricks'. One example among many is in the video 'The Artist Project: Wayne Thiebaud', *The Metropolitan Museum of Art*, 7 December 2015: https://www.metmuseum.org/perspectives/the-artist-project-wayne-thiebaud (accessed 1 March 2025).

20 Josef Albers, *Interaction of Color*, New Haven: Yale University Press, 2013 (originally published 1963), p. 4.

21 Thiebaud film 1971, 8'47"–9'04".

22 Thiebaud film 1971, 8'11"–8'15".

23 Benson with Shearer 1969, p. 66.

24 Ibid, p. 70.

25 Calvin Tomkins, 'Art or Not, It's Food for Thought', *Life Magazine*, 20 November 1964, p. 143.

26 Coplans 1962, p. 27.

27 Andrew Deener, *The Problem with Feeding Cities: The Social Transformation of Infrastructure, Abundance, and Inequality in America*, Chicago: University of Chicago Press, 2020, p. 74.

28 Coplans 1962, p. 27.

29 Ibid.

30 Donald Judd, 'In the Galleries: Wayne Thiebaud' (September 1962), in Judd 2005, p. 60.

31 Artist's statement, 1962, reproduced in Teagle 2018, p. 150.

32 Michael Kimmelman, 'Art Review. Wistful Joy in Soda-Fountain Dreams', *The New York Times*, 29 June 2001, Section E, p. 31.

33 Artist's statement, 1962, reproduced in Teagle 2018, p. 150.

34 Adam Gopnik, 'The Art World. Window Gazing', *The New Yorker*, 29 April 1991, pp. 78–80, at p. 78. Gopnik summed up Thiebaud's situation: 'his commitment to an art mediated through the eye and the mind rather than through the pervasive clichés of advertising quickly made him look *retardataire* – like a charming provincial who didn't really get it.'

35 The exhibition *Wayne Thiebaud: Art Comes from Art*, Fine Arts Museums of San Francisco, 22 March–17 August 2025 explored Thiebaud's process, which openly drew ideas from and reinterpreted old and new European and American artworks.

36 One example of Thiebaud's contemporary impact is the exhibition *Wayne Thiebaud Influencer: A New Generation*, Manetti Shrem Museum of Art, UC Davis, 3 June–12 November 2021. The exhibition presented Thiebaud's work in the context of nineteen contemporary artists.

37 Rebecca Mead, 'Steal, Adapt, Borrow: Jonathan Anderson's Designs at Loewe', *The New Yorker*, 24 March 2025, pp. 40–53, at p. 40. In his address, Anderson noted, 'This speech contains a lot of theft', a reference to the fact that the adage was in fact a re-statement from the film director Jim Jarmusch, itself borrowed from Jean-Luc Godard. It is worth noting the regression of quotes to demonstrate alternate artistic definitions of originality sourced from other traditions, which was in fact Thiebaud's practice and instruction to his students.

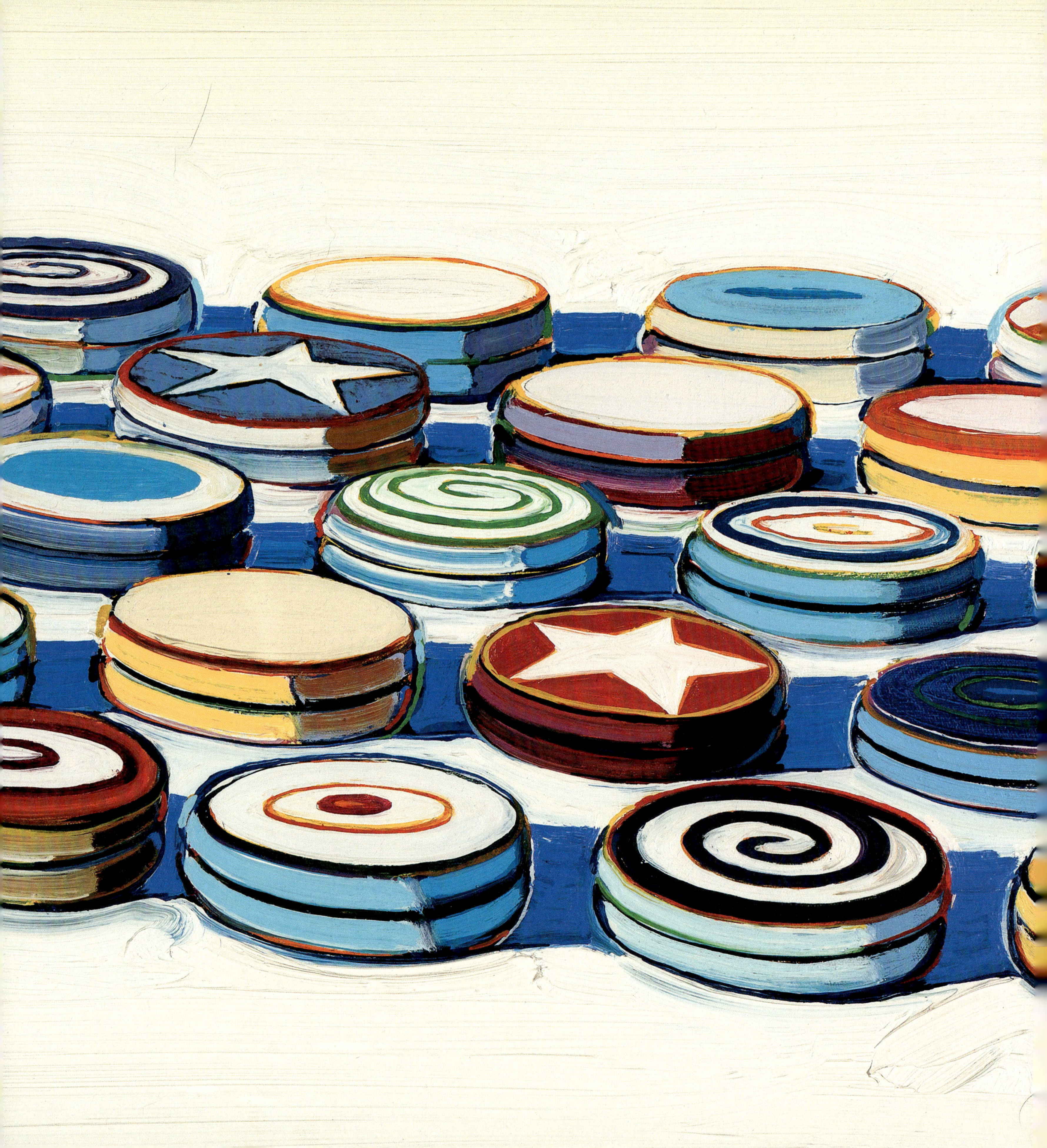

Wayne Thiebaud's Common Objects

Lucy Bradnock

In a review of Wayne Thiebaud's (1920–2021) solo exhibition at the De Young Museum in San Francisco in 1962, the visionary curator Walter Hopps (1932–2005) catalogued at some length in the pages of the newly founded contemporary art magazine *Artforum* the artist's vernacular subject matter:

> Pies, singly and in groups, sectioned and whole; layer cakes, singly and in groups, sectioned and whole; pie a-la-mode; ice cream sundaes in groups, soft drink syrup dispenser; delicatessen counter of confections, delicatessen counter of meats and cheeses; fresh meat counter; lunch counter with condiment bottles, hamburger and French fries; hamburger singly; whole barbecued chickens; barbecued ribs; lollipops in various groups; slot machines, singly and in groups; pinball machines, singly and in groups.[1]

The litany of familiar foodstuffs reads like the menu of a celebratory cook-out or a leisurely weekend wander down main street. The simplicity of Hopps's list and the familiarity of Thiebaud's subjects did not lead critics to recognise them easily, however. Indeed, those who encountered Thiebaud's work in the early years of the 1960s struggled to name and define his practice despite, or perhaps because of, its apparent straightforwardness.

Hopps emphasised not only Thiebaud's familiar subjects, both savoury and sweet, but also his tendency to isolate or present in repeated rows or groups the items he depicted, attentive to structure and pattern as well as to the object. In his loose, pen-drawn sketches and his finished painting alike, Thiebaud delineated his anecdotal subjects via particular visual strategies: clear outlines and heavy shadows that render objects at once isolated and monumental; an elevated viewpoint that invokes the sense of looking down at produce on a tabletop or lunch counter; and a tendency to abstract those surfaces, rendering them flat compositional devices more than realistic settings that recede. In the 1962 painting *Delicatessen Counter* (cat. 13), for example, the close viewpoint removes any contextualising information for the viewer, so that the horizontal lines of the shelves bisect the picture plane and flatten the pictorial space. In *Cold Cereal* (cat. 4), the angular lines of what are presumably the edges of a breakfast table trifurcate the canvas, creating a zig-zag pattern of pale blue, beige and cream triangles, resisting easy legibility as a three-dimensional object in space. It may have been this spatial ambiguity that gave critics pause regarding Thiebaud's Pop Art credentials. His paintings seemed to them at once to insist upon the three-dimensional mass of their common objects and yet, to present these objects arranged in curiously flattened pictorial spaces that tip towards the viewer or against blank and inscrutable backgrounds.

Across 1962 and 1963, Thiebaud's work would be frequently exhibited in New York and California, as critics and curators attempted to pin down quite what these compelling paintings of everyday things ought to be called. Thiebaud's work was situated variously in relation to different and sometimes contradictory styles, subjects, categories and critical debates about a broader tendency towards what appeared to be a distinctly post-war vernacular. And it appeared in group exhibitions alongside other artists whose subject

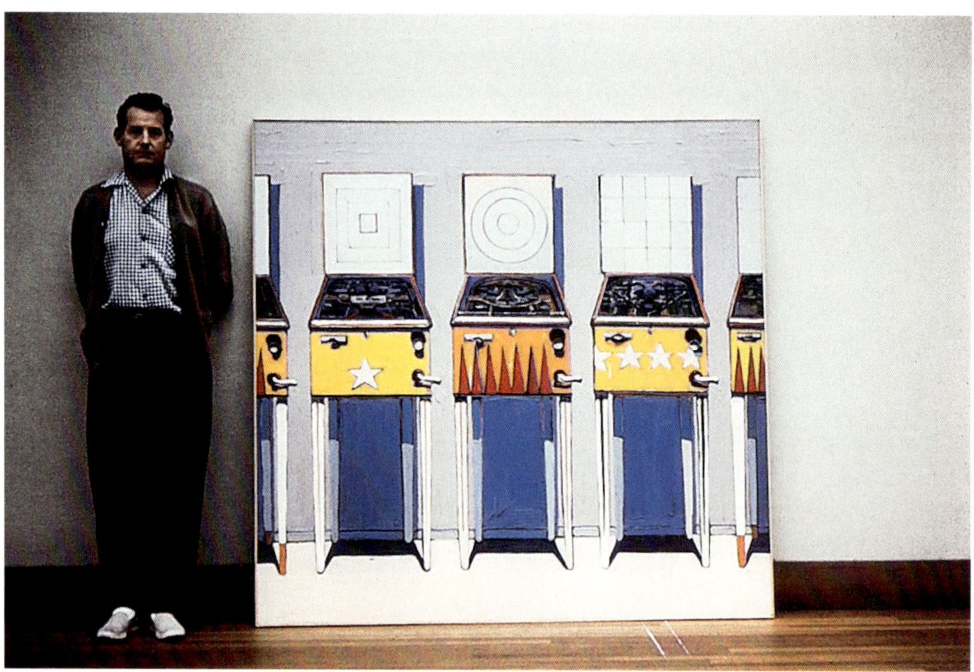

appeared drawn from the consumer landscape that Americans could see booming around them. Several critics sought to explain Thiebaud's work via recourse to the terminology of 'Pop Art', a phrase coined as early as 1954 by the British critic and curator Lawrence Alloway (1926–1990) to describe art that drew from popular culture. Pop, and the critical debates that raged around it, reached American shores via several landmark exhibitions in the first years of the 1960s, in which Thiebaud's work was a regular fixture, even as he had significant solo exhibitions of his own at the Allan Stone Gallery in New York (see fig. 5 and 6), and the De Young (fig. 11). Yet, an examination of this early critical reception reveals that Thiebaud's relationship with Pop was complicated and ambivalent, and that the matter of common objects featured in contemporary art was far from settled.

Factual artists and common objects

Around the time of Thiebaud's San Francisco exhibition, New York gallerist Sidney Janis included a single painting by Thiebaud, *Salads, Sandwiches and Desserts* (fig. 12), in his *International Exhibition of the New Realists*, where it appeared alongside Pop paintings and three-dimensional assemblage sculptures comprised of found objects. In including Thiebaud in this quite broad-church group of artists from the United States and Europe, notwithstanding the very different contexts of Sacramento and Paris, Janis counted the painter among those 'factual artists' who also went by numerous

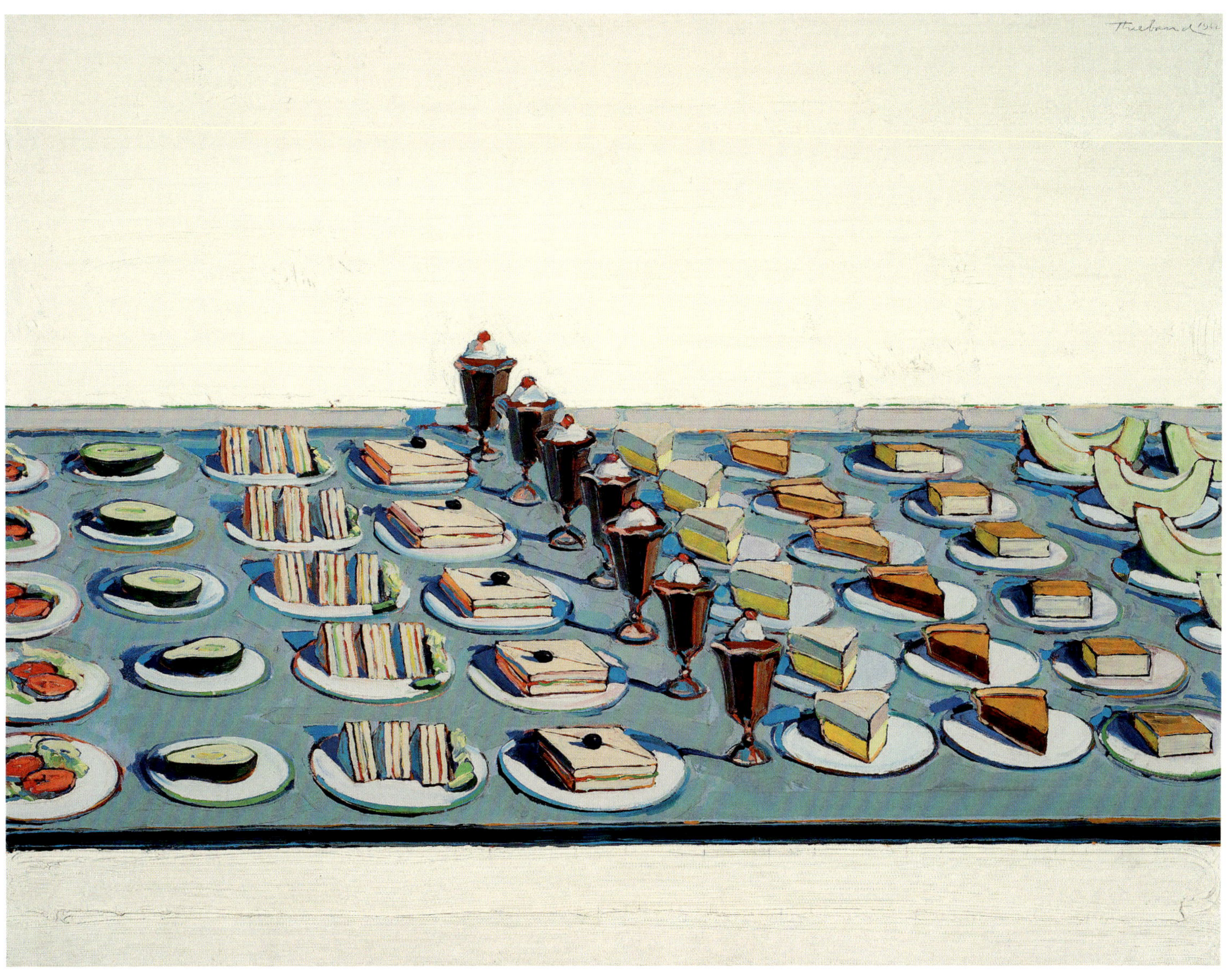

12 Wayne Thiebaud, *Salads, Sandwiches and Desserts*, 1962, oil on canvas, 140.18 × 183.36 cm, Sheldon Museum of Art, Lincoln, Nebraska

other categorisations: 'As the Abstract Expressionist became the world recognized painter of the 50s,' Janis outlined in his slim catalogue, so 'the new Factual artist (referred to as the Pop Artist in England, the Polymaterialist in Italy, and here as in France, as the New Realist) may already have proved to be the pacemaker of the 60s.'[2] Unable to settle on just one moniker to describe the work of the artists in his exhibition, he listed even more potential descriptors in an addendum: 'Other titles applied to artists with this point of view: Commonists; Neo-Dadaists; Factualists; Artists of Pop Culture and Popular Realists.' Betraying Janis's struggle to unify the works included in his exhibition, this multiple terminology also suggests that many of the works were in and of themselves difficult to classify. Indeed, Thiebaud's large painting, which depicted plates of salad leaves, avocado halves, sandwiches, chocolate pudding, pie slices and melon segments, all arranged in rows, feels anything but 'factual'. Rather, this array of dishes feels less convincing as a real-life occurrence than other arrangements that focus on a single food type or that place objects within a more clearly delineated space. Here, the tabletop upon which the rows are placed feels somehow too big and the assortment too varied to be plausible, the familiarity of the painting's contents undercut by its ambiguous quality.

Just weeks after Hopps's review of Thiebaud's work in *Artforum*, the curator opened a group show that included Thiebaud at the Pasadena Art Museum in Southern California, the first of a number of landmark exhibitions on the West Coast that are often considered the first Pop shows in the United States. The simplicity of its title, *New Painting of Common Objects*, belied the complex and sometimes contradictory impulses represented by the eight artists on display. Hopps included in the exhibition works by a combination of New York- and California-based artists, each of whom presented vernacular objects and imagery in their work. As well as works by Thiebaud, he selected paintings by Jim Dine (born 1935), Robert Dowd (1936–1996), Joe Goode (1937–2025), Phillip Hefferton (1933–2008), Roy Lichtenstein (1923–1997), Ed Ruscha (born 1937) and Andy Warhol (1928–1987), whose first solo exhibition Hopps had held at his Ferus Gallery in Los Angeles earlier that year. Although Hopps did not use the term 'Pop' explicitly, the poster designed for the exhibition by Ruscha (fig. 13) announced its consumer culture reference points in both its strident tri-colour appearance and its means of manufacture. Infamously, Ruscha opted not to design the poster himself, instead phoning in an order to a commercial printer of prize-fight posters, with the stylistic instruction to 'make it loud'.[3] Although *New Painting* 'wasn't a Pop show, per se', according to Hopps, the exhibition was quickly hailed as such by critics and has been accepted into established histories of American Pop Art.[4]

Following his assessment that Thiebaud's 'carbohydrate and starchy items seem superior to the protein, with the curious exception of the conspicuous success of hot dogs' and that his 'pies are the very best of all, even ahead of cakes', Hopps selected Thiebaud's *Five Hot Dogs* (cat. 6), *Lemon Meringue Half* (fig. 14) and *Pie a la Mode* (fig. 15), all from 1961, for inclusion in the exhibition. The trio represented Thiebaud's quintessential American subjects, as well as betraying formal tropes that would come to define his work: groups of repeated objects, and subjects that devolve into flattened bands of colour or shapes. In *Lemon Meringue Half*, for example, the biscuit base, lemon curd and soft meringue layers of the cut pie appear simultaneously as stripes that approach abstraction and as the more familiar constituent parts of the pie in its tin. That Thiebaud painted pies in full, half and individual slices suggests an interest both in shape and geometry, as well as an awareness of the act of slicing and serving.

No catalogue was published for the Pasadena exhibition, and it attracted only a few critical reviews, despite its subsequent heralding as a landmark Pop exhibition.[5] Among those that appraised the show at the time, the critic John

13 Poster for the exhibition *New Painting of Common Objects*, Pasadena Art Museum, 1962, woodtype letterpress on paper, 107.6 x 71.1 cm, Ed Ruscha Studio

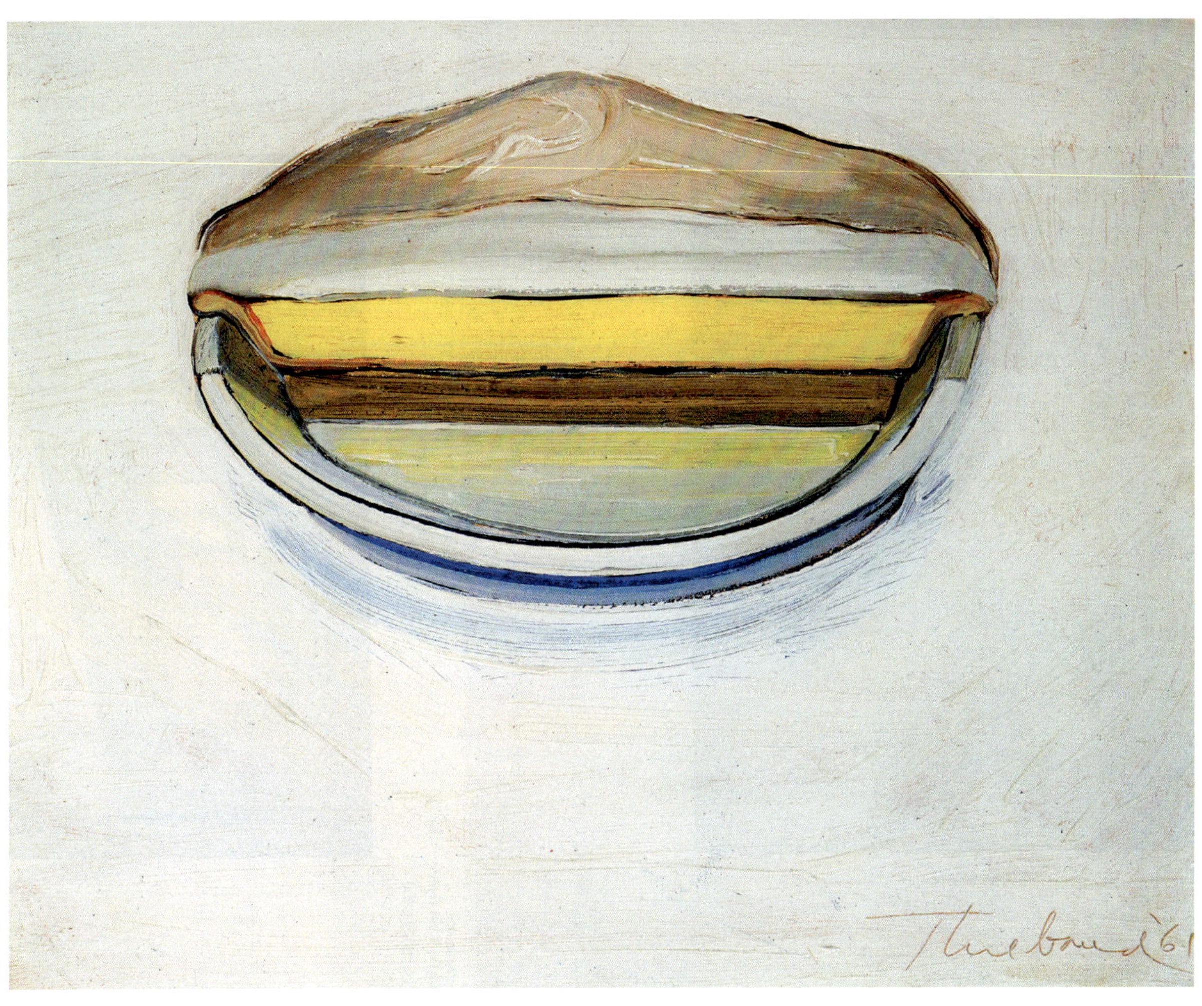

14 Wayne Thiebaud, *Lemon Meringue Half*, 1961, oil on canvas, 41 x 51.1 cm, private collection

Coplans (1920–2003), writing in *Artforum*, cited Thiebaud as a kind of odd man out, distinct from the punchy critique of consumerism that Coplans discerned in Lichtenstein's brash reproduction of advertising imagery.[6] The quietness and relative painterliness of Thiebaud's works of the early 1960s clearly seemed to Coplans to place him apart from his more obviously Pop Art peers. Certainly, they embodied a quieter and slower pace than Ruscha's garish, commercially produced poster, which feels slightly ill-suited to the timeless Americana of Thiebaud's hot dogs and pies. Recalling the show in an interview towards the end of his life, Hopps also expressed reservations about the links that his inclusion of Thiebaud implied, saying, 'I think I was quite wrong about putting Wayne Thiebaud in "New Painting of Common Objects". Thiebaud's work really relates more to the Bay Area painterly tradition of David Park and Richard Diebenkorn.'[7] Thiebaud moved in the same circles as both painters, key figures in the so-called San Francisco School, and there are clear affinities with both.

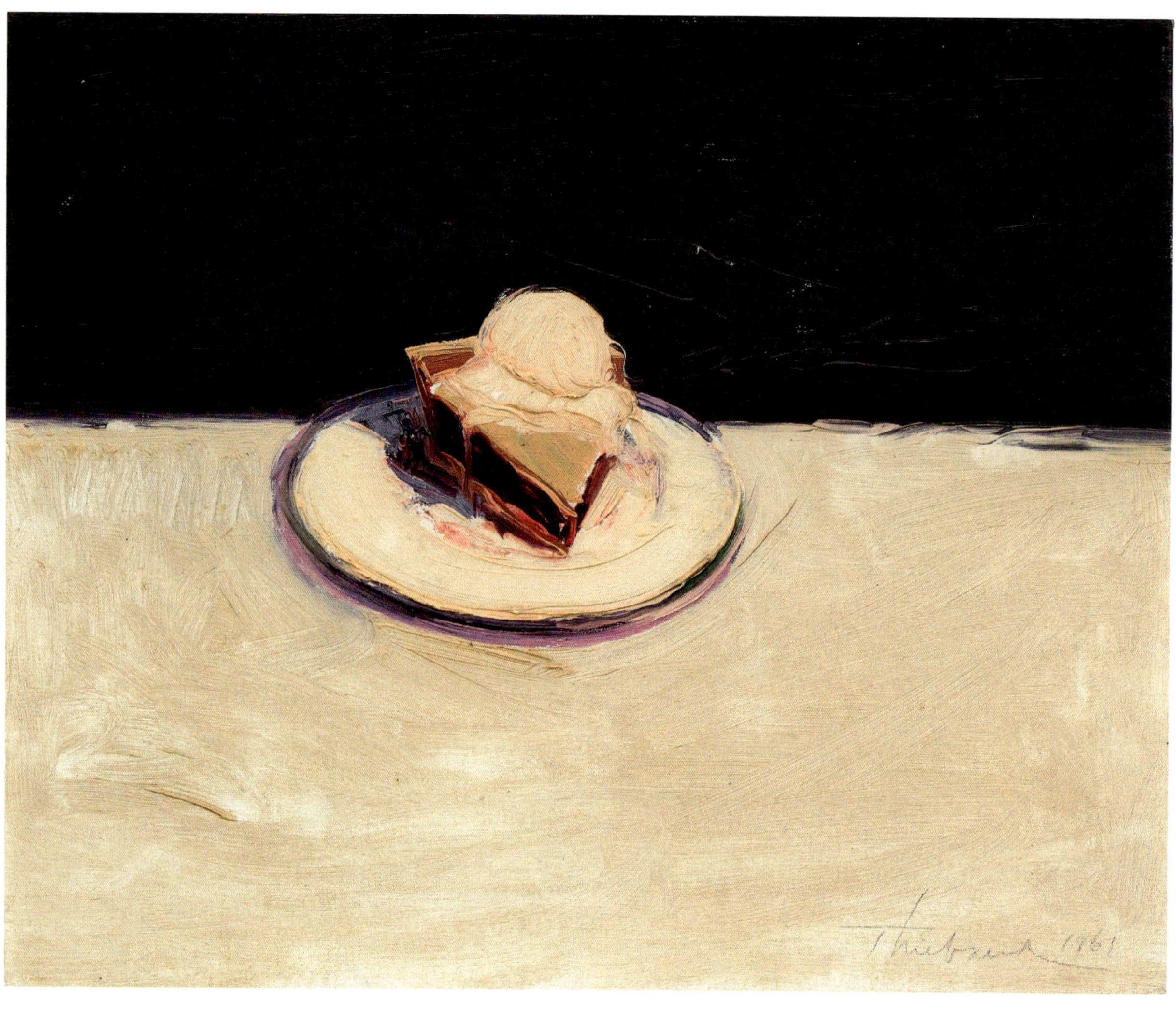

15 Wayne Thiebaud, *Pie a la Mode*, 1961, oil on canvas, 43.2 x 53.3 cm, private collection

Park (1911–1960) and Diebenkorn (1922–1993) represented an aesthetic that was a far cry from the loud design of the *New Painting* poster and many of the artists included in that exhibition. Instead, they belonged to the more subdued and painterly San Francisco School of painting. Park, a generation older than both Diebenkorn and Thiebaud, produced figurative paintings of vernacular subjects, including a small number of still-life subjects, in which Thiebaud recognised 'the feeling of bigness in very small things'.[8] In paintings such as *Brush and Comb* and *Still Life with Hammer and Pliers* (both 1956, private collection), and *Still Life with Butter Dish* (1957, private collection), Park described objects and surfaces in thick and sometimes sketchy paint strokes that render hazy the boundaries between subject and ground. In Thiebaud's *Cold Cereal* (cat. 4), similarly thick strokes delineate the shallow bowl and breakfast cereal box, rendering the edges of these objects indistinct as they

Detail of cat. 4

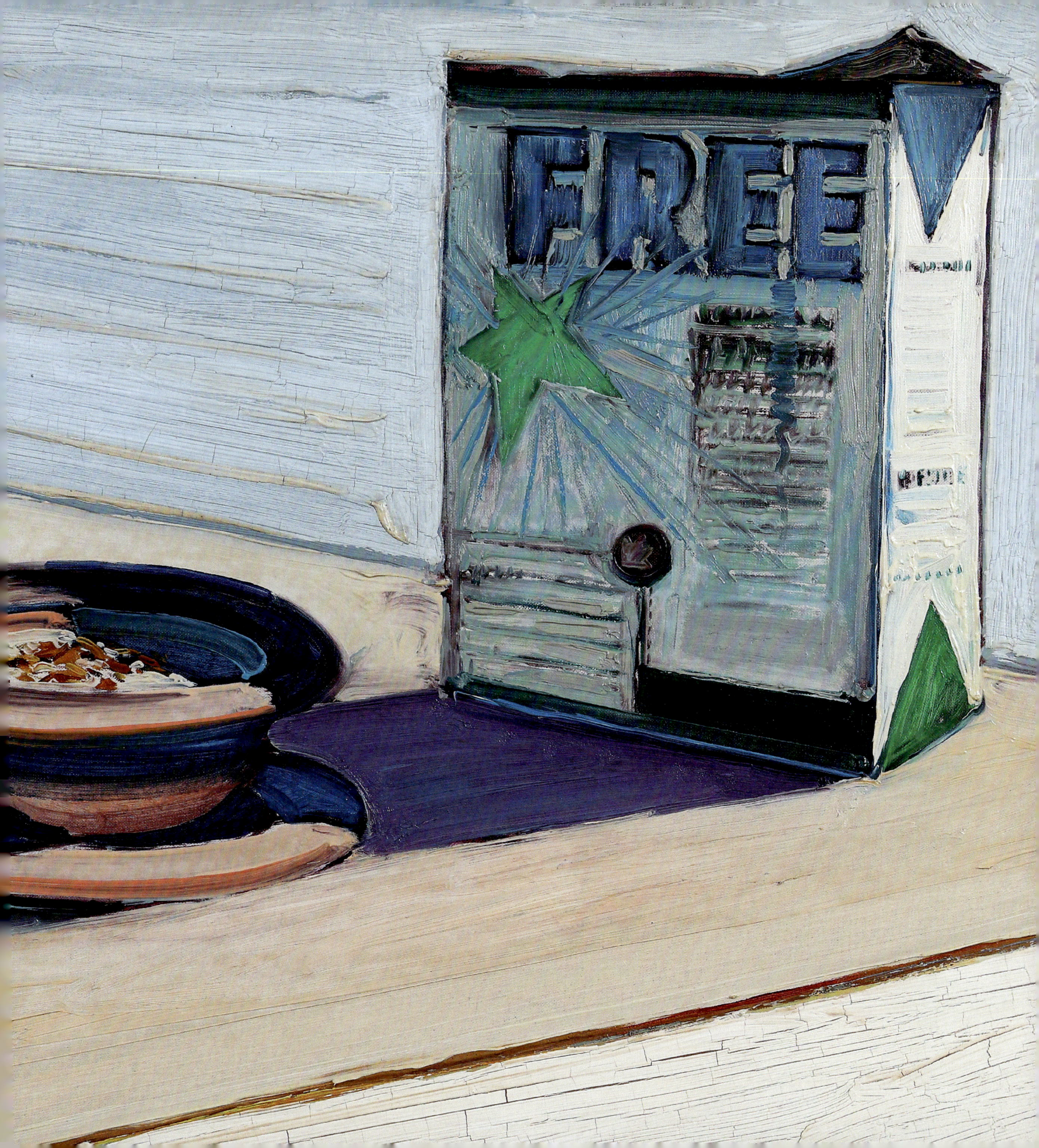

FREE

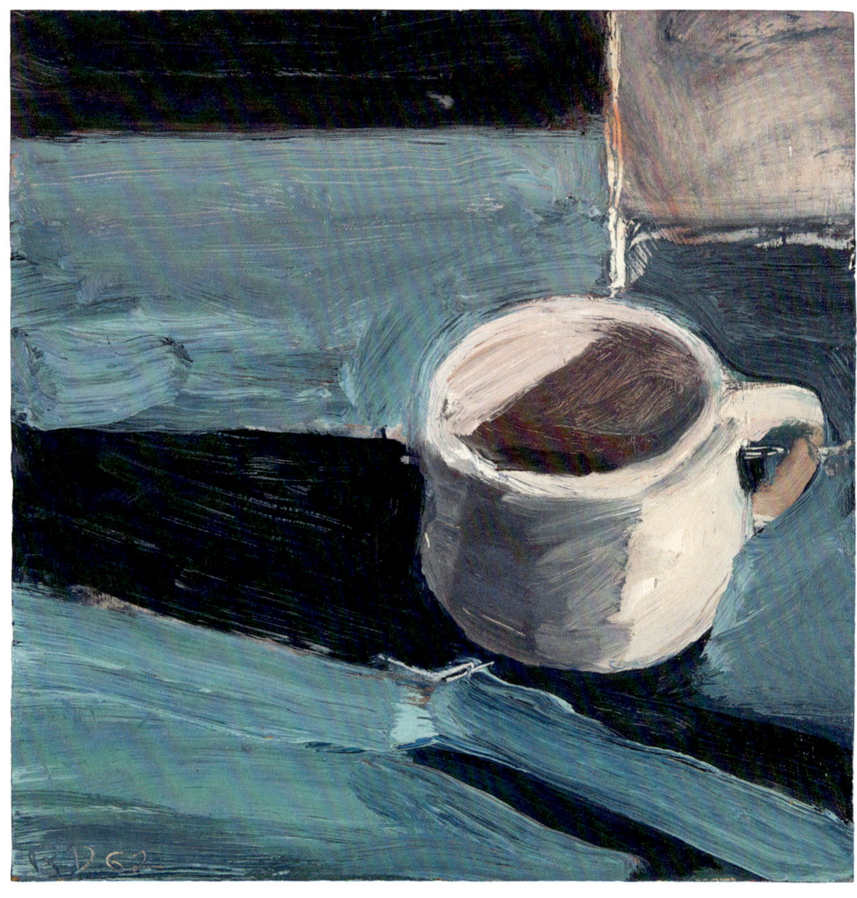

come into contact with the space of the tabletop. Diebenkorn also produced in the early 1960s several small-scale paintings of everyday objects: scissors, cups and bottles, a cigar box, a matchbook, an ashtray. These are often depicted from a high viewpoint, delineated by solid shadows and isolated on flat surfaces that tilt towards the viewer to fill the whole picture plane. In the small, square painting *Cup* (fig. 16), for example, the form of a basic white ceramic coffee cup is described in broad painterly strokes of grey and pink amidst a mid-blue ground bisected by a swatch of ink-dark green. Diebenkorn's handling of the paint is looser and more suggestive than is evident in Thiebaud's paintings of common objects from the same years, including his own small-scale *Cup of Coffee* (cat. 7). But there are clear stylistic similarities with works such as *Boston Cremes* (cat. 10), which indicate a shared interest in the way in which paint can form objects in space and in the relation between figures and ground, or objects and space. If Hopps recognised in Park and Diebenkorn Thiebaud's thick paint strokes – his ability to conjure in impasto the sweet and sticky frosting of the cakes that he depicted – the comparison might also suggest the precarious nature of Thiebaud's figuration, in which the familiarity of vernacular subject matter is belied by a concern with colour, line and balance across the picture plane. 'I don't make a lot of distinction between things like landscape or figure painting,' Thiebaud claimed, 'because to me the problems are inherently the same – lighting, color, structure, and so on.'[9]

And yet, Thiebaud did not regard the formal concerns of painting as necessarily separate from Pop's apparent interest in commercial and consumer contexts. On the one hand, he clearly understood the connection between light and space in the consumer environment: in a 1962 artist's statement later published under the title 'Is a Lollipop Tree Worth Painting?', Thiebaud pointed to the apparatus of the commercial display and shop floor to draw attention to the contemporary particularities of light, colour and space in his paintings. He invoked the

> strong display lights … which can do all kinds of goofey and wonderful things … make an object cast colored shadows, change its local color before your eyes, glow and develop a halo or imbue it with a pulsating effect. Often these things have ten, twenty, or more light sources to heighten them … used cars, diamonds, and candied apples are displayed and sold to us in this way.[10]

Similarly, he described the question of how to render space in terms of an 'ultra clear, bright, air-conditioned atmosphere that might be stirred up around the objects and echo their presence'. In line with broader twentieth-century shifts in commercial architecture and product styling,[11] Thiebaud thus understood consumerism as an inherently visual mode in which objects are shaped by their environment, which is in turn defined by light, space and colour, albeit rendered in his still-life works in thick painterly impasto.

On the other hand, several of the so-called Pop artists included in *New Painting of Common Objects* also used painterly techniques as Thiebaud did, eschewing the flat acrylic paints and screenprint reproductive technologies that are today more commonly associated with Pop. This was especially true of those based on the West Coast such as Goode, whose painting *Happy Birthday* (fig. 17) was included in the exhibition and would feature on the cover of *Artforum* to accompany that magazine's review of the show. In its unusual combination of abstraction and realism, Goode's work provides a useful comparison with Thiebaud's for the way in which it appeals both to avant-garde innovation and to old-timey Americana. *Happy Birthday* comprises a large, monochromatic painting in lilac pink in front of which a real glass milk bottle, also painted, sits on a low plinth, the work invoking at once the abstract painting prevalent in the United States in the post-war decades and the familiar sight of milk on a doorstep. In a similar manner, Thiebaud's subjects feel quintessentially American: hot dogs, pumpkin pie, gumballs. If gesturing towards a cosy American scene, however, Goode's painting does so in a rather detached, deadpan manner, sharing a sense of ambivalence with Thiebaud's work.

This sense of narrative strangeness and painterly solidity sets Thiebaud and Goode apart not only from New York artists such as Warhol and Lichtenstein but also from West Coast peers such as Ruscha, whose work was included in *New Painting of Common Objects* alongside Thiebaud's, but depicted signage, logos and

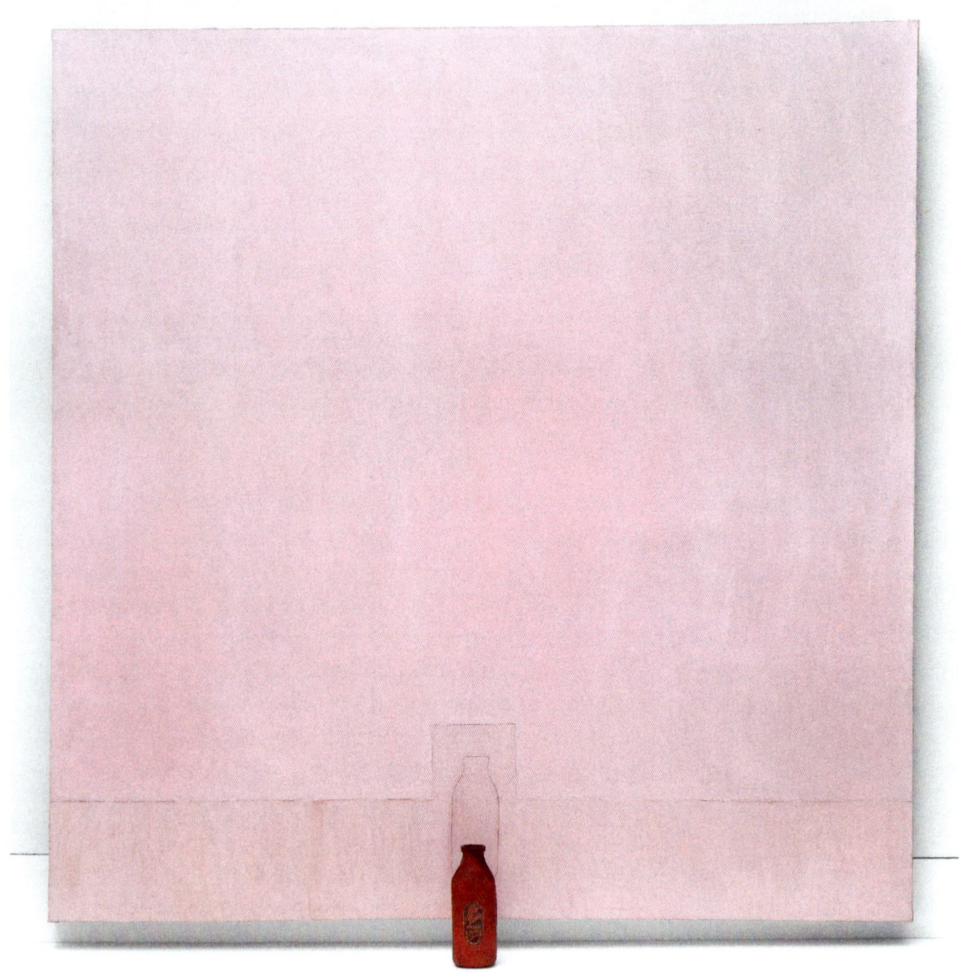

consumer packaging (see fig. 7). More akin to the kind of work that Thiebaud was producing, though notably absent from the exclusively male roster of *New Painting of Common Objects* and subsequent Pop exhibitions, was the work of the Los Angeles-based artist Vija Celmins (born 1938), who, between 1962 and 1965, painted functional objects against plain grey backgrounds in her Venice Beach studio. Works such as *Eggs* (fig. 18) sit somewhere between the expressive domestic paintings of Park and Diebenkorn and the more brightly coloured lunch counters invoked by Thiebaud, even as Celmins's frequent depiction of small electric appliances (heater, fan, desk lamp, television, frying pan) emphasised the quotidian efficiencies of modern domestic existence. Just as

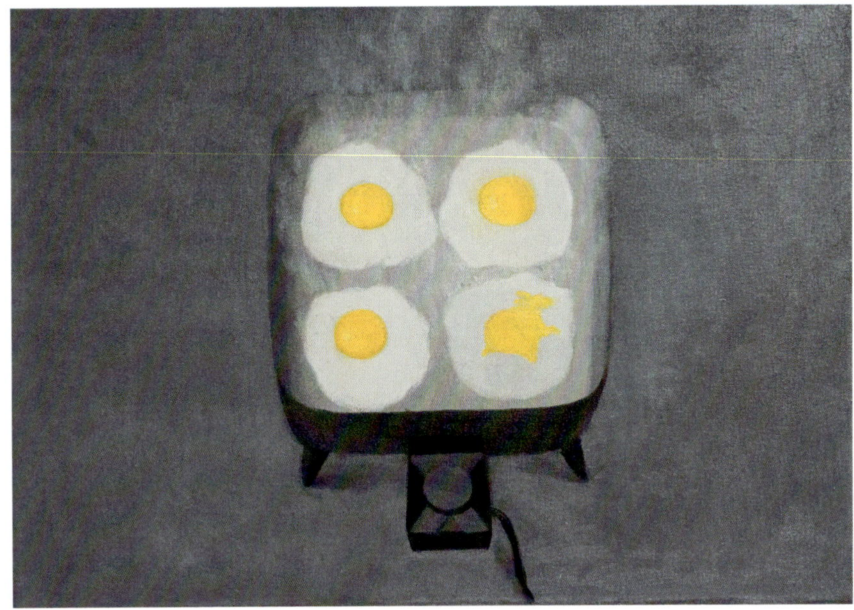

18 Vija Celmins (born 1938), *Eggs*, 1964, oil on canvas, 61.6 x 89.5 cm, Museum of Contemporary Art San Diego

Thiebaud's works stage foodstuff on plates, in dishes and arrayed behind glass in lunch and delicatessen counters, so Celmins contains her frying eggs within the borders of the shallow electric frying pan, flattening them for display to a viewer or consumer by adopting a high viewpoint that reminds us, as Thiebaud's works do also, of the intimate link between food product and its tempting display. In Celmins's hands, the dramatic tilt of the square pan and its cord trailing to the bottom edge of the painting mimic the form of the vertical electric signage ubiquitous in 1960s California. Yet, the blank background offers little in the way of context or scale, so that we remain uncertain whether these eggs are being cooked at home or for commercial diners.

Six Painters and the Object, and Six More

The year after Thiebaud's work was included in *New Painting of Common Objects*, it appeared in another early Pop Art show alongside many of the same names as in the Pasadena exhibition. Mounted at the Los Angeles County Museum of Art by Alloway, *Six More* was intended as an addendum to the exhibition *Six Painters and the Object*, which travelled to Los Angeles from the Solomon R. Guggenheim Museum in New York.[12] While the New York iteration had included such East Coast artists as Warhol, Lichtenstein and James Rosenquist (1933–2017), the Los Angeles addition showcased West Coast artists in whom Alloway observed a parallel interest in everyday subjects, including Thiebaud. In the slender catalogue that accompanied the exhibition, Alloway used the term 'Pop Art' to describe their work and invoked the democratising impulse of that artform, writing that, 'By using signs and objects from the man-made environment, pop artists are evoking that part of the culture that we all share, and have all grown

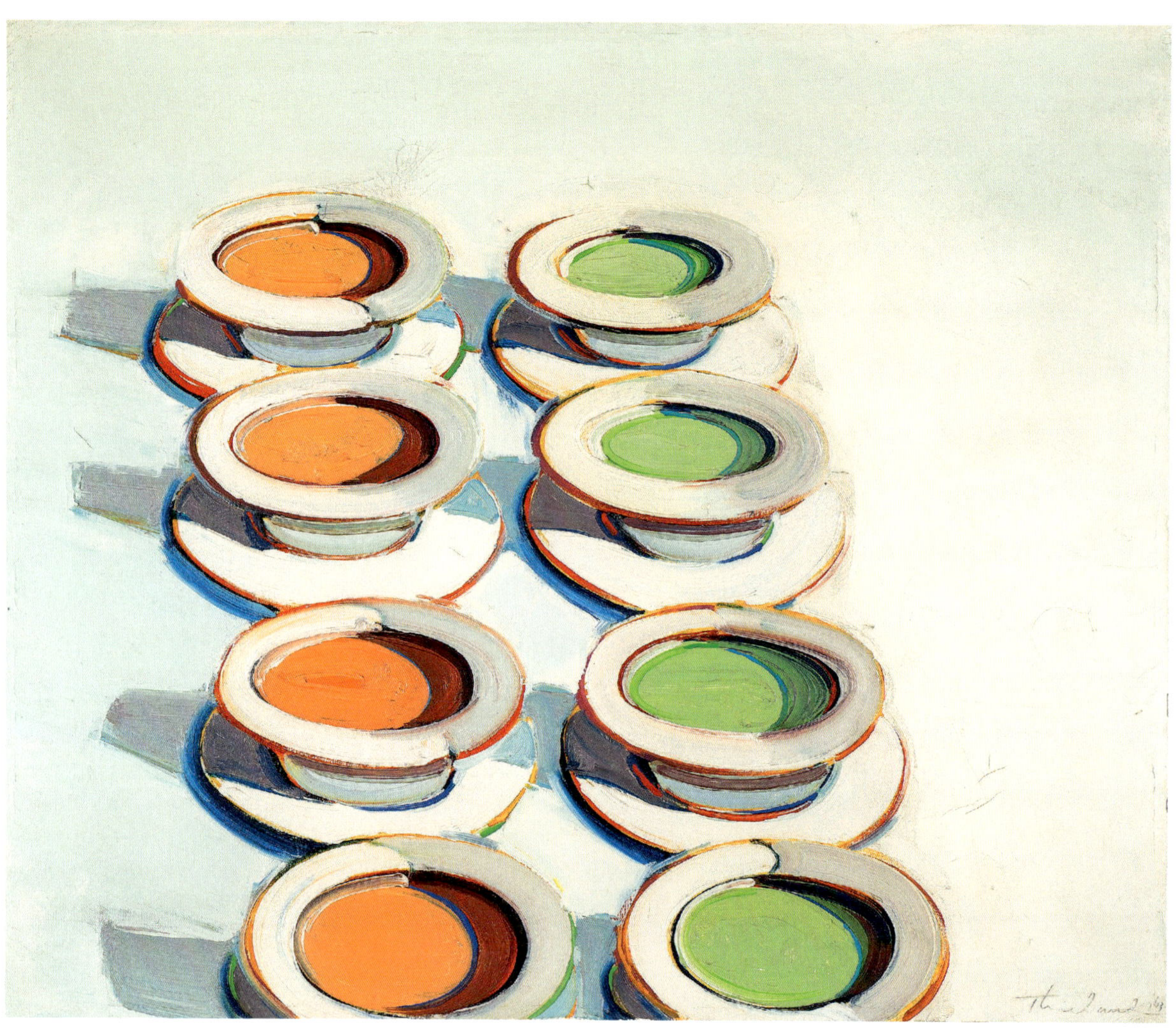

19 Wayne Thiebaud, *Cream Soups*, 1963, oil on canvas, 75.6 x 91.4 cm, private collection

up with.'[13] The seven paintings by Thiebaud that were included in the exhibition appeared to conform to this definition in their depiction of quotidian and economically accessible objects: delicatessen and cake counters (cat. 14 and 17), a jawbreaker machine and coin-operated supermarket horse, cream soups (fig. 19), sugary-looking yo-yos and cold cereal (cat. 4). In his essay, Alloway accordingly hailed Thiebaud 'a laureate of lunch counters and diners' – an improvement on the more banal moniker given by critic Alfred Frankenstein, who had flippantly labelled Thiebaud the 'hungriest artist in California'.[14] Alloway situated Thiebaud within a European lineage, drawing out dual reference points: the first in the historical still-life paintings of Jean-Siméon Chardin (1699–1779) and Pierre Bonnard (1867–1947), the second in a quintessentially American landscape, the banal non-places of 'the anonymous, continuous highway culture that crosses the United States'.[15] Thiebaud's work was thus positioned as at once

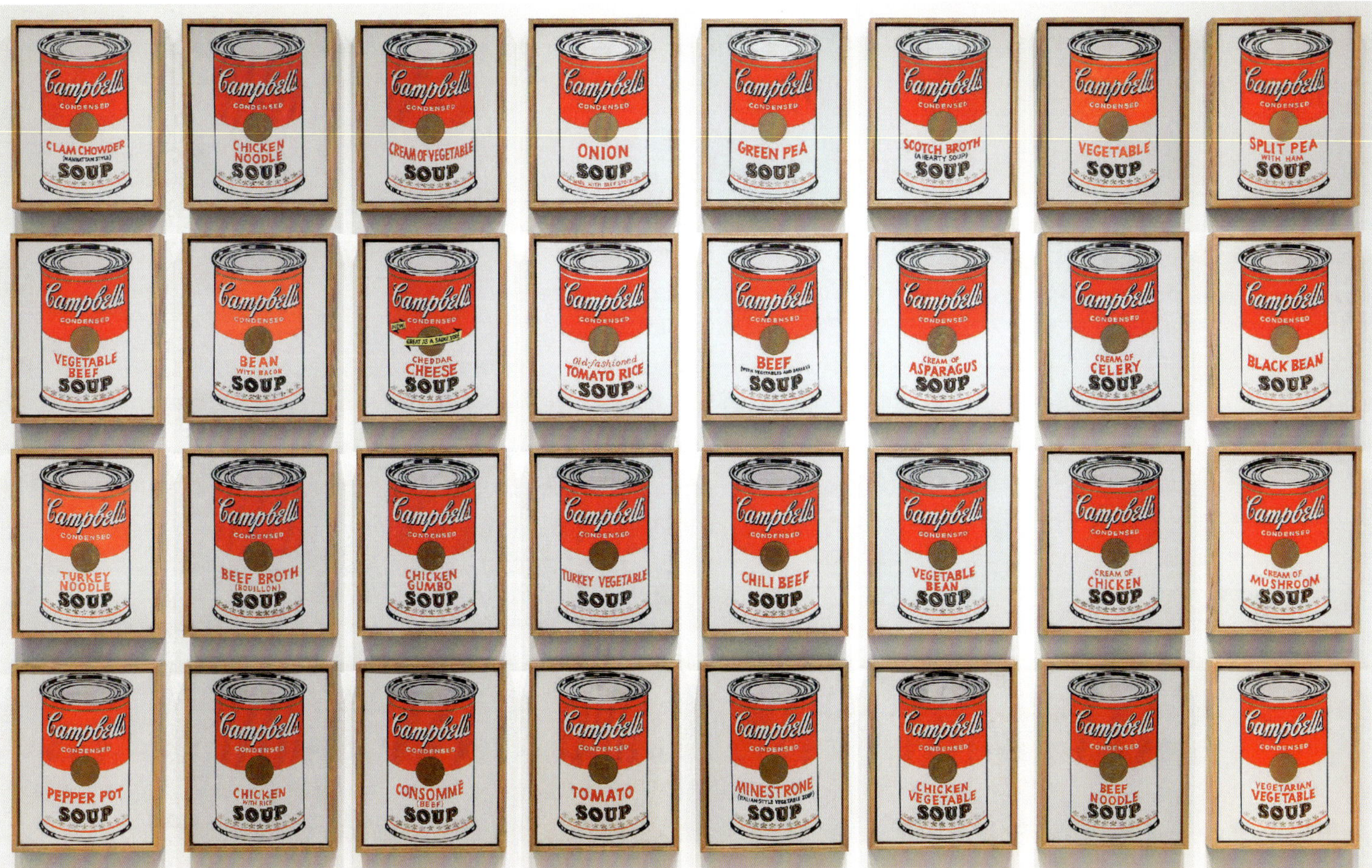

20 Andy Warhol (1928–1987), *Campbell's Soup Cans*, 1962, acrylic with metallic enamel paint on canvas, 32 panels, each panel 50.8 x 40.6 cm, Museum of Modern Art, New York

timeless and quintessentially of its time and place, both universal and distinctly local. Herein lay some of the tensions and contradictions that Thiebaud's inclusion in these early Pop Art exhibitions laid bare.

As other critics had done in their responses to *New Painting of Common Objects*, so reviewers of Alloway's exhibition expressed reservations about the unifying claims being made: addressing *Six Painters and the Object* and *Six More*, the writer Don Factor concluded that 'the generalizations made about "Pop Art" have very little to do with the work exhibited'.[16] Looking back on those early years of the decade from the position of 1966, Philip Leider reiterated those contemporaneous voices who had expressed doubt about the usefulness of the term 'Pop Art' to describe works made by painters working in California. In a reflection published in *Artforum*, he reminded readers that 'all of the Pop artists might make "new paintings of common objects" but not all of the new painters of common objects could easily be classified as Pop artists'.[17]

As Leider suspected, Thiebaud's work of the early 1960s was at odds with many of his New York Pop peers, despite their inclusion in many of the same exhibitions. The distinction is evident in a comparison of Thiebaud's painting *Cream Soups* (fig. 19), which was shown in *Six More*, and Warhol's contemporaneous *Campbell's Soup Can* paintings (fig. 20), two of which had featured in *New Painting of Common Objects*, and all 32 of which had comprised the artist's first solo exhibition, held at Hopps's Los Angeles Ferus Gallery in 1962. Then as now, soup represented the quintessential ordinary foodstuff, ubiquitous and accessible to most Americans, purchased for roughly ten cents a can in grocery stores and served – either canned or homemade – at most lunch counters and diners across the country. Each of Warhol's soup can paintings depicts one of the well-known brand's 32 soup flavours, delineating in acrylic paint and metallic enamel Campbell's signature red-and-white label with gold seal design. The graphic lines emphasise the cans as flat images rather than three-dimensional objects, making the paintings' subject advertising posters as much as actual cans. Where Warhol was interested in packaging and marketing, Thiebaud's viscous soups are shown already decanted into individual bowls, the flavours discernible not via logo and labelling but colour: the orange on the left we might assume to be cream of tomato, while the green soup on the right of the painting could be cream of asparagus or green pea (all three Campbell's flavours, though Thiebaud's soups might just as well be homemade). Thus, Warhol and Thiebaud implicitly locate their subjects in different spaces: one, the brightly lit supermarket aisle, the other, the diner or luncheonette. Warhol even invoked the supermarket display in his Ferus Gallery exhibition, in which his soup can paintings were placed on a shelf that ran the length of the gallery, allowing visitors to peruse the paintings just as they would products in a store. Thiebaud, by comparison, favoured in his solo exhibitions of this period a conventional display style more akin to traditional still-life works.

To 1960s audiences, by comparison, Thiebaud's subjects might well have read as nostalgic, given the vast visual and material shifts in the consumer landscape, the 'plastic postwar world' heralded by *Newsweek* in 1943.[18] In Alloway's terms, they seemed to represent 'the culture that we … have all grown up with',[19] rather than the new cultural forms emerging rapidly in the 1960s. Indeed, Thiebaud himself was well aware that his paintings captured a moment in time, observing that 'commonplace objects are constantly changing'.[20] The 1950s and 1960s in America were characterised by a close attention to and reimagining of the common objects of American domestic and consumer existence, driven by economic boom and new material technologies. The demand for ease and efficiency in modern homes and eateries was manifested in the increased popularity of melamine tableware, wipeable Formica and vinyl surfaces, and moulded and vacuum-formed plastics shaped into display cases and advertising signage. Glass milk bottles on doorsteps began to be replaced by new paperboard cartons lined with plastic. These new consumer technologies are largely absent from Thiebaud's paintings, and he rarely referenced explicitly this new economic landscape of things, tending to depict instead more traditional forms of food presentation, including glass and ceramic tableware and vessels. But it is nonetheless possible to view Thiebaud's still-life works in the context of this backdrop of consumer change and a close post-war attention to the role of everyday objects in shaping modern living. His repeated plates and rows of standardised food items might thus be read in relation to abundance and the increased mass production of food in the post-war period, one in which consumers found themselves between the homey domesticity of traditional lunch spots offering homemade fare and the new and more homogenised mass cultural eatery that augured the arrival of fast food. Thiebaud himself pointed to this potential interpretation, writing in his artist's statement that, 'Painting a row of cakes the way they are displayed on a lunch counter suggests some rather obvious notions about conformism, mechanized living, and mass-produced culture.'[21]

Some critics also interpreted Thiebaud's still-life works in terms of their capacity for critique. Writing in *Art News* on the occasion of Thiebaud's first New York exhibition in 1962, the critic Thomas Hess interpreted his work as a biting social commentary aimed at America's bland and artificial consumer culture in which 'layer cakes troop down air-conditioned shelving like cholesterol angels'.[22] For Hess, Thiebaud's bright colouring and the viscosity of his paint were directly related to the sickliness of his subjects, designed to encourage disgust in their viewers, faced with seductive but ultimately unsatisfying products: 'He preaches revulsion', Hess wrote, 'by isolating the American food habit.' Yet, Thiebaud resisted this singular and too-easy interpretation, emphasising instead the potential for his vernacular subjects to encourage a form of uncertainty, even empathy, with his subjects. 'In addition,' he wrote, 'there are some surprising things which are present ... how alone these endless rows can be ... a kind of lonely togetherness ... each piece of pie has a heightened loneliness of its very own giving it a uniqueness and specialness in spite of its regimentation.'[23] Far from the 'endless anonymity of mass production'[24] that Factor had recognised in Warhol's soup can paintings, then, Thiebaud invokes a sense of personal, even moral, investment in the products and objects that he painted.

Thiebaud also described his approach to vernacular subjects in terms of an investment in their potential to become disquieting: 'Common objects', he declared, 'become strangely uncommon when removed from their context and ordinary way of being seen.'[25] The everyday objects in his paintings are isolated from their surroundings, presented in what critic Nancy Marmer would describe as 'hygienically vacant settings'.[26] This has the effect of both elevating them and rendering them odd, an effect reinforced by the heavy outlines and blue-tinged shadows that feature in many of the paintings from the early 1960s. Goode's works have a similar effect, according to Ruscha, who wrote of his peer that 'Joe realized that lowly, mundane objects could be funny and terrifying at the same time, and could be beautiful devices for making paintings.'[27] There is in both painters' work the unsettling sense of a strange story lurking just beneath the surface, although Thiebaud's feels less ironic than Goode's.

Pop in common

With his work linked firmly to the bicoastal development of Pop Art by means of its inclusion in Hopps's and Alloway's exhibitions, it is perhaps unsurprising that Thiebaud would feature in a further landmark exhibition of Pop Art in the autumn of 1963: *Pop Art U.S.A.*, curated by Coplans at the Oakland Art Museum. Once again, the curatorial logic behind the Oakland exhibition, elucidated in a catalogue essay by Coplans that was concurrently published in the pages of *Artforum*, broke down in relation to Thiebaud's work, or at least resolved into a distinctly baggy category: Coplans identified in American Pop Art an emphasis on mass media (the comic strip, advertising, Hollywood) and a determined dissociation from the European artistic tradition that Sidney Janis had proposed just a year earlier.[28] Neither could reasonably apply to Thiebaud's paintings and, although Coplans's article included a reproduction of Thiebaud's *Jawbreaker Machine* (1963, private collection), his work was not discussed in the essay itself, an acknowledgement perhaps that definitions of Pop were already narrowing and becoming more concretely tied to fast-paced and superficial consumer signs and reproductive technologies. Yet, even in 1965, as Marmer described California Pop for a survey publication edited by the curator and art historian Lucy Lippard, she included Thiebaud as central to this regional manifestation of the tendency, firmly aligning Thiebaud's 'cafeteria goodies and his neon-lit bakeshop specials' with Pop Art even as she acknowledged their equal relation to the Bay Area figurative school.[29] If Pop more conventionally came to marshal the commercial reproductive technologies of commercialism to depict commercial subjects (think Ruscha's *New Painting* poster), Thiebaud, Marmer explained, took paint as close to the matter of his subjects as it could go – as Thiebaud put it, 'white, gooey, shiny, sticky oil paint spread out on top of a painted cake "becomes" frosting'.[30]

Even as Thiebaud's work was central to the early staging of Pop Art in the United States, via its inclusion in landmark exhibitions like *New Painting of Common Objects*, *Six More* and *Pop Art U.S.A.*, it bore an uneasy relationship to the commercial tendencies often associated with Pop Art, resisting Pop's investment in a landscape of signage that delineated the communications network. His work was both painterly and carefully drawn, his paint thick but his outlines crisp, his colours bright yet his tone nostalgic. Thiebaud's early, if brief, experience drawing animations for Walt Disney Studios might at first blush invite us to align his practice with the work of artists such as Lichtenstein, whose scaled-up paintings of comic books meticulously reproduced the sharp lines, bright colours and Ben Day dots of newsprint comic strips. Thiebaud's fondness for seriality and repetition both within and across different works might also align him with Pop Art. Despite these affinities, however, Thiebaud professed himself less interested in the decorative flatness of his subjects or their participation in an economy of signs than in what he termed their 'positional relationship',[31] that is, a deep exploration of objects' relation to each other and of our relation to them. Thiebaud's common objects function first and foremost as exercises in painting and in object-centred empathy, an invitation to the viewer to read emotion, memory and personal narrative into simple objects. Thiebaud elaborated to explain that 'a positional relationship, what a shift of weight does, how near or far something is, those judgments depend upon our capacity to transfer our empathy into objects and allow us to "feel" their form and structure'.

The positions of Thiebaud's still-life works in relation to Pop Art was one of ambivalence rather than opposition, and his inclusion in these landmark American Pop exhibitions in California represents more than a curatorial misstep. Rather, it suggests that, in the early 1960s, the category of Pop was a nebulous and expansive one that could include expressive, ambiguous and even semi-abstract works as well as more slick depictions of logos, products and signs. Although it would later become associated with mechanical reproduction – screen-printing in particular – Pop was predominantly associated, in its early manifestations, with painting and Pop exhibitions often included works by artists who did not align themselves with the term or whose work, like Thiebaud's, had affinities with several different styles. This was perhaps particularly the case on the West Coast, where painters' interest in common objects was informed by earlier painterly traditions and a merging of abstraction and figuration, and where artistic practice was arguably less subject to the vicissitudes of the market. Such creative expansiveness, in which familiar things could carry multiple meanings, was characteristic of a moment in which the intertwined status of art and of common objects alike remained unresolved.

Notes

1 Walter Hopps, 'Wayne Thiebaud', *Artforum*, vol. 1, no. 4, September 1962, p. 43.

2 Sidney Janis ed., *International Exhibition of the New Realists*, exh. cat. Sidney Janis Gallery, New York, 1962, n.p.

3 Walter Hopps and Hans Ulrich Obrist, 'Walter Hopps Hopps Hopps: Talks with Hans Ulrich Obrist', *Artforum*, vol. 34, no. 6, February 1996, p. 106.

4 Hopps interview with Jim Edwards in Brauer 2001, p. 43.

5 The museum produced a portfolio of mimeographs by five artists (Dine, Dowd, Goode, Hefferton, Ruscha) to accompany the exhibition but Thiebaud was not included. The Pasadena Art Museum purchased just one work from the exhibition, by Dowd.

6 Coplans 1962.

7 Hopps interview with Jim Edwards in Brauer 2001, p. 45.

8 Nancy Boas, *David Park: A Painter's Life*, Berkeley: University of California Press, 2012, p. 189.

9 Tsujimoto 1985, p. 41.

10 Artist's statement, 1962, reproduced in Teagle 2018, pp. 149–50. Originally submitted to the Museum of Modern Art, New York, as part of the museum's acquisitions process, the statement was published in the *San Francisco Sunday Chronicle* on 15 July 1962, p. 29.

11 Jim Heimann ed., *Shop America: Midcentury Storefront Design, 1938–1950*, Taschen, 2007.

12 *Six More*, Los Angeles County Museum of Art, 24 July–25 August 1963.

13 Alloway 1963, n.p.

14 Alfred Frankenstein, 'Impressive Shows at Legion of Honor', *San Francisco Chronicle*, 29 December 1961, p. 23.

15 Alloway 1963, n.p.

16 Factor 1963, p. 13.

17 Philip Leider, 'Joe Goode and the Common Object', *Artforum*, vol. 4, no. 7, March 1966, p. 24.

18 'Test-Tube Marvels of Wartime Promise a New Era in Plastics', *Newsweek*, cited in Stephen Philips, 'Plastics', in Beatriz Colomina, Annmarie Brennan and Jeannie Kim eds, *Cold War Hothouses: Inventing Postwar Culture from Cockpit to Playboy*, Princeton: Princeton Architectural Press, 2004, p. 97.

19 Alloway 1963, n.p.

20 Benson with Shearer 1969, p. 70.

21 Artist's statement, 1962, reproduced in Teagle 2018, p. 150.

22 Hess 1962, p. 17.

23 Artist's statement, 1962, reproduced in Teagle 2018, p. 150.

24 Factor 1963, p. 13.

25 Tsujimoto 1985, p. 51.

26 Nancy Marmer, 'Pop Art in California', in Lippard 1966, p. 153.

27 Edward Ruscha, 'Appreciation', in Bruce Guenther ed., *Joe Goode*, exh. cat. Orange County Museum of Art, Newport Beach, California, 1997, p. 9.

28 John Coplans, 'Pop Art, USA', *Artforum*, vol. 2, no. 4, October 1963, p. 28.

29 Nancy Marmer, 'Pop Art in California', in Lippard 1966, p. 153.

30 Ibid, citing Thiebaud's 1962 artist's statement.

31 Lewallen 1989, p. 2.

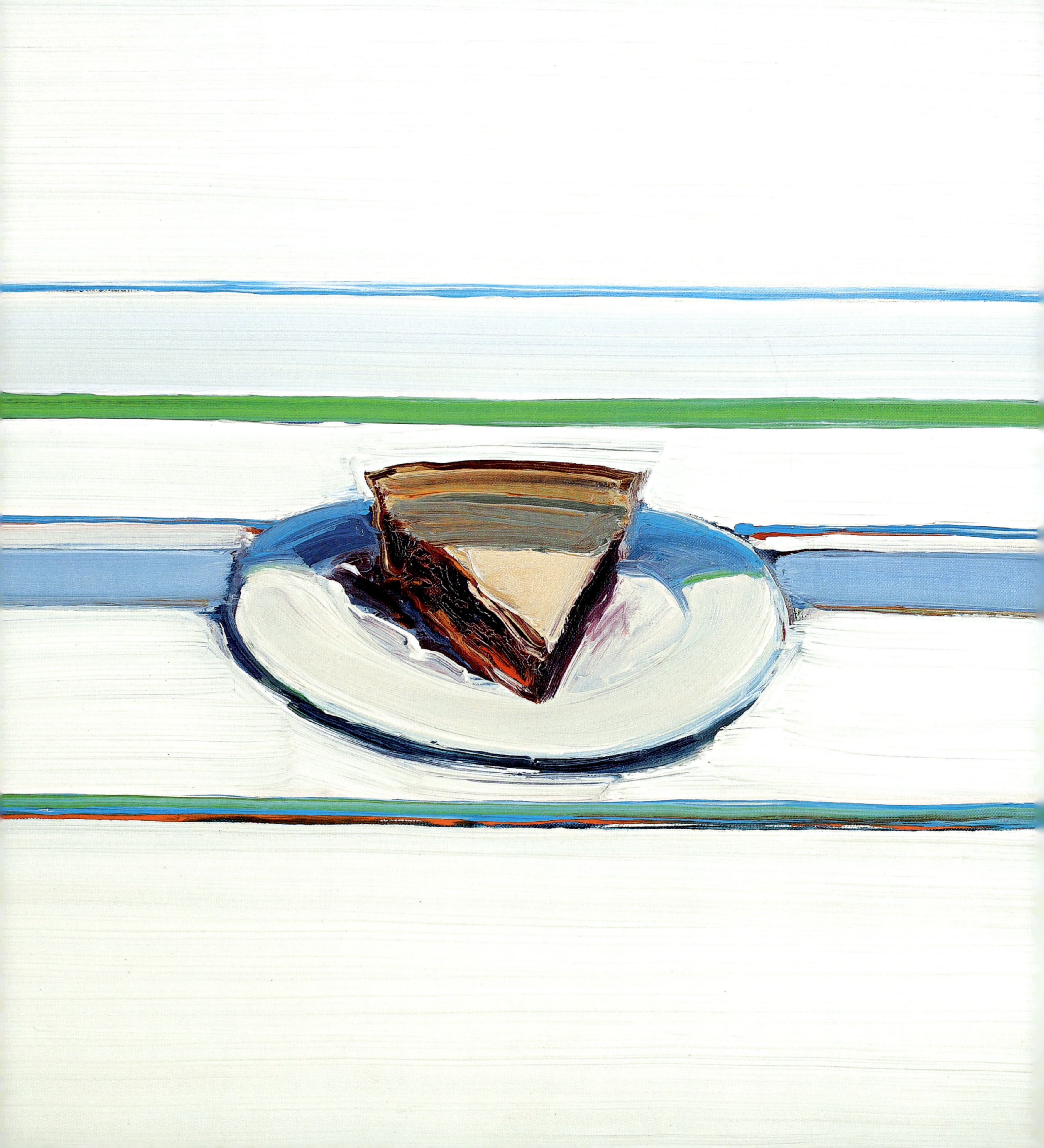

The Very Being of the Image

Richard Shiff

'I didn't think of myself as a Pop artist', Wayne Thiebaud (1920–2021) insisted.[1] Yet, many viewed him as Pop, given his bold presentation of commonplace objects.[2] Thiebaud reasoned that the primary exemplars of the Pop style worked from sources in photography; more specifically, they adopted commercial imagery that had itself been disseminated through photomechanical and photoelectronic media. 'I think Pop art … is a kind of appropriation of commercial art and for that reason I find little interest in it.'[3]

Ironically, Thiebaud's initial training and early employment were in commercial design – experience for which he remained extremely grateful.[4] It enabled him to represent objects convincingly, out of his head: 'I never worked directly in front of the object. Probably it was by working as a commercial artist for such a long period that made this possible.'[5] When painting his Pop-like arrays of pies and cakes, he preferred to work from his memory-store of direct observation, forgoing the aide-mémoire of a photograph or any other preexisting depiction. He had memories of the restaurants in which he worked as a young man; memories of roadside diners from trips by automobile; and memories of the Horn & Hardart Automats in New York, where pies and cakes appeared in brightly illuminated glass boxes, ready for self-serve, inspiring futuristic fantasies of an entirely automated society (fig. 21).[6] The visual analogy to Thiebaud's paintings of pies and cakes of the 1960s is obvious: appealing treats in orderly array, already framed, with the artificial colours of fillings and frostings enhanced by bright lighting. To regard the Automat as an experiential point of creative origin is tempting but Thiebaud himself referred to a more general desire to represent aspects of the daily environment that artists had ignored: 'to paint something that I have not seen painted and keep it very basic'.[7] Like the display cases of the Automat, those of the local delicatessen and candy store became worthy targets of study (cat. 12 and 14). Gumball vending machines, statuesque when isolated within a painter's rectangular format, evoked an Automat in miniature (cat. 18).

Although some people have a 'photographic' memory, Thiebaud stated that memory in art lacks photographic precision and stability, for the imagination continually adjusts the mental picture. To paint from memory is to inform an emerging representation creatively, through a series of imaginative changes.[8] 'I think using the memory is a wonderful thing … it may be one of the bases of style. That's because the memory depends on human interjection.'[9] A photographic image, the kind stored in an album or a smartphone rather than in a mind, substitutes for living memory. An image painted does not reproduce memory but is constructed from or of memories. Thiebaud elaborated, 'A photographer in a way starts with everything and gets a little something; a painter has to start with zero, nothing, and make something.'[10] Yet, in perceiving an image already created, this difference registers only if the viewer attends to the physicality of the medium. Otherwise, the presentation of a theme in a photograph will seem equivalent to the same theme conveyed by a painting, as if every picture of pies were merely a picture of pies. Perhaps the near-instantaneity and mechanicity of photography render it superior for capturing thematic material, like a

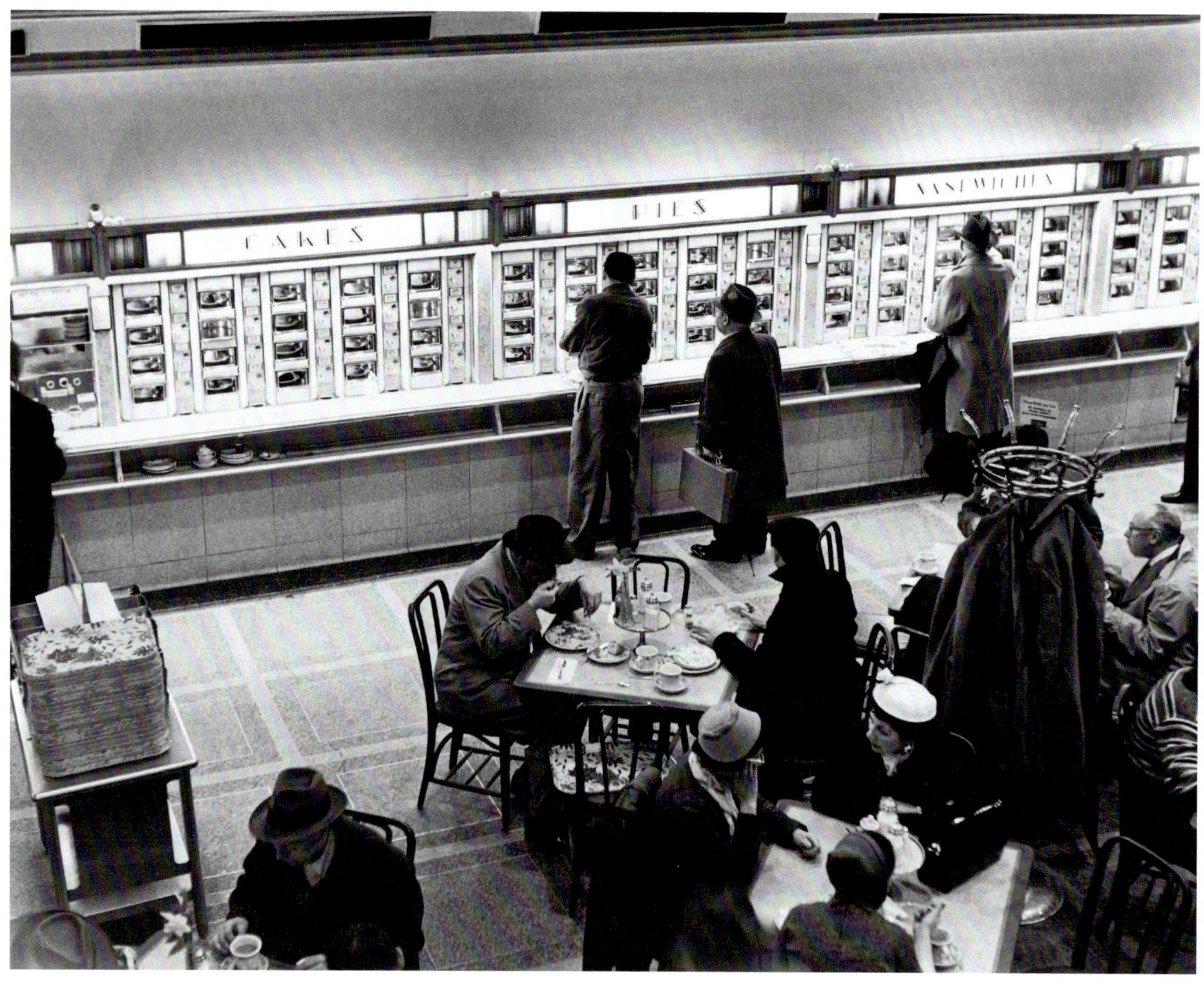

21 Albert Mozell (1918–2009), *Horn & Hardart Automat, NYC*, 1957, photograph

wedding ceremony or the scene of a crime. Although a photograph can be edited after the fact, no editing is necessary (photography 'starts with everything'). Painting, in contrast, consists entirely of editing; its process of give and take develops a theme rather than presenting it whole as if already established elsewhere.[11]

Roland Barthes suggested as much when analysing what he regarded as the zero-degree of professional photographic practice, the anonymous press photo, intended to convey information without implicit commentary – starting with everything, ending with the same, net gain zero. Yet, even press photos prove to be connoted by their context and the captions that accompany them (a gain in meaning). To illustrate what might separate painting from photography when the two appear to bear similar messages, Barthes resorted to an example from the pre-photographic history of art:

In a picture by a [Renaissance] Primitive, 'spirituality' is not a signified but, as it were, the very being of the image [*l'être même de l'image*]. Certainly there may be coded elements in some paintings, rhetorical figures, period symbols, but no signifying unit refers to spirituality, which is a mode of being and not the object of a structured message.[12]

While a photograph can refer to spirituality by selective pose and lighting, certain paintings possess spirituality as their motivating force.

Thiebaud's earthbound images of pies and cakes hardly seem to project spirituality in the manner of a Fra Angelico. Is there some other factor that sets his paintings of common objects apart from photographic studies as well as from the imagery of photo-based Pop to which his constructions were likened? For him, what constitutes 'the very being of the image'?

A Thiebaud teleology

In April 1962, at his first solo exhibition in New York, Thiebaud met a degree of success unexpected. His paintings of pies and cakes, promoted by the gallerist Allan Stone (1932–2006), sold quickly to enthusiastic collectors, as if precisely what this sophisticated segment of the public had been seeking, although not quite consciously. The most distinguished of the initial purchasers was the curator Alfred Barr, acquiring works of contemporary art on behalf of the Museum of Modern Art; he chose *Cut Meringues* (fig. 22). In accordance with museum policy, Barr subsequently requested a statement for the acquisition file, which gave Thiebaud the opportunity to articulate a philosophy of art. Practised as a university instructor and a skilled writer, he was adept at explaining himself without lapsing into arty clichés.

'Each era produces its own still life', Thiebaud wrote, as if cognisant of the early twentieth-century theories of the art historians Aloïs Riegl and Erwin Panofsky, 'My interest in painting is traditional and modest in its aim. I hope that it may allow us to see ourselves looking at ourselves.'[13] Thiebaud's array of pies, a testament to American post-war abundance, would reflect viewers through the everyday environment that the viewers themselves participated in creating – an actualised product of their fantasies and desires. Such was Thiebaud's official statement of origin: he was representing the aesthetic consciousness of his moment in history, as had the two predecessors in still life he cited, Jean-Siméon Chardin (1699–1779) and Paul Cézanne (1839–1906). Chardin's 'copper pots and clay pipes'[14] (fig. 23) had represented late eighteenth-century culture, and Cézanne's spreads of apples, pears, oranges and peaches had (somehow) represented late nineteenth-century culture. In Cézanne's case, the peculiarities of his exploratory mode of depiction and anonymous, repetitive brushstroke were more indicative of his modernising times than his commonplace subject matter (though Cézanne was hardly devoted to modernity). The tables of both Chardin and Cézanne featured a domestic context with comestibles remaining close to their state in nature, whereas Thiebaud represented confections produced by industrialised kitchens. The quantity of the items in Thiebaud's art connotes a difference in

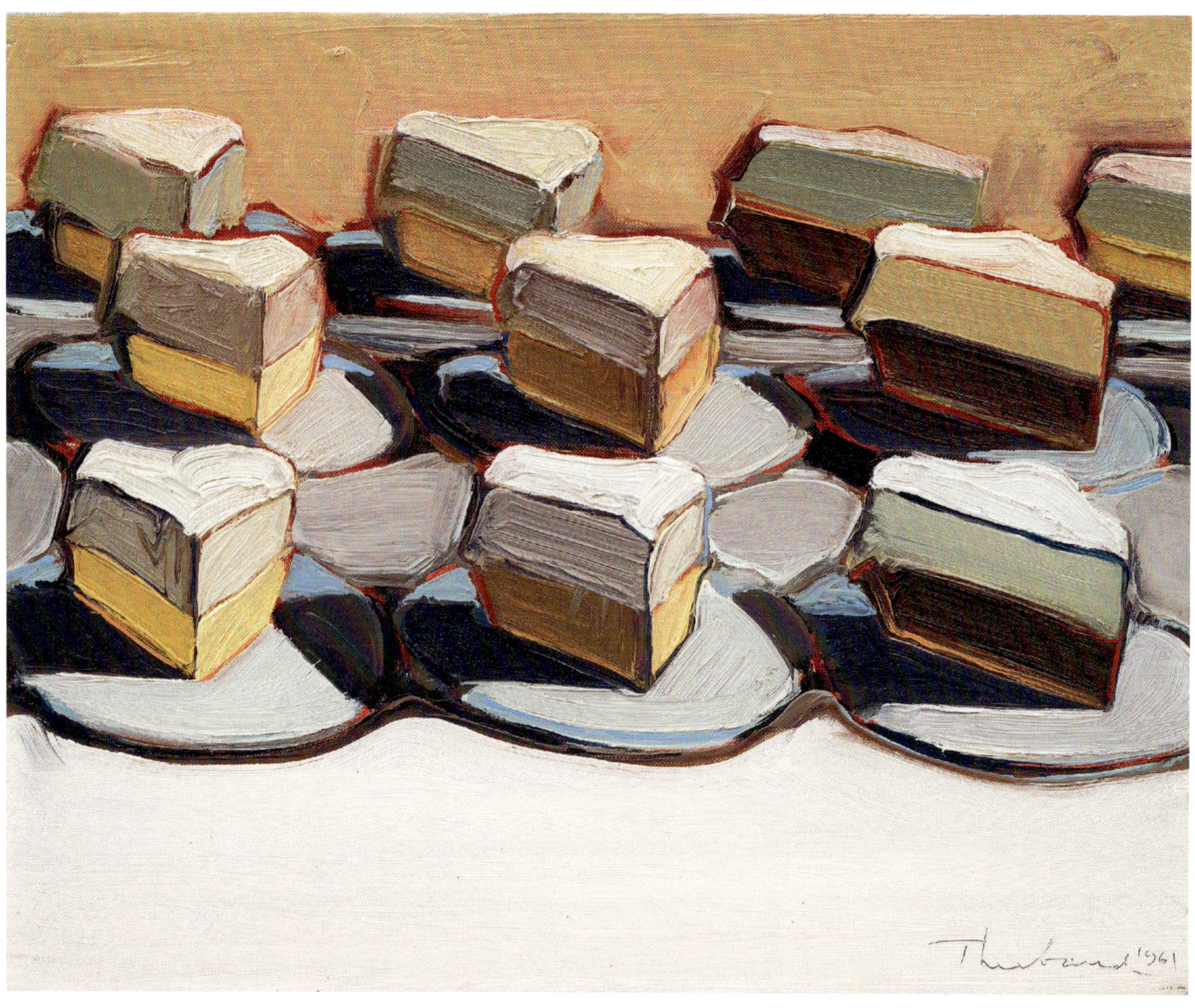

22 Wayne Thiebaud, *Cut Meringues*, 1961,
oil on canvas, 40.6 x 50.6 cm, Museum of
Modern Art, New York

the quality of the culture. He recognised that this feature of his still life –
its assembly-line character, itself amplified by his production of many similar
compositions – might bear social significance, whether in celebration or
critique of post-war America. No wonder that many who concentrated on this
aspect of Thiebaud's art concluded that he was aligning his place in history
with Pop.

At that moment in 1962, the fundamental notion that 'each era produces its
own still life' became Thiebaud's official justification for his imagery, including
its distinctive colouration, sense of artificial illumination and frequent choice
of abrupt, frontal display. He avoided the cliché of linking a critique of popular
mass culture to the economics of industrialised mass production. If a painting

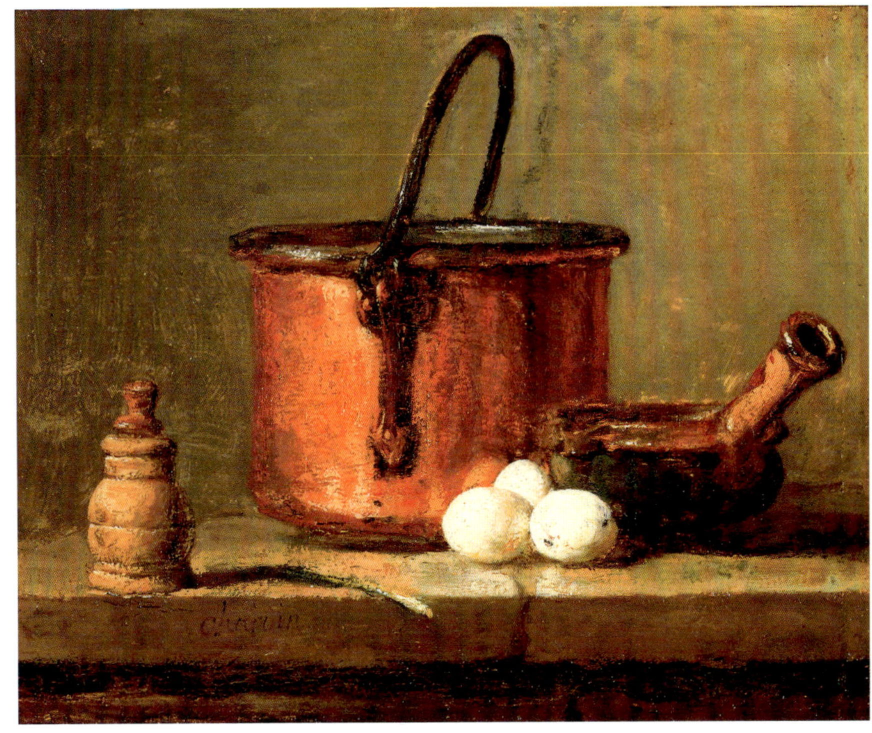

23 Jean-Siméon Chardin (1699–1779), *Still Life,*
c. 1732, oil on wood panel, 17.1 × 21 cm,
The Detroit Institute of Arts

represents a still life that in turn represents an era, it must symbolise an entire
culture rather than just the taste of a social class within a hierarchy of classes.
Thiebaud took the trappings of mass culture and industrial-scale production
as an endemic condition to be observed rather than resisted. In any case, the
condition was evolving. He noted that certain salt and pepper shakers, for years
ubiquitous across the country, were disappearing (see cat. 30): 'Commonplace
objects are constantly changing and when I paint the ones I remember I am
like Chardin tattling on what we were.'[15] His observation required no theory
of fashion and planned obsolescence. A bit reluctantly it seems, Thiebaud
nevertheless acknowledged the broad sociocultural meaning projected by
his imagery of relative sameness: 'Painting a row of cakes [or pies] the way
they are displayed on a lunch counter suggests some rather obvious notions
about conformism, mechanized living, and mass produced culture' (cat. 5).[16]
To this familiar notion, he added a challenging corollary: 'how alone these
endless rows can be … a kind of lonely togetherness … each piece of pie has
a heightened loneliness'. Thiebaud's airy surrounding enhanced the effect:
'The space inference that I want is one of isolation. Ultra clear, bright, air-
conditioned atmosphere.' Imagine each chilled slice of pie waiting to be chosen,
as if joining in a murmuring chorus of 'pick *me*' – each one an individual and
yet alike. A decade earlier, the art historian Meyer Schapiro hit upon the same
allegorical figure to account for the impassive look of Cézanne's card players,
each awaiting the right card while engaged in 'collective solitaire' (fig. 24).[17]

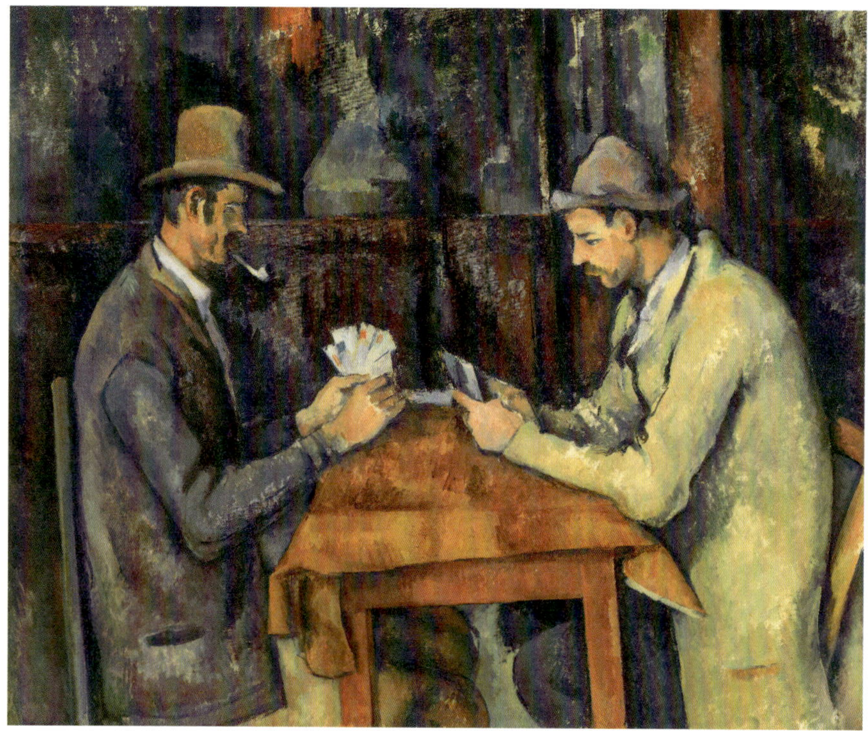

24 Paul Cézanne (1839–1906), *The Card Players*, c. 1892–96, oil on canvas, 60 x 73 cm, The Courtauld, London (Samuel Courtauld Trust)

The sociologist David Riesman, in *The Lonely Crowd* (1956), called on card-playing as well: 'The poker game in the back room, with its praise of masks, fits [the inner-directed person's] habituation to social distance, even loneliness.'[18]

Concepts of conformity, individuality and isolation circulated within what Harold Rosenberg, channelling Nietzsche, dubbed 'the herd of independent minds': 'There is a mass culture of "individuals" too.'[19] For his part, Thiebaud took his sense of the separation of units within a communal whole to a moral realisation: 'None of us can escape our responsibility however totalitarian or utopian our world may be.'[20] Here, he extended the connotations of the compositions of pies and cakes from social anomie to the problematic politics of the Cold War era, where one person's totalitarianism might be another person's utopianism. A few years later, ever modest in his judgments, he remarked that no one knows 'enough about the world to be able to say with finality what is happening in it'.[21] Acting responsibly applies whether one fully understands a situation or not. Morality becomes guesswork, an existentialist of the time might conclude. Thiebaud happened to reprise his statement of higher purpose some years later when he wrote a paean to the bottles and vases of Giorgio Morandi (1890–1964): 'Morandi suggests we are all single in this world, hoping for independent repose. But our best opportunity, for a community of excellence, depends upon a collection of enlightened individuals.'[22]

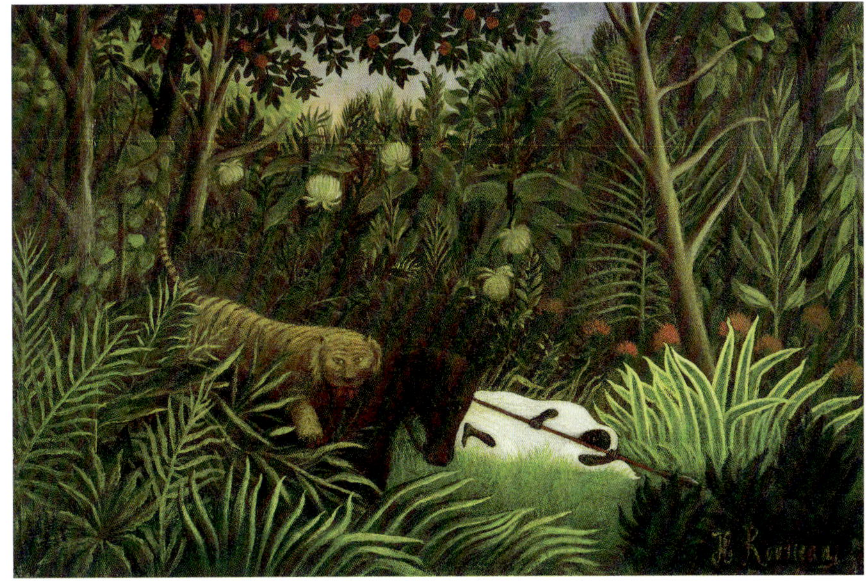

25 Attributed to Henri Rousseau (1844–1910), *Arab Rider in the Jungle Unhorsed by a Tiger*, c. 1904, oil on canvas, 42.9 x 65.1 cm, Collection of the Wayne Thiebaud Foundation

To pass from the microcosm of a few brushstrokes (Thiebaud's pies, Morandi's bottles) to the macrocosm of a philosophy of everything – 'our world' – is a stretch, even if the interpretive gesture leaves ample room for doubt. As a critical ploy, however, what Thiebaud did in 1962 was hardly unusual; and he may have believed that the request from the museum solicited a statement of moral gain through art. In associating a direct manner of painting with the general condition of life in a modern consumer society, Thiebaud had been preceded by numerous socially oriented critics, including Rosenberg, Herbert Read and, notably, Clement Greenberg (the latter's observational formalism ended at the artwork's edge, beyond which he sounded like Theodor Adorno). One of Greenberg's most trenchant statements appeared in 1946, at the start of the post-war period of rapid economic gain and middle-class affluence, conditions that expanded the market for art or at least the public interest in art as a signifier of cultural status. Grounding his analysis in the specifics of artistic process, Greenberg linked 'the palpability of oil pigment' to 'our society's growing impotence to organize experience in any other terms than those of the concrete sensation, immediate return, tangible datum'.[23] The public favoured imagery that required little interpretive effort, no detour from their enjoyment of the cultural product. Greenberg keyed his assessment of the degraded state of American sensibility to the popular vogue for the art of Henri 'Le Douanier' Rousseau (1844–1910). Thiebaud himself was not immune to Rousseau's charm; eventually, in 2010, he acquired an example that featured a daring introduction of stark black and white into an environment of greens (fig. 25). For Thiebaud, the black and white may have constituted an agreeable 'surprise element' or 'anomaly', the 'human element' he appreciated in 'what they call naïve painting or primitive painting'.[24] Greenberg extended his own interpretive stretch: Rousseau's 'flat, direct, almost crass colors, contours, and modelling gave to many painters the first real impression they ever got of what life, reduced to solely empirical considerations … looks like in art.'[25] Greenberg followed the sociological reasoning that Thiebaud himself would apply: art 'allow[s] us to see ourselves looking at ourselves.'[26]

Thiebaud had no need of Rousseau or similar aesthetic models to justify the empirical fact of his colourful pies and cakes. With his experience of the readily legible imagery of commercial illustration, cartoons and animation cells, he was at home generating 'direct, almost crass colors, contours, and modelling'. His statement for the Museum of Modern Art includes this: 'My time spent as an advertising art director, cartoonist, and illustrator some years ago is partly responsible for the look of some of the things.'[27] The residual cartoonist is present in *Boston Cremes* (cat. 10); with its dramatic perspective and sense of animation, a left-right-left march, it requires only a caption to liberate a visual pun, 'Advance of the Boston Cremes'. Thiebaud admitted that his manner was more emphatic than subtle: 'I don't think I am much of a colorist. My interest is with contrasts of great intensity. This effect exemplifies the idea of starkness and glare that I am trying for.' Glare is as 'crass' as the 'flat, direct' colouration Greenberg observed in Rousseau. It was also a feature of the environments that especially impressed Thiebaud, like the glassed-in deli counter and the Automat.

Thiebaud may have replied to the Museum of Modern Art more thoroughly than required; he linked a moral philosophy to what captured his aesthetic interest in the everyday environment – 'still lifes taken from window displays, store counters, supermarket shelves, and mass-produced items'.[28] He established the indirect social significance of this imagery, its suggestion of 'lonely togetherness' leading inescapably to the recognition of collective and personal responsibility. But what if Thiebaud had chosen not to add the philosophical and moralistic part with its suggestion of ultimate meaning or purpose, the teleological element? What if he never went beyond the example of his era's 'own still life', the version of it that he simply enjoyed painting? This would amount to a variant account of the origin and motivation of the Museum's *Cut Meringues* – more sensuous, less cerebral, more affect, less critique. Several years later, he remarked, 'A painting as such is neither a better nor worse painting because of the amount of social comment it contains.'[29]

A Thiebaud phenomenology

Thiebaud understood that less can be more: 'Unfortunately, we don't have a history of painting … where you focus *just* on painting. Not about sociality, not about wars, not about the relationship of kings to courtesans and all of that.'[30] Once a critic eliminates the potential references to social conditions and scandal, what remains, to use Thiebaud's term, is 'a painting as such', art as such. The great nineteenth-century critic Théophile Thoré, despite his pronounced political sensitivities, argued that certain paintings

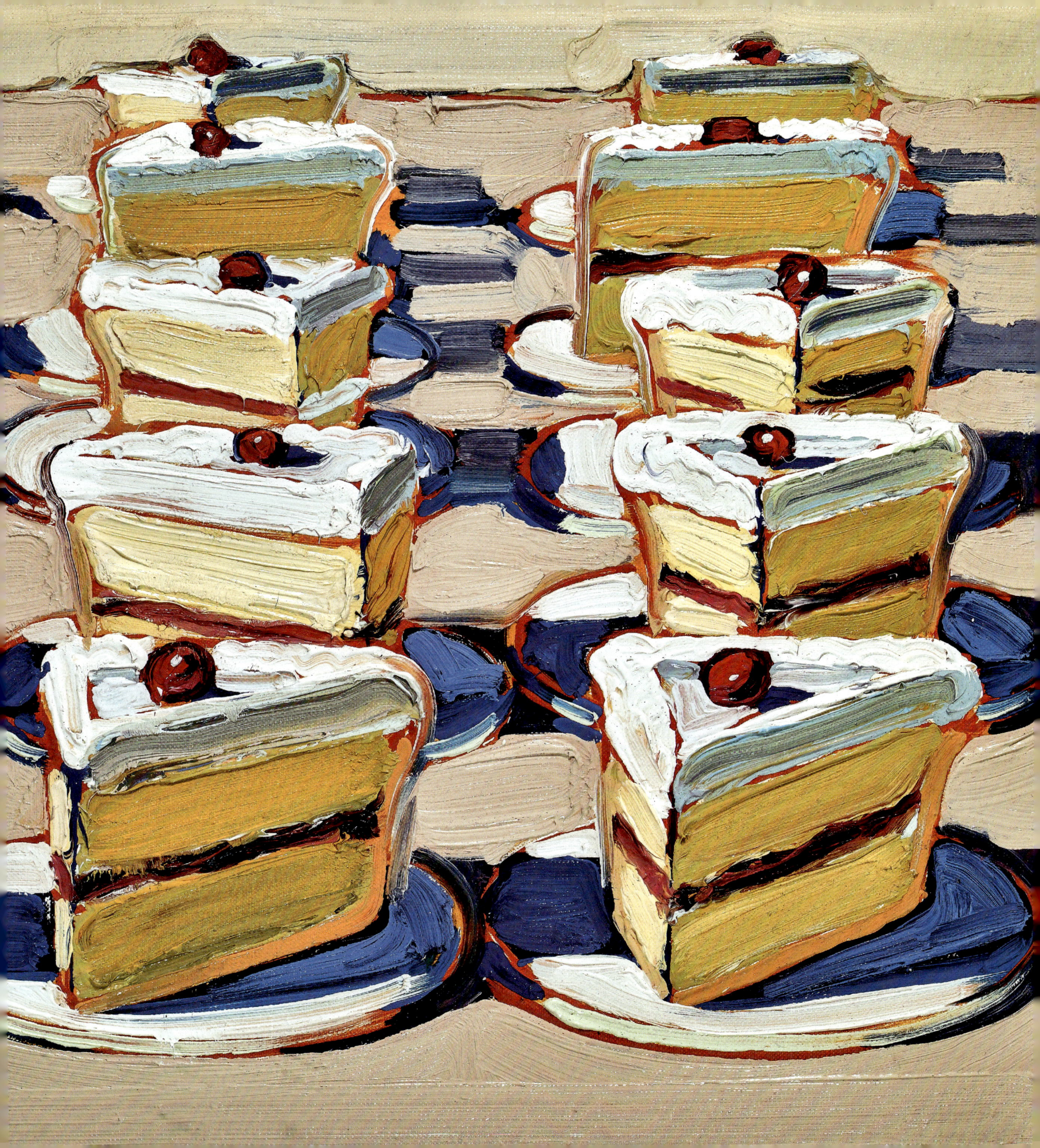

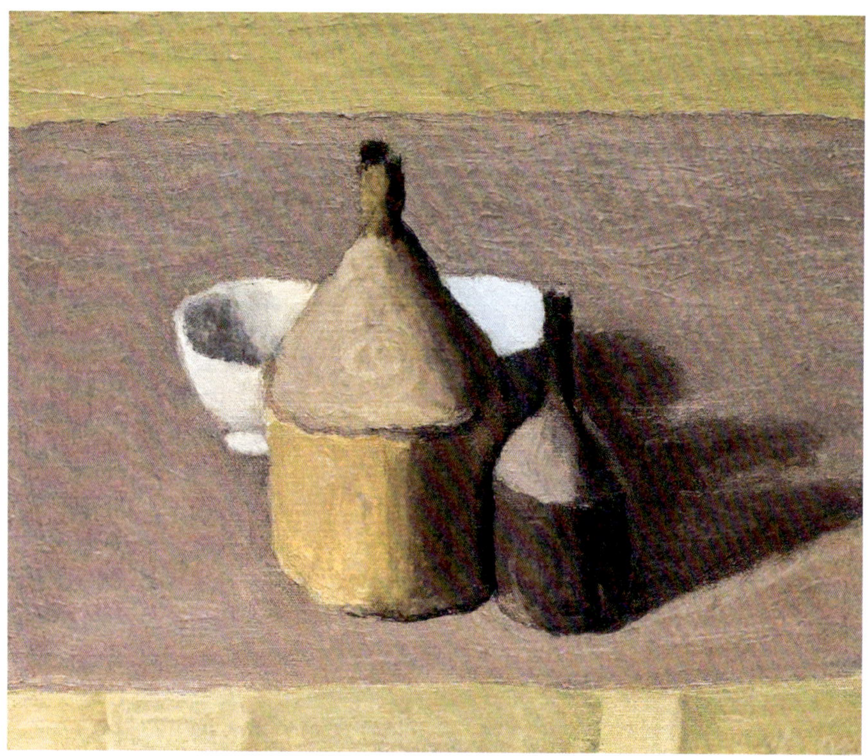

impress a viewer with 'the value of art itself', as if all possible supplemental connotations were rendered irrelevant for all time.[31] Such statements mystify those who doubt that anything has inherent value in isolation, as opposed to acquiring value by the politics of exchange or, as with antiquities, by mere historical survival. For his part, Thiebaud believed that value in art derives from its practice, a value he perceived in the art of predecessors whose practice guided his own.[32]

In Chardin and Cézanne, Thiebaud could observe intensified visual textures, the materiality of paint, the factor of *matière*. Closer to his own time, in Morandi, he found a precedent for his animated edges. Through the physicality of Morandi's paint, the delineation of his objects merges with their nominal background, which does not remain 'back' (an effect found also in Cézanne, whose sequences of faceted marks continue into walls, skies and other background elements, counteracting the expectation of atmospheric perspective). Thiebaud stated that Morandi 'pressures' his still-life objects against each other and 'compacts' them into their pictorialised spatial environment (fig. 26).[33] Thiebaud's metaphor, like Morandi's imagery, conveys a tactile force. 'You feel painting in your body', he said. 'Empathy ... for me is crucial.'[34] As his own empathetic and caricatural response, he painted five packaged sandwiches leaning against each other in a row (fig. 27).[35] Their hint of glossy wrapping, connoting automated production, contrasts with

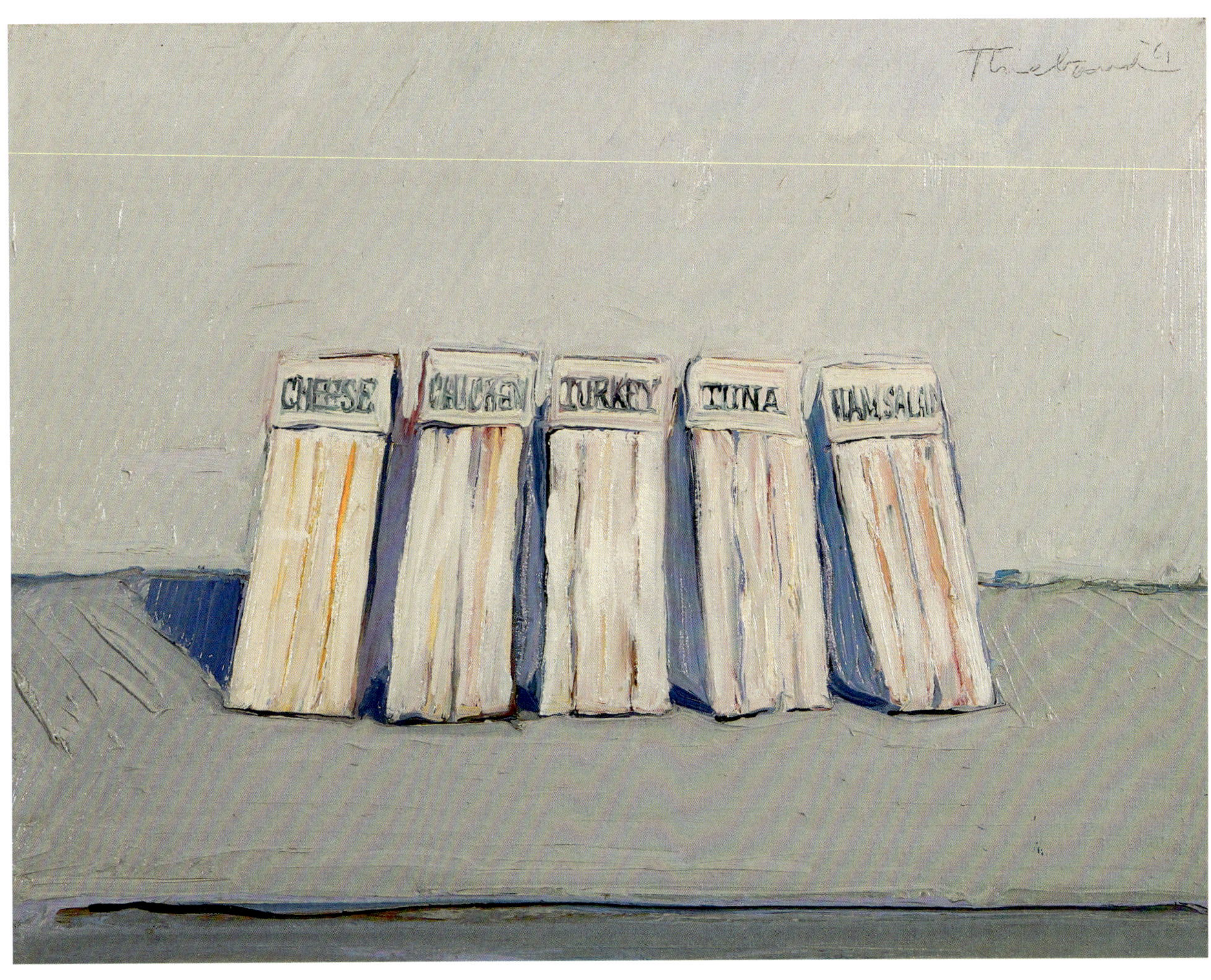

27 Wayne Thiebaud, *Sandwich Group*, 1961, oil on canvas, 49.5 x 59.7 cm, Collection of the Wayne Thiebaud Foundation

the homely, worn surfaces of the objects Morandi collected. Yet, as paint, a Thiebaud sandwich, a commercial illustrator's subject, enters Morandi's world.

Instead of sandwiches, Thiebaud might have depicted five people leaning into each other while lacking signs of mutual response. The illustrious precedent of Édouard Manet (1832–1883) may have encouraged Thiebaud's attitude toward figure painting, where people often appear impassive, with a surprisingly affectless expression: compare Manet's *A Bar at the Folies-Bergère* (fig. 28) to Thiebaud's *Girl with Mirror* (fig. 29). Thiebaud spoke of the 'expressionlessness' of his tired-out models as a depictive aim: 'This mask develops … to try still, in spite of that, to turn the figure into some kind of animated object.'[36] Paint provided the animation. If Manet's barmaid remains impassive, the bottles on the countertop, like those on Morandi's table, project feelings that originate in the manipulation of paint. Because figures and objects in Manet's art seemed to elicit equal interest, his critic Thoré

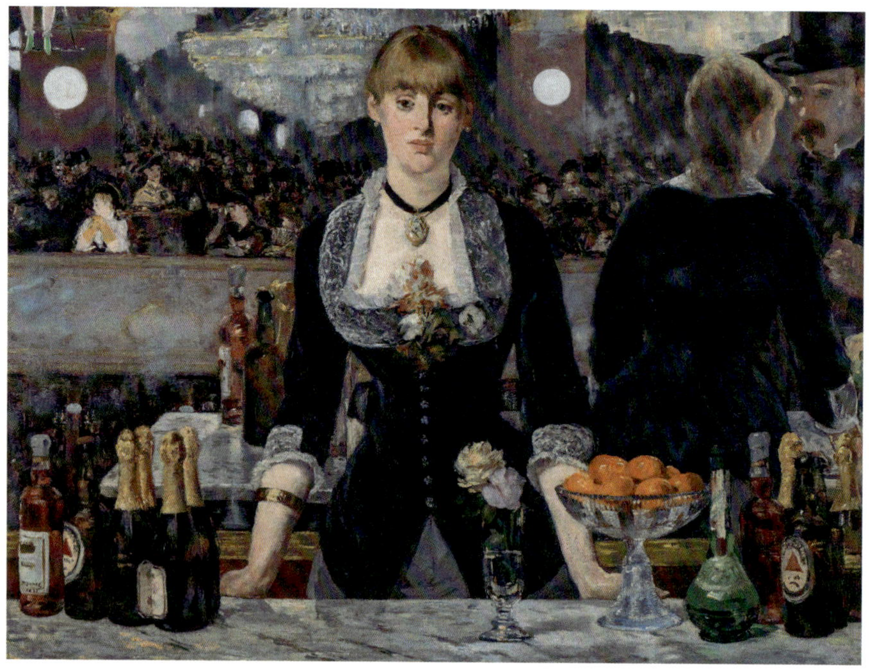

ascribed the condition to pantheism, 'valu[ing] a human head no more than a slipper'.[37] Some years later, it became a commonplace to comment that Cézanne's portrait heads expressed no more personality than his apples.[38] To artists of the twentieth century, such ironic observations – in their initial context, usually derogatory – indicated that Cézanne, far from being confused about moral values, had liberated himself from hierarchies of *pictorial* values. A still life that symbolised the era, as Thiebaud imagined it, had the same symbolising force as a paradigmatic portrait. Despite traditional conceptual hierarchies, he and Manet treated the human image as a still life, each genre becoming equivalent to the other when animated by paint-matter. Thiebaud, using live models for figure compositions, reiterated that 'all painting is memory painting. In working from life, the duration interval [between observation and representation] is simply shortened.'[39]

By the late 1950s, capitalising on his training in commercial practice, Thiebaud committed himself to representational art. Nevertheless, among older Americans he admired, Franz Kline (1910–1962) had shifted to abstraction, and Willem de Kooning (1904–1997) appeared at that moment to be doing the same. While on teaching leave during the 1956–57 academic year, Thiebaud sought out Kline and de Kooning in New York. What subject to paint was the question. If he had had the option, he mused in 2009, 'I could say to myself, "I love painting so much and the chance to do painting, why don't you just tell me what to do? And come and pick it up next Thursday. Tell me something else you want me to paint, and come back." And that would be a life I think I could enjoy. That's how far away I am from a serious painter who works to be an

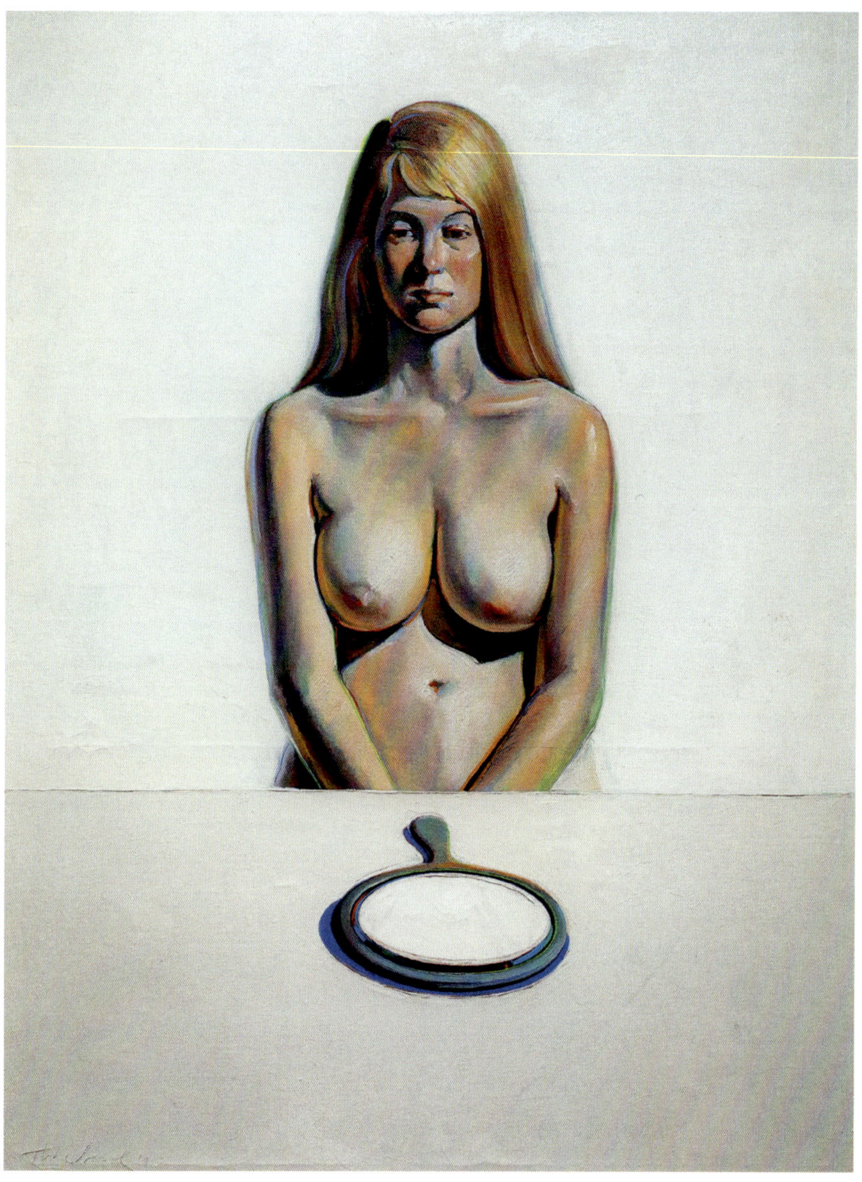

artist.'[40] Thiebaud always regarded de Kooning as serious. Both believed that art comes from art; cultural critics do social and political analysis, while painters paint.[41] If others, by their example, were teaching Thiebaud how to paint, de Kooning instructed him in how a painter should live. His basic advice: 'What matters with painting is to do something you *want* to do and not to do anything that you think you should do'[42] and 'You should find something that you really feel genuine in terms of your experience.'[43] Go for genuine feeling.

Thiebaud followed de Kooning's direction, deciding to paint what he simply liked, whether culturally celebrated or not. In this approach to practice, the tactile feel specific to paint might precede concerns for its final look. Hence Thiebaud's aversion to art that mimicked a photographic model: 'There's no textural immediacy.'[44] As for subject matter, pies and cakes were to Thiebaud what the woman was to de Kooning: 'I was always kind of interested in the way in which [pies in a restaurant] formed these nice patterns. I said, alright, I'll go ahead with this and I'll make [basic geometric forms] into pies. I was really enjoying myself … and as I finished, I looked at it, and said, my God, I just painted a bunch of pies. That's going to be the end of me as a serious painter.'[45] *Doubly* unserious: first, the specific subject hardly matters; then, when it's chosen, it's just pies.

The public proved forgiving. The modernist project either reversed or flattened the old hierarchies; painting an apple instead of a human head was good enough, just as serious as anything else, and the many who went fully abstract represented nothing at all. Thiebaud often said that he wanted to reduce the gap between representation and abstraction: 'There's not very much of any interest that separates abstract and figurative painting.'[46] Painting remained painting, either way. Thiebaud's pies, conceived as geometry, occupied a middle ground: 'I took three basic shapes to work with: a rectangle, an ellipse or a circle and a triangle. Well, that's a piece of pie.'[47] In a review of his exhibition at the Allan Stone Gallery in 1962, Max Kozloff generated an off-the-cuff proposal suited to Thiebaud. Still life, like abstraction, serves the release of feeling:

> Frequently it happens that artists who experience an impasse with their habitual motifs turn to still life as a means to discharge energy, and to work through their problems without the distractions that ambitious themes imply. Because of its very neutrality, the still-life subject can be all the apter a vehicle of feeling, and the clearer a crystallizer of tension. No more natural pretext for the display of structure and/or expression is available – short of the non-representational.[48]

Contemporary still life provided representational cover for indulging in the advantages of abstract art: heightened expression of feeling, limitless structural invention, liberated handling of the paint, with its colours, textures and varieties of illumination. When Thiebaud used ellipses and triangles to paint pies, it was the geometry that he felt and not the pies, for they were imaginary to begin with. A mental abstraction guided his pseudo-representation.

Some of Thiebaud's early still-life compositions play with principles of design associated with articulating flat surfaces; these representations mimic abstraction. *Around the Cake* (fig. 30) is a play on concentric circles, evoking a representational target by Jasper Johns (born 1930) or an abstract one by Kenneth Noland (1924–2010).[49] *Half Cakes* (fig. 31) divides its near-square format diagonally, implicating the framing edges in the general composition, as if the representation were devolving into two right triangles.[50] Here, as elsewhere in Thiebaud's art, the sense of perspectival recession contradicts the planarity of the inherent geometric order, its obviousness exaggerated to the point of caricature. Thiebaud dared to violate an unwritten rule of representational

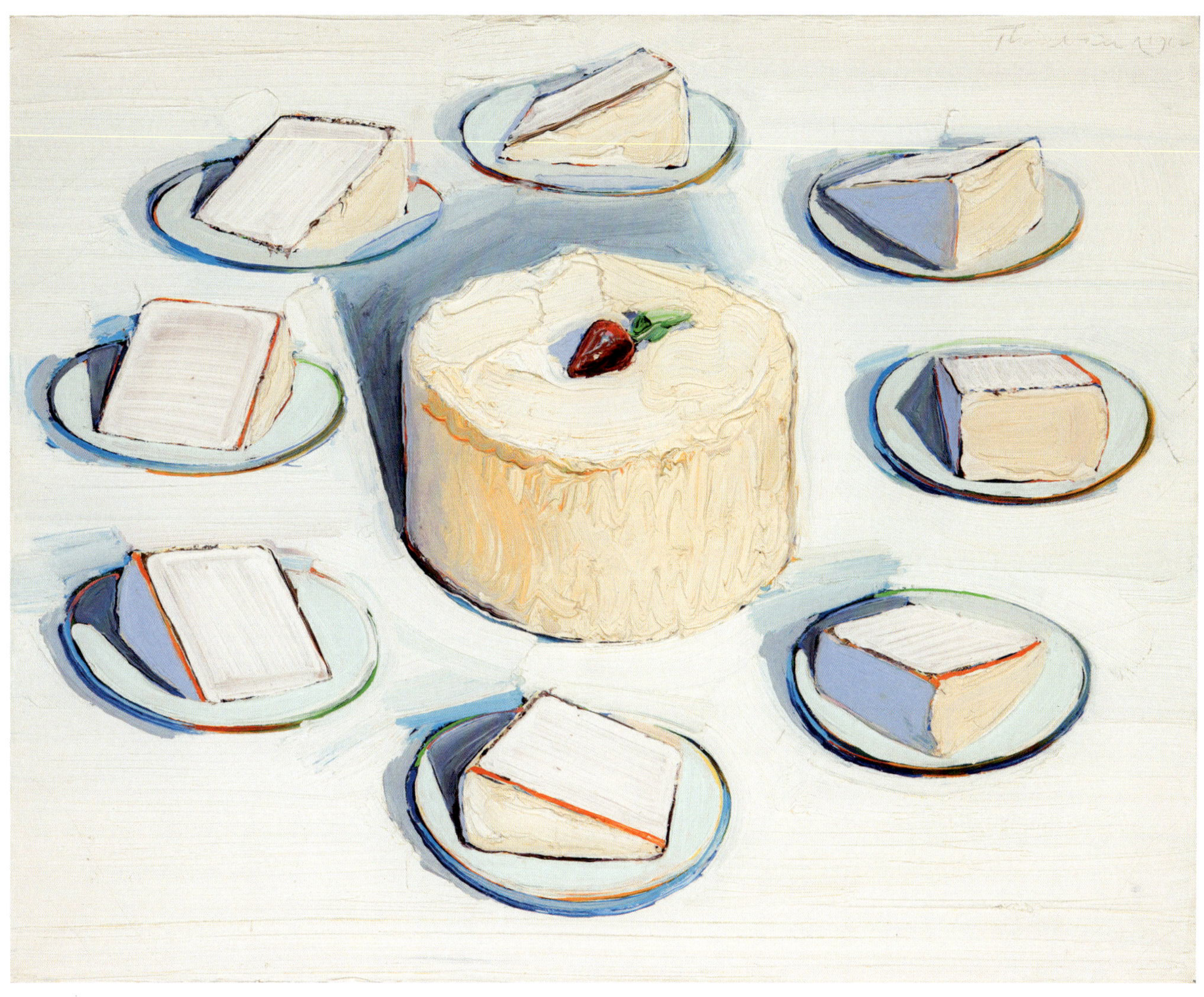

art: avoid the flattening effects of centering and symmetry. These paintings exemplify how *not* to arrange a representational scene within a standard pictorial format; they generate a condition of perpetual tension in which the pictorial order (representation) and the graphic order (abstraction) vie for dominance. Thiebaud's shortcuts to simplicity and unabashed aesthetic pleasure often masked formal mischief. Another take on the situation: he maintained representation while gaining the emotive advantages of formal abstraction, its direct appeal to feeling (regardless of a viewer's interest in cake).

'I'm going to just start as directly as I can', Thiebaud said, recalling his strategy, 'And I took the canvas and made some ovals, thinking about Cézanne – the cube, the cone, and the sphere – and put some triangles over them and thought, well, that maybe could represent a pie on a plate.'[51] Having set the

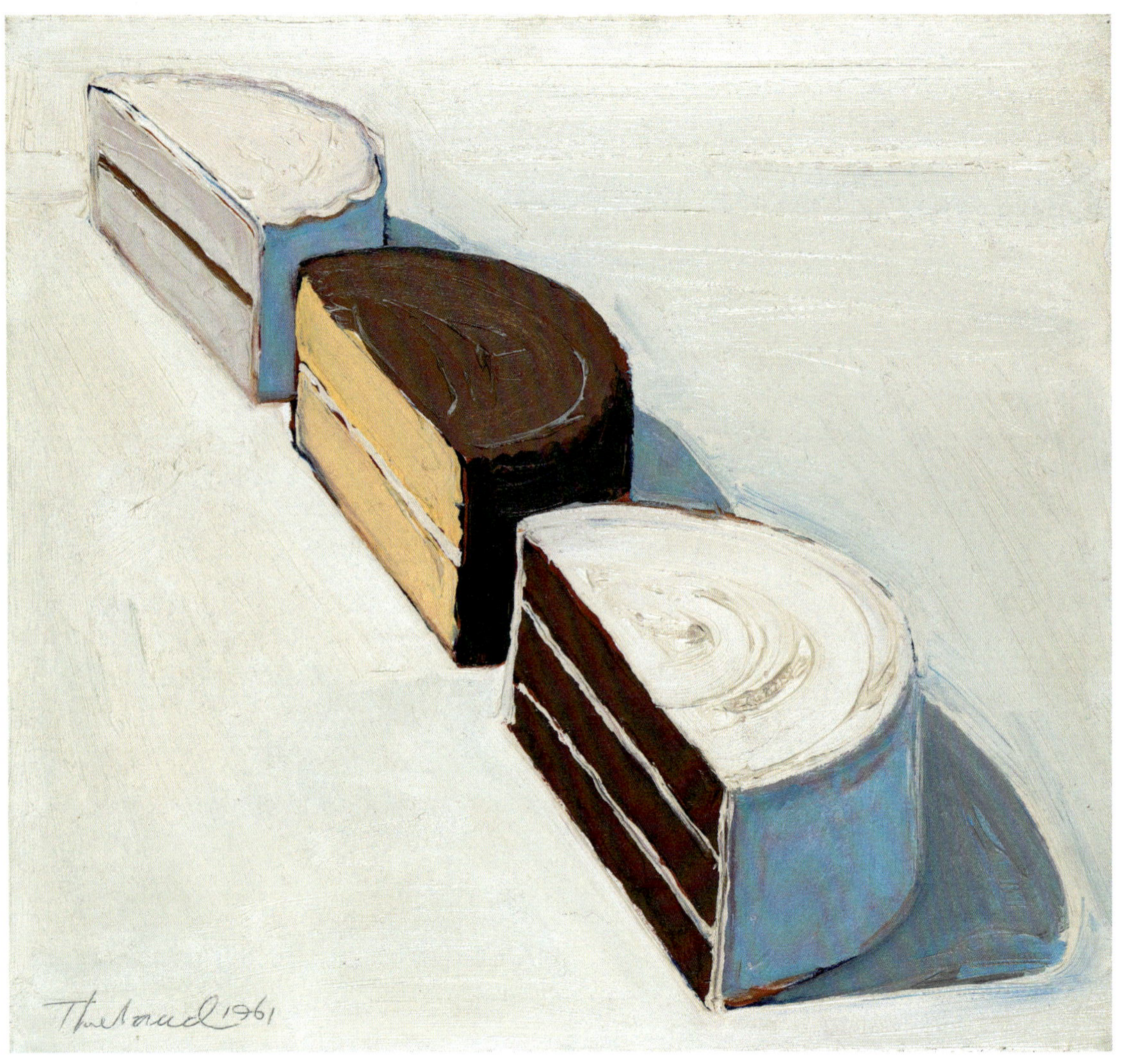

31 Wayne Thiebaud, *Half Cakes*, 1961, oil on canvas, 50.8 x 56.5 cm, Wadsworth Atheneum Museum of Art, Hartford

social and political aside, he created a representational art of still life from invented geometric forms, abstraction-like, in coordination with his memory of pies and other foodstuffs; his use of memory superimposed a mental abstraction upon a visual one. Two modes of abstraction were yielding Thiebaud's representations. This process distinguished him not only from conventional still-life painters but also from the new Pop artists. For his still lifes (but not his figure paintings), he typically had no model with a physical or material presence – no group of objects painstakingly arranged in the studio, as with Cézanne and Morandi, and no set of photographic images as an alternative source.[52]

In a sense, Thiebaud followed the imperative that Rosenberg had announced in 1952 when considering de Kooning and other post-war painters

in New York: as 'a gesture of liberation, from Value – political, esthetic, moral …
[they decided] just to PAINT'.[53] Rosenberg alluded to the abandonment of still
life, pointedly Cézanne's, as a legendary site of avant-garde practice: 'The apples
[were] brushed off the table', an action that left the table as a tabula rasa on
which 'just to paint'. Thiebaud, an oddity within this New York scenario, painted
with gestural bravado while letting his apples – in his case, pies – remain.
The subject lent itself to memory-work in no need of continuous observation.
'With a triangle or a circle or an oval', Thiebaud remarked, 'there's not much to
remember.'[54] Both Thiebaud and Cézanne used multicoloured halation at the
edges of represented objects, indicating the effect of light as well as the sense
of a volumetric form turning around its edge in the represented space (see the
edges of the plates in Thiebaud's *Pie Counter*, cat. 16; the cup handle in his *Cup of
Coffee*, cat. 7; and the contours of the fruit in Cézanne's *Pot of Flowers and Fruit*,
fig. 32). The halated edges imply a threefold presence: solid object, intangible
illumination and surrounding spatial void. Thiebaud remarked: 'In Cézanne
there is always this swelling, like the volume trying to get away from the plane,
even though there is also a linear matrix.'[55] The halated contour marked the site
of this tension. Given the value Cézanne placed on immediate sensation, one
imagines him discovering the phenomenon of halation anew with every studio
session, whereas Thiebaud, with his designer's memory, already knew of 'those
auras and those vibrating halations … not seen so much as sensed'.[56] For him,
paint itself was the object of immediate sensation, a phenomenological factor
of his representational process. His concentration on the potential of paint
became especially evident in landscape works of his later years, which display
all possible textures, opacities and translucencies. In *Downhill Intersection*
(fig. 33), Thiebaud's willful variation in paint quality animates the imaginative
configuration of hillside streets and apartment blocks.

So, yes, to think back to the regimentation of the rows of pies with their
irregular variation is to approach allegories of consumer society and the 'Lonely
Crowd', and perhaps, ultimately, a statement on individual responsibility, as
Thiebaud articulated it for the Museum of Modern Art. He justified his practice
as exemplifying a moral teaching for those who might benefit from it. In this
respect, he followed the modernist impulse to social critique, already apparent
in Manet's era. Critique of cultural and political norms, as well as resistance
to institutional censorship: all this constitutes a modernist trope that can
result in caricature or allegorical pronouncement. Many modernist paintings
have reflected on consumer culture and the confected aspects of the social
environment. Around 1910, Pablo Picasso (1881–1973) referenced popular songs
and branded products; in 1924, Stuart Davis (1892–1964) constructed a still
life of a drinking glass accompanied by a light bulb. As in Manet, Picasso and
Davis, so in Diego Rivera (1886–1957) and David Alfaro Siqueiros (1896–1974),
so also in Philip Guston (1913–1980) and Mark Rothko (1903–1970), and in
more contemporary figures such as Robert Colescott (1925–2009), Peter Saul
(born 1934) and Dana Schutz (born 1976), where the focus might turn from the
consumer economy to the politics of racism and war.[57]

But to stop short of pursuing such critique – paradoxically distracted by
one's own physical and material engagement – allows an artist to concentrate

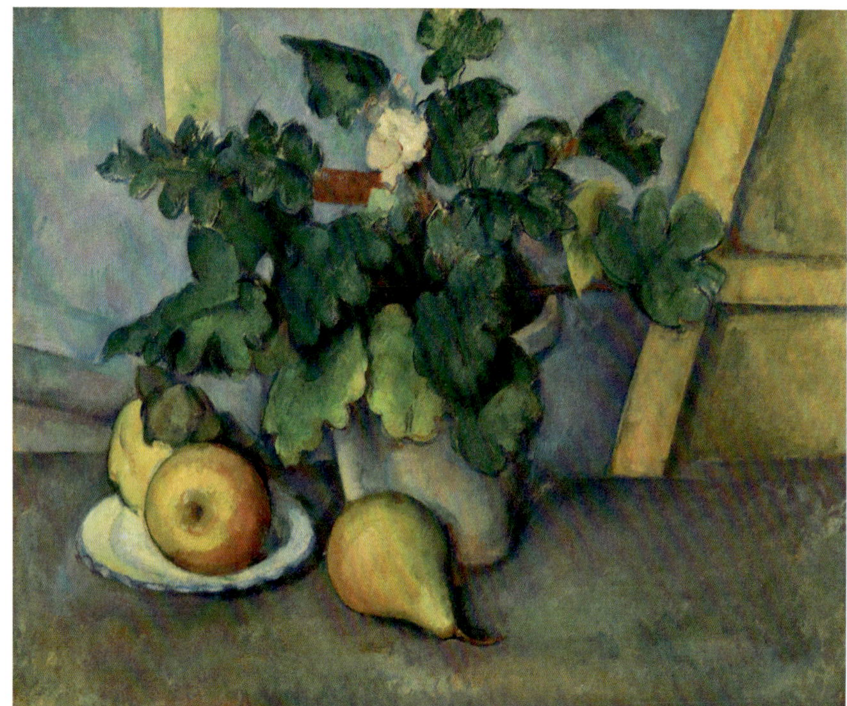

on the imaginative invention-in-process rather than on a message intended. Such was Rosenberg's argument for 'action painting', an exploration of feeling through gestural brushwork, textural variation and a range of effects of colour. Rigorous composition, plotting a theme, ceased to be of paramount concern. Hence, speculation on the possibilities of alloverness, non-composition and minimal, reductive or repetitive order on the part of artists and critics of the 1960s. Thiebaud's multi-object still lifes, though representational, seem additive, rather like the paratactic one-thing-after-another of a stripe painting by Frank Stella (1936–2024) or a 'stack' of rectangular prisms installed by Donald Judd (1928–1994). Thiebaud had a way of being of his time and 'serious' despite being neither Pop nor minimal nor polemical. As he said, 'Each era produces its own still life.'[58] And so he did.

Over the top

For whatever reason, Thiebaud chose not to end his statement for the Museum of Modern Art with his inspiring philosophical reflection on 'lonely togetherness'. He returned instead to his procedure for depicting commonplace objects, as if intent on giving technique the last word. His use of impasto, he wrote, 'experiment[s] with what happens when the relationship between paint and subject matter comes as close together as I can possibly get them ... white, gooey, shiny, sticky oil paint spread out on the top of a painted cake "becomes" frosting' (cat. 17).[59] The analogy is problematic: oil paint when

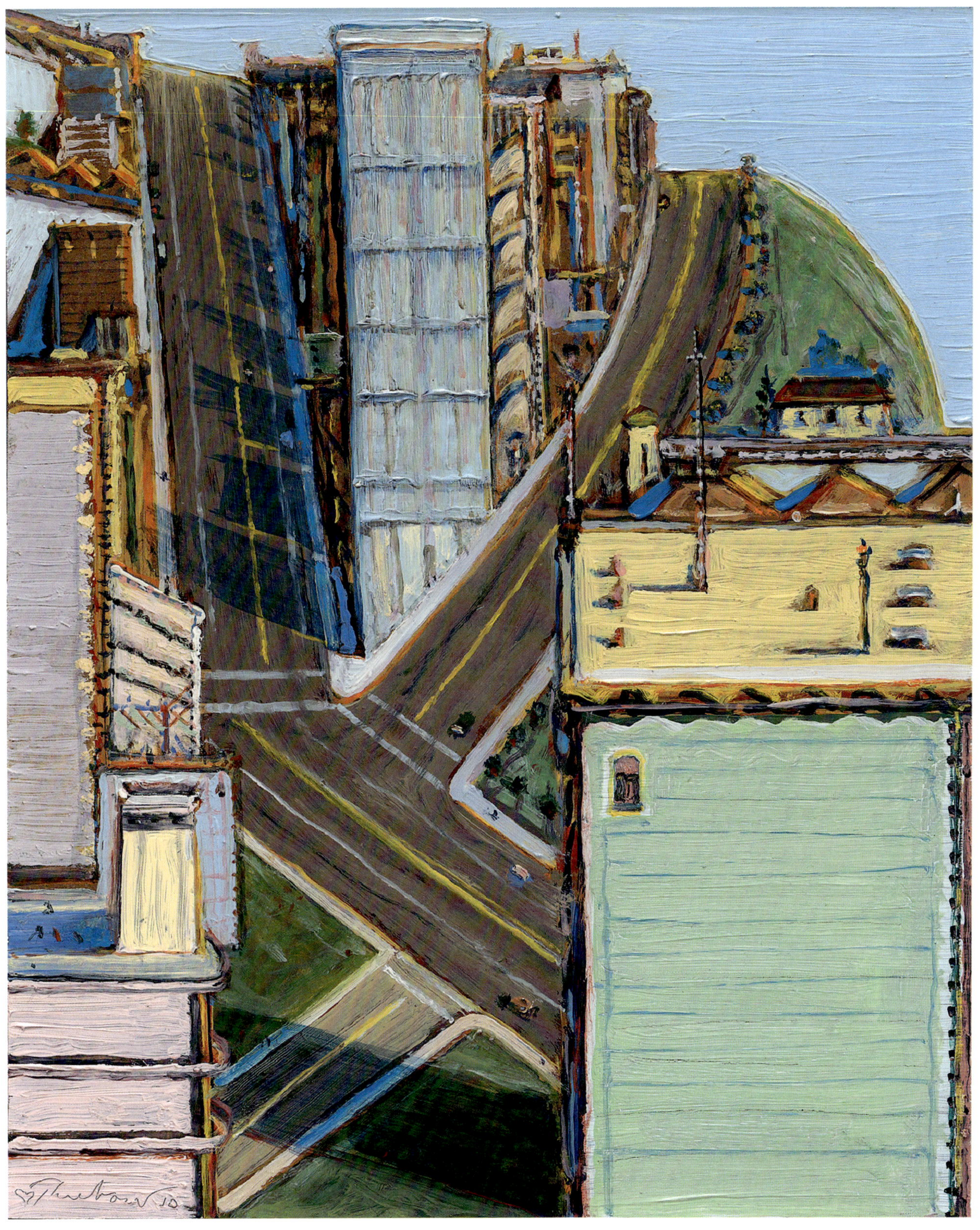

applied can be gooier and stickier than any frosting composed of sugar, butter and milk; when dried, the paint *looks* somewhat gooey and sticky but isn't. Despite the realities, critics have been seduced by how appetising Thiebaud's frosted 'cakes' appear.[60] Yet when one quality approaches sensory equivalence to another, representation to model, the relationship is liable to flip like an image in a concave mirror. It may seem that the imagined cake exists only as a template for applying paint.

Kozloff's review of the 1962 exhibition at the Allan Stone Gallery noted the transformative ambivalence: 'This uncanny mimetic quality of Thiebaud's handling is the essence of his wit, because the paint apes the edible, while obviously asserting itself as inorganic matter.'[61] 'Obviously' indeed, for wit hinges on exaggeration, which entails obviousness. Here, the dominant quality of Thiebaud's manner of rendering belongs more to the paint than to the object represented. One might counter that such is true of any planometric representation of a volumetric form (a cake, a pie, a human body); a tension always exists between the referent and its rendering. Yet, for the wit, pun or irony to register requires stressing an element of divergence beyond what is typical. Caricature highlights a feature of the represented subject to the point that nothing else attracts comparable attention. In the case of a Thiebaud cake, the representation of the icing becomes so exaggerated that it reduces to – or rises to – a condition of utter materiality, to which a viewer reacts empathetically with a sense more tactile than gustatory. To find the paint appetising represents a certain blindness to the rhetoric of visual wit. In planning Thiebaud's opening, Stone ordered cake to be served in the gallery (fig. 6), a clever scheme that backfired: 'People said that my painting of a cake looked very realistic. However, when we posed a real cake near the painting, the real cake looked so different that we decided not to offer the comparison.'[62]

This anecdote informs the interpretive confusion that Thiebaud's art incited – Pop or not Pop, verism or caricature, seriousness or blague. Such dilemmas evoke one of his contemporaries, whose issues were similar: 'I am an admirer of Claes Oldenburg [1929–2022]', Thiebaud said, 'particularly his drawings and early plaster sculpture.'[63] He knew Oldenburg from his 1956–57 New York sojourn and later brought students from California to his studio.[64] The two artists shared food imagery – pies, cakes, hamburgers, ice cream cones – though Oldenburg developed these nominally Pop subjects as sculpture. Thiebaud approved.[65]

In 1962, Judd was switching from abstract painting to sculptural construction (he would call it three-dimensional work). Concurrently, he composed concise, laconic art reviews, punctuated by caustic humour. As he exposed aesthetic principles in operation, he often mentioned one artist at the expense of another. Reviewing Thiebaud at Allan Stone, he alluded to both Oldenburg and Roy Lichtenstein (1923–1997) to Thiebaud's detriment. Yet the account was hardly dismissive, for 'in the protected circle of representational art [Thiebaud] is one of the best .... He has done something rather than ape old art.'[66] Apparently, Judd appreciated the innovation of a cafeteria still life. What annoyed him, however, was the sense that Thiebaud was illustrating, that is, his imagery and brushwork were

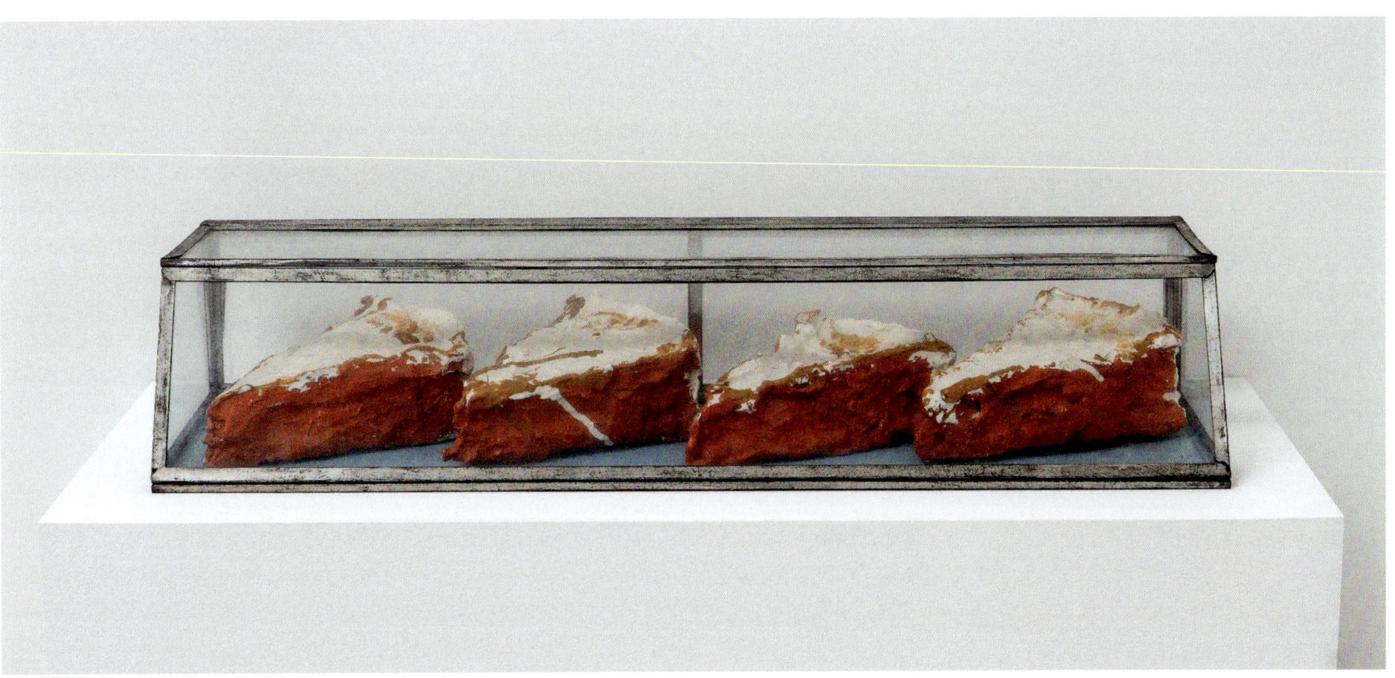

'communicative of the object' (impasto imitating frosting); his painting reflected a model rather than existing independently. In Judd's view, Thiebaud's exaggeration did not go far enough to be transformative: 'The juiciness of the paint is a little gross; a little grossness … is a little impossible.' In full grossness, Oldenburg 'makes his [plaster] cakes and pies and other foods and articles actual objects, which is different epistemologically from illustration'. An 'actual object' is complete as is. Oldenburg's *Four Pies in a Glass Case* (fig. 34) adds no nuance to the red filling; this is grossness, an exaggeration of a sensory property that distracts from particularising the representational reference. Is the filling cherry? No, it's red.

Let's say that Judd was correct in his assessment of Oldenburg. He may nevertheless have been wrong to contrast Oldenburg's total grossness to Thiebaud's 'little' variant; he might instead have perceived that their results were analogous, one in three dimensions, the other in two. As I've been implying through examples, Thiebaud's direct manner, relying on a memory-store of geometric forms and material textures, presents the physicality of his paint at least as much as it renders the general appearance of his objects. A viewer's attention is likely to shift from illustrative values to material values and from these material values to emotive ones. In this respect, Thiebaud perceived in Morandi's compositions the trembling edges of objects and the compression of the whole – empathic intimacy rather than detached description. Thiebaud's own representations began and ended as abstractions, which is ironical given his status as consummate illustrator. When he said, 'I love painting so much', he was alluding to the process, not the product; hence, his fantasy of working on successive commissions entailing any subject whatever.[67] All subjects become equivalent when converted to paint and the forms it configures; in *Downhill Intersection*, the apartment blocks manifest cake-like qualities.

This line of interpretation calls for elaboration. As an abbreviated mode of graphic representation, illustration is tantamount to caricature; by comparison with lens-based verism, it verges on the non-representational, the abstract. Arguing the case for Oldenburg's manner of volumetric illustration, Judd wrote of a concentration on 'shapes that are emotive'; Oldenburg isolated and stressed such forms so that the represented object communicated the feeling of the emotive shape as its salient property. 'Three fat layers with a small one on top are enough': this was Judd's account of Oldenburg's ludicrously enlarged *Floor Burger* (fig. 35), which conveys less the sense of bun, burger and pickle, and more the sense of bulging slabs of pliant material.[68] As representation, the form passes over the top of its retaining wall of normative reference; the caricature is so gross that the depiction reduces to a feeling that never existed before Oldenburg created its embodiment. Such an emotional effect is not expressive, not a release of an artist's internal emotion, but, as it were, impressive, a feeling sensed only in the invented object. Oldenburg's representations, Judd wrote, 'are objects as they're felt, not as they are' – not as their fixed classification would identify and characterise them.[69] He continued, 'It's the interest in the object that is the main thing, not the object

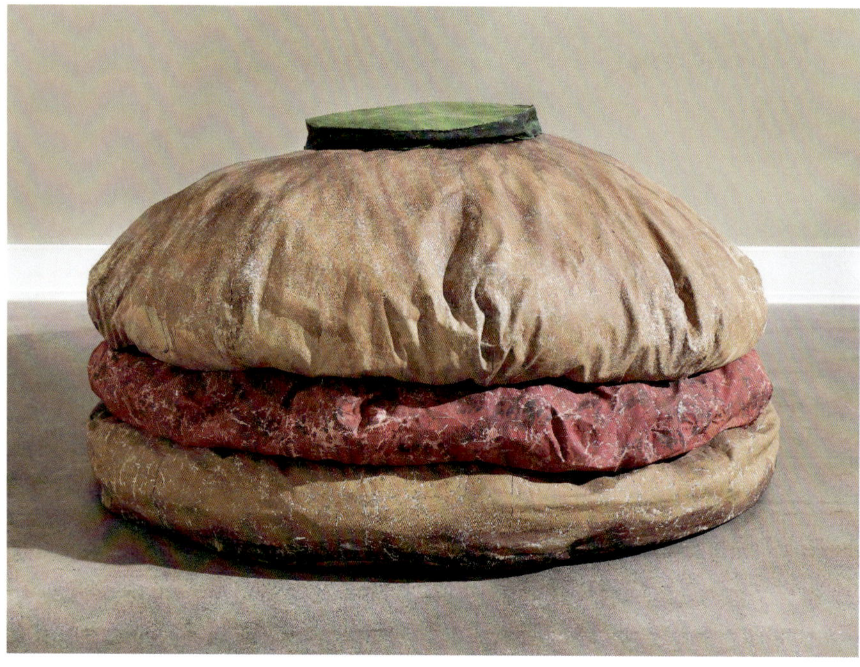

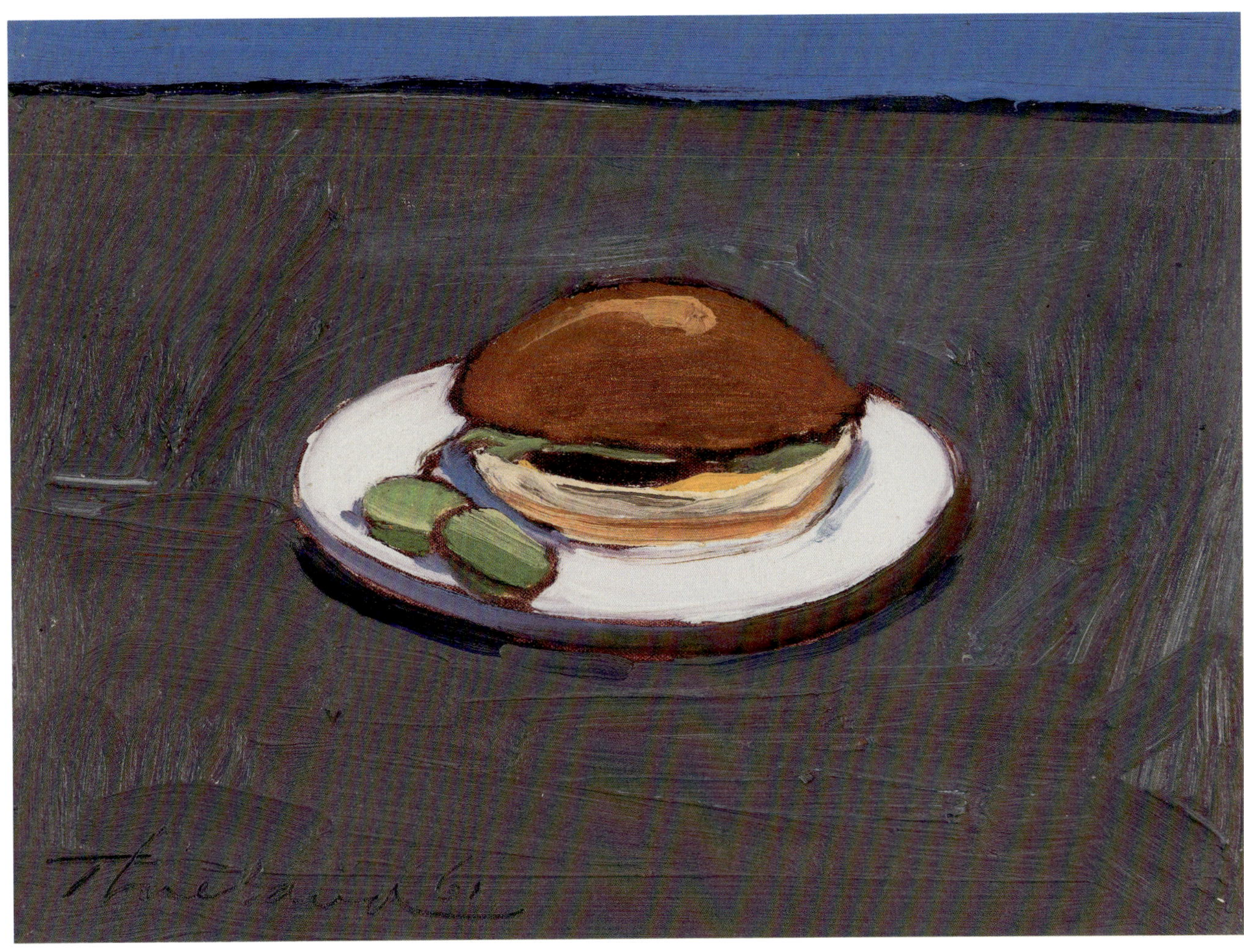

36 Wayne Thiebaud, *Hamburger*, 1961, oil on canvas, 30.4 x 41.2 cm, Collection of the Paul LeBaron Thiebaud Trust

itself .... The sense of objects occurs with forms that are near some simple, basic, profound forms you feel .... The reference to objects [merely] gives them a way to occur.'

As in Judd's understanding of Oldenburg, so in Thiebaud's understanding of Thiebaud, who created an abstract art that avoided abstracting from anything; it engaged instead in a constructive process that generated representations ('I laid out these triangles and started turning them into pies').[70] Thiebaud's love of painting-as-painting took him over the top – perhaps he was already there at the start. As I have stated, he perceived little distinction between painting as representation and as abstraction: 'I'm basically always convinced that my work is abstract.'[71] His version of a hamburger (fig. 36), no more naturalistic than Oldenburg's, amounts to a sliding action from left to right with some added spin, a movement felt in paint that passes through both the representational figure and its representational ground. Asked what was so interesting about a hamburger, Thiebaud replied, 'Its shape, its architecture. A hamburger is like a corny imitation of a Frank Lloyd Wright building.'[72] Abstraction, materiality, feeling: in Thiebaud's case, these are the aspects of 'the very being of the image'.

I suppose that a similar argument might suit many artists of the modern period, from Piet Mondrian and Kasimir Malevich to Gerhard Richter and Jack Whitten. But Oldenburg and Thiebaud go over the top by stealth; their blatant pretence to representation disarms suspicions of emotive abstraction. The punchline of the cake anecdote at the Allan Stone Gallery proves utterly revealing: 'When we posed a real cake near the painting …. Only then did I realize how little my painted object resembled a real object.'[73] Using a conventional mode of representation, Thiebaud made something other than a representation. It had its own being within its own category, one still lacking an appropriate name.

Notes

For essential aid in research, I thank Barnaby Wright, Rachel Teagle, Maria Bult, Jeannie McKetta, Chloe Nahum and Erin Gordon.

1   Aschheim and Daubert 2014, p. 25.
2   Jan Butterfield, 'Wayne Thiebaud: A Feast for the Senses', *Arts Magazine*, October 1977, p. 137: 'The Pop Art thing happened to me as a label about 1962.'
3   Pardee 2019.
4   Kaufman 2023, p. 139.
5   John Coplans, 'Wayne Thiebaud: An Interview', in Coplans 1968, pp. 23–36, at p. 30. In Bult 2012, however, Thiebaud stated that he occasionally used a studio set-up for a still life: 'I'm not always relying on memory'.
6   Bult 2012.
7   Ibid.
8   Kaufman 2023, p. 146.
9   Pardee 2019.

10   Alessia Masi, 'Interview to Wayne Thiebaud' in Masi 2011, p. 51 (punctuation regularised; reference courtesy Chloe Nahum).
11   Aschheim and Daubert 2014, p. 70 gives details of Thiebaud's process: 'I pretty much always make some preliminary drawings. It's just that when I begin to paint … I just start painting with a light color. But that's really drawing with a brush. You know, figuring out, and then wiping it and changing it. … there's always lots of overpainting or wiping out what's underneath.'
12   Roland Barthes, 'Le Message photographique', *Communications*, vol. 1, no. 1, 1961, pp. 127–38, at p. 133. English edition: 'The Photographic Message', in Roland Barthes, *Image, Music, Text*, Stephen Heath trans., London: Fontana Press, 1977, pp. 15–31, at p. 24.
13   Artist's statement, 1962, reproduced in Teagle 2018, p. 149. See Aloïs Riegl, *Late Roman Art Industry*, Rolf Winkes trans., Rome: Giorgio

Bretschneider, 1985 (originally published 1901) and Erwin Panofsky, *Perspective as a Symbolic Form*, Christopher S. Wood trans., New York: Zone Books, 1991 (originally published 1924–25).
14   Artist's statement, 1962, reproduced in Teagle 2018, p. 149.
15   Benson with Shearer 1969, p. 70.
16   Artist's statement, 1962, reproduced in Teagle 2018, p. 150.
17   Meyer Schapiro, *Paul Cézanne*, New York: Abrams, 1988 (originally published 1952), p. 16.
18   David Riesman with Nathan Glazer and Reuel Denney, *The Lonely Crowd: A Study of the Changing American Character*, New Haven: Yale University Press, 1961 (originally published 1956), p. 138.
19   Harold Rosenberg, 'The Herd of Independent Minds: Has the Avant-Garde Its Own Mass Culture?', *Commentary*, vol. 6, no. 3, September 1948, pp. 242–45.

20   Artist's statement, 1962, reproduced in Teagle 2018, p. 150.

21   Benson with Shearer 1969, p. 70.

22   Wayne Thiebaud, 'A Fellow Painter's View of Giorgio Morandi', *The New York Times*, 15 November 1981, p. 37.

23   Clement Greenberg, 'Henri Rousseau and Modern Art' (1946), in O'Brian 1986–93, vol. 2, p. 94.

24   Aschheim and Daubert 2014, p. 27.

25   Clement Greenberg, 'Henri Rousseau and Modern Art' (1946), in O'Brian 1986–93, vol. 2, p. 95.

26   Artist's statement, 1962, reproduced in Teagle 2018, p. 149.

27   Ibid, p. 150.

28   Ibid, pp. 149–50.

29   John Coplans, 'Wayne Thiebaud: An Interview', in Coplans 1968, pp. 23–36, at p. 28.

30   Pardee 2019 (original emphasis).

31   Théophile Thoré, 'Galerie de M. le Comte de Morny', *L'Artiste*, vol. 10, 1847, p. 52 (author's translation).

32   Benson with Shearer 1969, p. 65: 'I have such a proclivity towards art history and its uses.'

33   *Thiebaud via Morandi* 2011 and Wollheim 1991, p. 66. On Thiebaud's early encounters with Morandi's art, see Dorothy Jean McKetta, *Giorgio Morandi: Los Angeles, 1961*, doctoral dissertation, The University of Texas at Austin, 2024, pp. 163–69 and 188–89.

34   'Wayne Thiebaud: "The Painted World"', Elson Lecture, National Gallery of Art, Washington, D.C., 1 March 2000: https://www.nga.gov/audio-video/audio/elson-thiebaud.html. See also Kaufman 2023, p. 144.

35   *Thiebaud via Morandi* 2011.

36   Wollheim 1991, p. 65. See also Kaufman 2023, p. 141.

37   Willem Bürger (Théophile Thoré), 'Salon de 1868', in Théophile Thoré-Bürger, *Les Salons: études de critique et d'esthétique*, 3 vols, Brussels: H. Lamertin, 1893, vol. 3, p. 532 (author's translation).

38   See, for example, Charles Morice, 'Le XXIe Salon des Indépendants', *Le Mercure de France*, vol. 54, 15 April 1905, p. 552.

39   Albright 1978, p. 86.

40   Aschheim and Daubert 2014, p. 30.

41   See Willem de Kooning, interview by Emile de Antonio, 1970, in *Painters Painting*, film produced and directed by Emile de Antonio, Turin Film Corp., 1972.

42   Thiebaud paraphrasing de Kooning's words in Aschheim and Daubert 2014, p. 8 (original emphasis).

43   Larsen 2001.

44   Pardee 2019.

45   Kaufman 2023, p. 140 (original ellipsis).

46   Wollheim 1991, p. 67. See also Kaufman 2023, p. 143.

47   Benson with Shearer 1969, p. 66.

48   Kozloff 1962, p. 406.

49   Albright 1978, p. 86: 'I'm interested in foods generally which have been fooled with ritualistically … There's something I find fascinating about making a circle of butter'.

50   Thiebaud later took this type of tension between image and format to an extreme in landscapes where a 'ridge' descends from an upper corner of a rectangular format, diagonally to a lower corner (see the pastel *Diagonal Ridge*, 1967, private collection).

51   Kaufman 2023, p. 140. Thiebaud's knowledge of Cézanne was enhanced by fellow West Coast artist Erle Loran's publication *Cézanne's Composition*, Berkeley: University of California Press, 1943, although Cézanne never referred to 'the cube'. In an alternative account of the early 'pies', Thiebaud recalled that he decided to 'paint some forms from the restaurant … the most sort of basic shapes. Triangles, squares, rectangles, ovals and circles and that's when I laid out these triangles and started turning them into pies': Bult 2012.

52   See note 5.

53   Harold Rosenberg, 'The American Action Painters' (1952), in Harold Rosenberg, *The Tradition of the New*, New York: McGraw-Hill, 1959, pp. 30 and 26.

54   Aschheim and Daubert 2014, p. 31 (order of phrasing reversed).

55   Albright 1978, p. 86. See also Aschheim and Daubert 2014, pp. 12 and 57–58.

56   Kaufman 2023, p. 142 and Albright 1978, p. 85. See also Wollheim 1991, p. 65 and Benson with Shearer 1969, p. 70.

57   Adolph Gottlieb, Mark Rothko and Barnett Newman, letter to *The New York Times*, 7 June 1943, at https://www.gottliebfoundation.org/blog/2022/9/23/from-the-archives-adolph-gottlieb-and-mark-rothko (accessed 23 March 2025): 'It is a widely accepted notion among painters that it does not matter what one paints, as long as it is well painted. This is the essence of academicism. There is no such thing as a good painting about nothing.'

58   Artist's statement, 1962, reproduced in Teagle 2018, p. 149.

59   Ibid, p. 150 (original ellipsis).

60   See, for example, Nicholas Fox Weber, 'The Pleasure of Craving the Bounties of American Life', in *Wayne Thiebaud: Updated Edition*, New York: Rizzoli, 2022, pp. 20–25.

61   Kozloff 1962, p. 407.

62   Benson with Shearer 1969, p. 68.

63   Pardee 2019.

64   Aschheim and Daubert 2014, p. 5.

65   Ibid, p. 25.

66   Donald Judd, 'In the Galleries: Wayne Thiebaud' (September 1962), in Judd 2005, p. 60.

67   Aschheim and Daubert 2014, p. 30.

68   Donald Judd, 'Specific Objects' (1964–65), in Judd 2005, p. 189. See also Donald Judd, 'In the Galleries: Claes Oldenburg' (September 1964), in Judd 2005, p. 133.

69   Donald Judd, 'Claes Oldenburg' (1966), in Judd 2005, p. 192.

70   Bult 2012.

71   Kaufman 2023, p. 143.

72   John Coplans, 'Wayne Thiebaud: An Interview', in Coplans 1968, pp. 23–36, at p. 30.

73   Benson with Shearer 1969, p. 68.

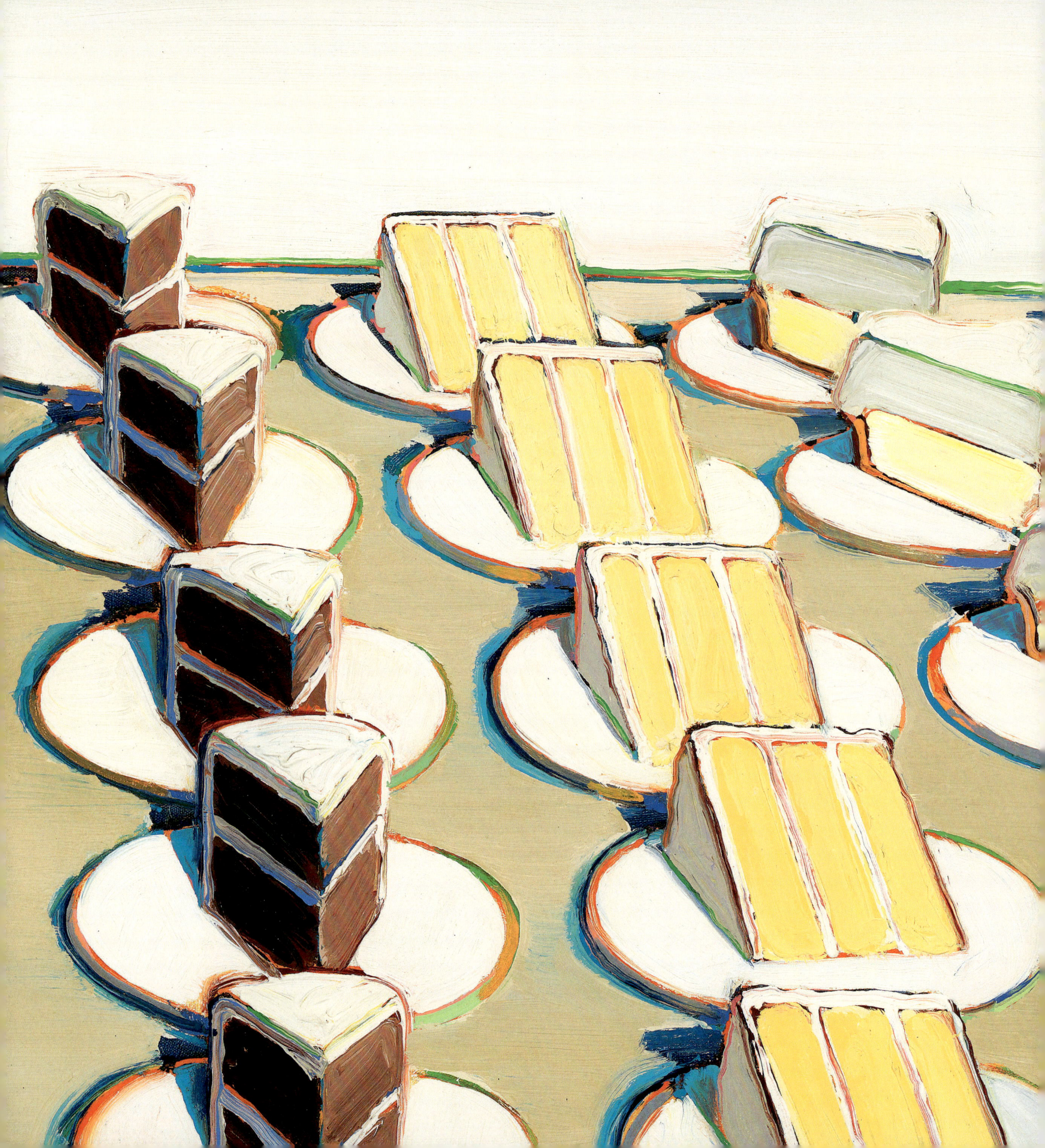

Catalogue

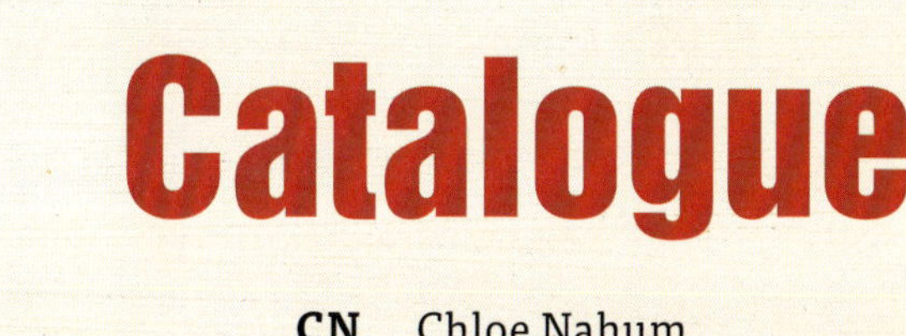

CN   Chloe Nahum
KS   Karen Serres
BW   Barnaby Wright

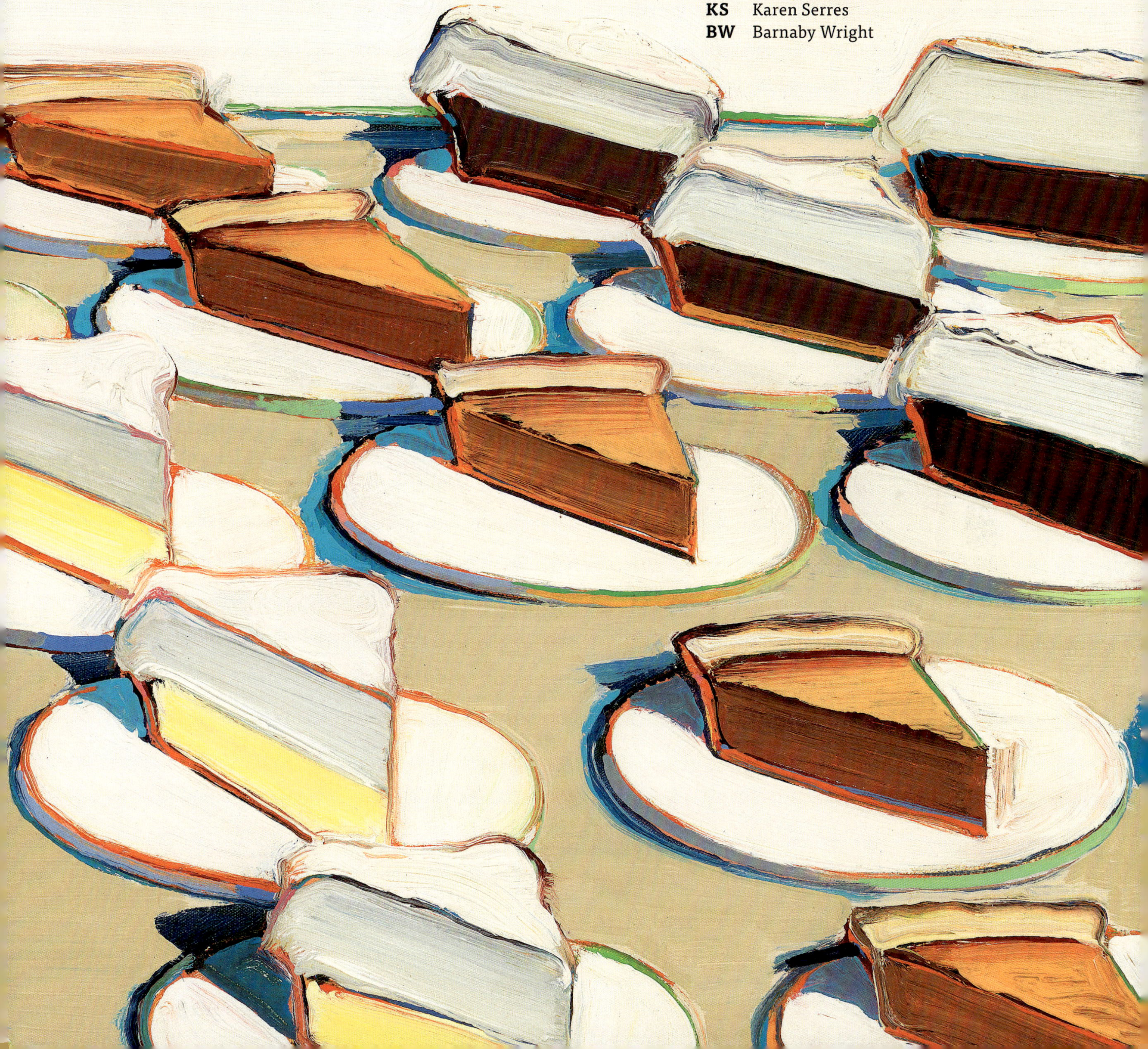

1
Pinball Machine

1956
Mixed media on board
91.5 x 121.5 cm
Collection of the Wayne Thiebaud Foundation

In 1956, Wayne Thiebaud took a year-long sabbatical from his post as chairman of the art department at Sacramento Junior College and travelled to New York. His aim was to meet artists developing abstraction and to encounter work that, until then, he had largely seen only in reproduction. As he put it, 'I had my heroes by then – Willem de Kooning and the whole fascination with Abstract Expressionism as an American movement … they became heroic to me, in terms of their quest.'[1] This painting dates from this period and readily announces the influence of its context in its abstracted setting and gestural, vigorous brushstrokes. As Thiebaud later put it, 'I just started imitating them, to see if I could sneak in some of their flourishes and drips and smears.'[2] Yet, in spite of his experimentation with the animated application of Abstract Expressionism, the work stands apart from the movement in its clearly defined subject matter formed of the vernacular Americana that Thiebaud had been depicting since at least 1953 – something that troubled him during this time. 'I felt sort of embarrassed by the fact that I had subject matter in there', he later recalled. 'I tried to cover it up with arty strokes and expressive lines'.[3] Yet, subject matter remained, bringing with it the corollary concern of depicting its interaction with light. Here, highlights of silver paint serve as early methods of producing the 'lively light' that would become one of Thiebaud's defining painterly enquiries.[4]

Placed on a stool at the left of the canvas is the iconic silhouette of a Coca-Cola bottle – a design created in 1916 following a brief for a shape 'so distinct that you would recognize it by feel in the dark or lying broken on the ground'.[5] Perhaps surprisingly, this quintessential totem of American design did not become commonplace in Thiebaud's repertoire, although other American artists, most prominently Andy Warhol, would embrace its symbolic riches in the years that followed. In contrast, pinball and gumball machines would long be favoured by Thiebaud, although taken latterly as isolated objects (see cat. 9 and 18). The gumball machine, seen at right, would become emblematic of his defence of the depiction of everyday objects. 'Look, gumball machines really are as beautiful as other things,' he would later say. 'Why can't they be painted?'[6] Dominating the painting is the pinball machine, which intrudes almost exaggeratedly into the picture plane. The thickly overlaid patterning of the machine may imply the presence of another painting below that Thiebaud both incorporated and worked over to create the dense final effect. This heavily decorated style was short-lived: in his later, celebrated painting of these highly ornamented machines, *Four Pinball Machines* (cat. 9), he would streamline the design of their decorative backglasses into clean grids and circles. Mirroring these newly legible designs, the later work views the machines front-on, employing dramatic foreshortening to create a linear pattern in a dramatically simplified environment.

Though the present painting plausibly depicts an interior scene, the sparser settings that Thiebaud would soon come to favour are prefigured in the solid divisions of red, light and dark blue that form the floor and walls – a construction that calls to mind the geometric abstractions of artists such as Piet Mondrian, one of Thiebaud's artistic heroes. Floating atop of this, the figurative elements appear almost as surreal intrusions, as still life, rendered in expressionistic style, collides with geometric abstraction. **CN**

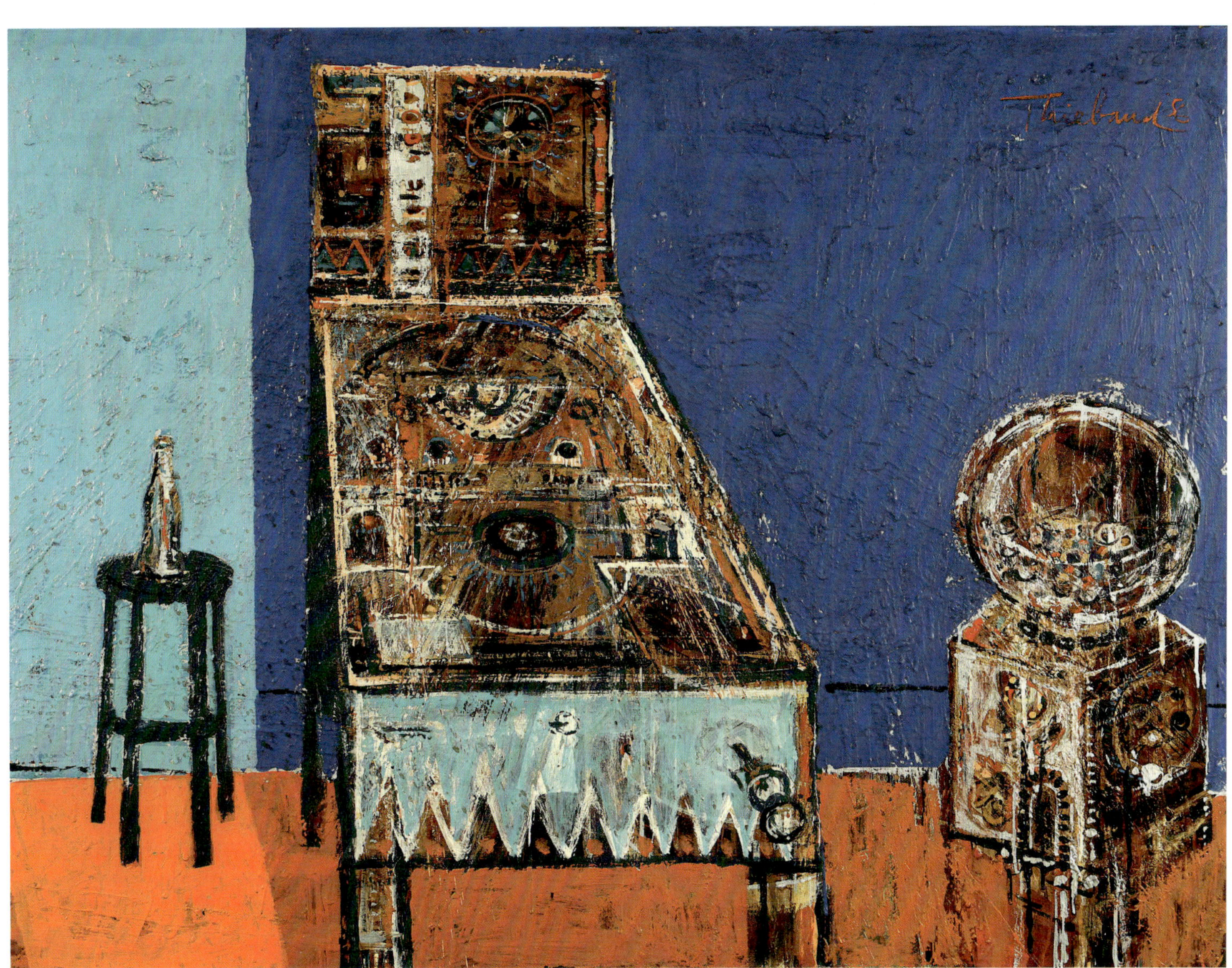

2

Meat Counter

1956–59
Oil on canvas
73 x 76.2 cm
The Kondos Collection

Like *Pinball Machine* (cat. 1), *Meat Counter* dates from around the time of Wayne Thiebaud's sojourn in New York. Though he dated the work '1957' on the bottom left of the canvas, he inscribed the dates 1956–59 on the stretcher, suggesting that he may have begun the painting in New York before finishing it in California, continuing to work on it after he had dated it. Around this time, Thiebaud developed an interest in shop windows and displays, and portrayed them in several works. In these, he experimented with various compositions, sometimes including people serving behind the counter and viewing displays through windows. The present painting comes closest to the composition that would remain his preferred mode of depicting shop displays: zoomed in on objects that are often presented in multiples. Here, these are the cooked meats that were one of the first products to be sold in American delicatessens from the late nineteenth century. In a 1962 *Time* interview, Thiebaud connected 'the luscious, fatty richness of oil paint and the greasiness of meats and buttery frostings'.[7] The latter would greatly outstrip the former as the favoured subject, perhaps due to Thiebaud's interest in foods that had been modified by human intervention. As he put it in 1968, 'I have only rarely painted steak …. I paint those foods which have mostly undergone some kind of a change or metamorphosis.'[8] Other, more obviously transformed kinds of meat, such as the hanging sausages seen in *Delicatessen Counter* (cat. 14), provided such a stimulus.

The painting is a significant early example of Thiebaud's interest in the commercial display methods used for prepared foods. Later paintings that engaged with the presentation of foodstuffs such as *Candy Counter* (cat. 12) and *Peppermint Counter* (cat. 15) are radically clarified and discharged of the busy brushstrokes that animate the present work. His treatment of colour here similarly sets the painting apart from his distinctive later style. Though Thiebaud would further develop an interest in the interplay of warm and cool colour, observable in the complementary orange and blue surfaces of the counter, this bold dialogue would largely be transposed onto objects and their highly coloured outlines, with their settings more typically rendered in cooler, neutral palettes suggestive of the 'stainless steel, porcelain, enameled, plastic world' that he sought to evoke.[9] Other aspects that would recur make an early appearance in the present painting. The hand-lettered 'show cards' that he would revisit in several later paintings (see cat. 13, 14 and 15) punctuate the counter.[10] Bold, deep blue shadows – another signature of his later works – also emerge in this canvas. Considered in combination with its early adoption of his favoured countertop composition, the painting can be understood as a statement of intent for what would follow as Thiebaud honed his style in the coming years. **CN**

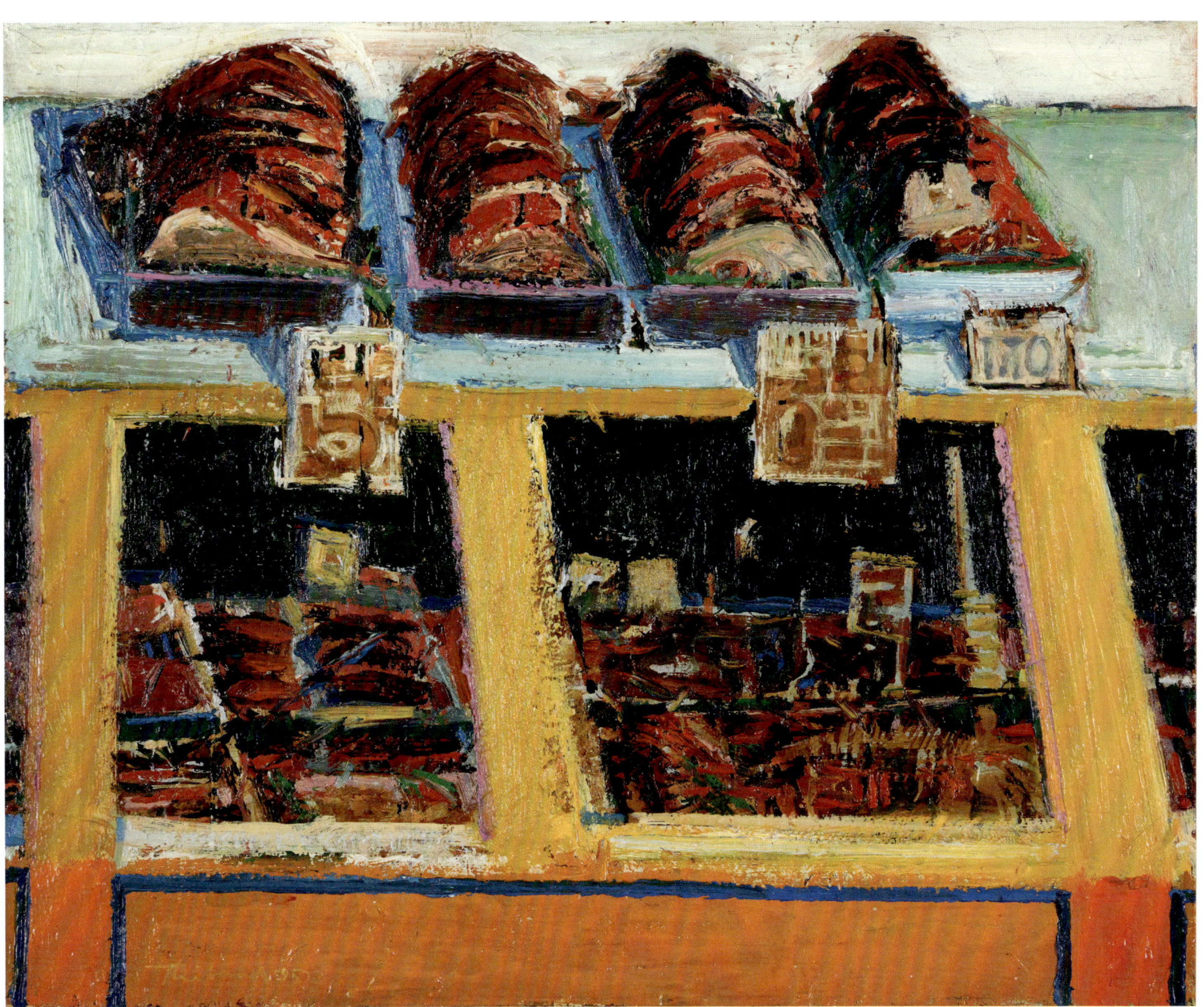

3

Penny Machines

1961
Oil on canvas
61 x 76.2 cm
Collection of John Berggruen

Penny Machines is an important work in the transitional phase between Wayne Thiebaud's early and mature styles. In it, the artist adopted much of the clarified, resolved approach that would win him renown when it and at least 45 other works, including *Cold Cereal* (cat. 4) and *Five Hot Dogs* (cat. 6), were exhibited at New York's Allan Stone Gallery in April 1962. Here, his subject is the candy vending machines that were ubiquitous in America, having first appeared in New York in 1888.[11] Due to their unreliable nature, they sold only penny items such as candy until the 1920s. Thiebaud had previously tried, in his words, to 'hide' the objects he depicted, leaving them 'lavishly overlayed with all kinds of abstract expressionist brushstrokes'.[12] Speaking of his earlier depictions of gumball machines (see cat. 1), he explained,

> they were so highly abstracted and I was so interested in being an artist. Then, as I got more and more interested in an object, as such, I began to feel that I wanted to get rid of the expressionist brushstroke, which jazzes up the surface, making everything active and busy. I decided to go back to very basic, formalistic concerns.[13]

Penny Machines demonstrates this embrace of the object and of a decidedly representational form of painting, produced mainly from memory, that had emerged in Thiebaud's practice towards the end of 1959. The gestural mode of mark-making with which he had experimented in earlier works was of less pertinence to this new undertaking, although the present painting sees it recalled for the newly representational purpose of rendering the striped throng of candy in the right-hand dispenser. Thiebaud's new, unabashed engagement with the motif is symbolically demonstrated by the frontal composition that he employs to observe the dispensers. He characterised this as a 'head on directness' and continued to favour it in depictions of similar objects, including the 1963 work *Three Machines* (cat. 18).[14] In so doing, he wished to interrogate their visual power, or aura, 'to figure out why the object attracted me'.[15] Consequently, he settled upon what he considered 'a neutral description with a minimum of interpretation … to present it as directly as I could'. Here, the inanimate objects seem to gaze out at the viewer with a somewhat anthropomorphic quality.

Though Thiebaud's instincts grew progressively more realist in terms of a direct articulation of his subject matter, his approach to paint increasingly exploited its physical properties in ways that, when viewed up close, could veer towards a more abstract idiom. He often spoke of his love of working with oil paint due to the relief brushwork that he could produce with it – an effect that he termed 'combing'.[16] Here, sweeping strokes of sensuous, thickly brushed impasto construct the blue wall and pink floor – bold colours that Thiebaud would largely move away from in breakthrough works of the same year, which instead employed a neutral, almost clinical ground of whites and creams. **CN**

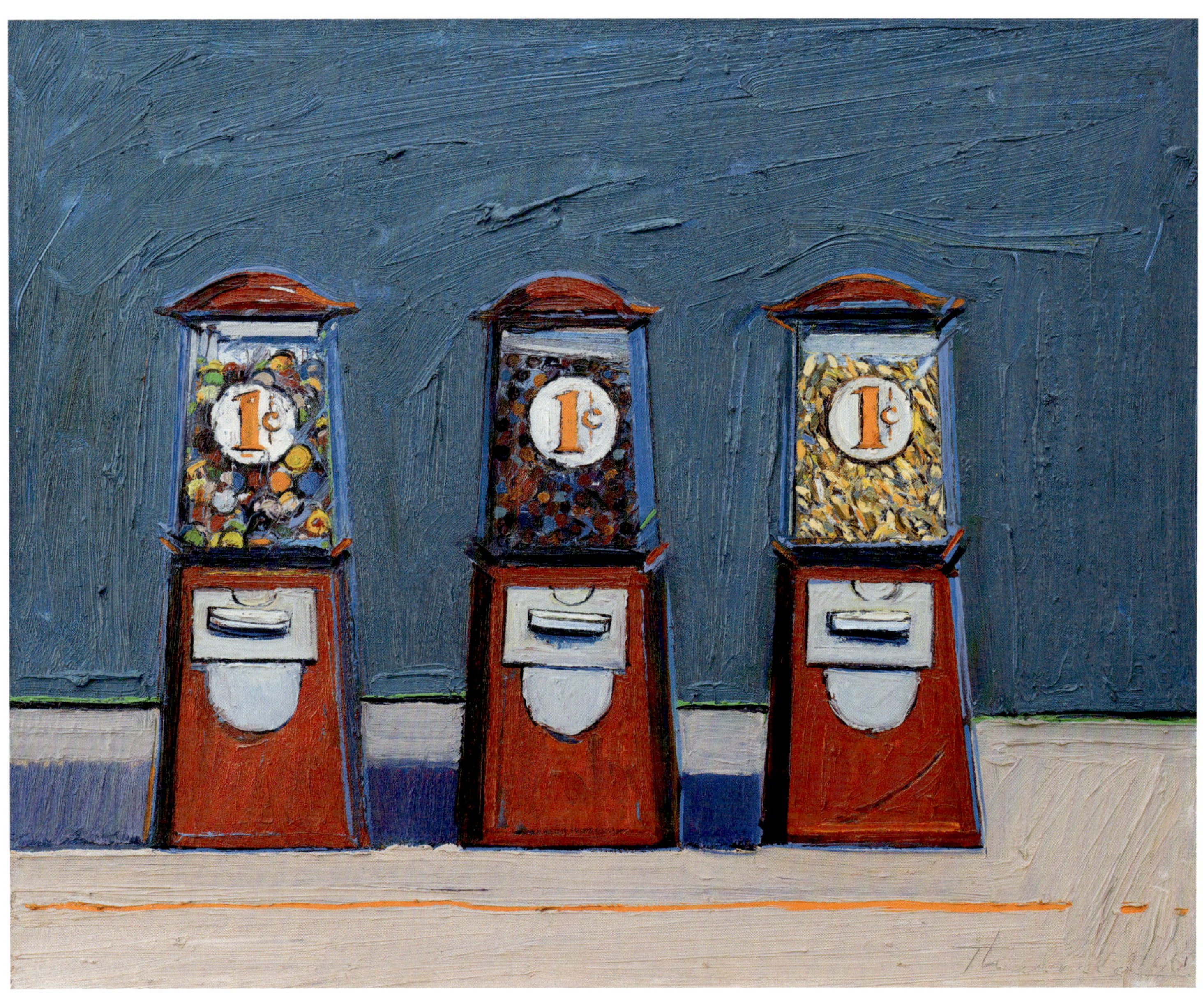

4
Cold Cereal

1961
Oil on canvas
61.5 x 76.5 cm
Collection of the Wayne Thiebaud Foundation

Cold cereal, so named in distinction from traditional hot breakfast fare such as porridge, was introduced in the United States in the 1880s and originally intended as a health food. By the mid-twentieth century, however, a plethora of high-sugar breakfast cereals were available, many of which were marketed towards children.[17] In the present painting, Wayne Thiebaud depicts the reverse of one such cereal box, across which the word 'FREE' is emblazoned in reference to the giveaways that had become a mainstay of cereal promotion by this time. The requisite coupon, surrounded by a dashed line and an arrow, occupies the bottom left of the box. With all other text eliminated, the word 'free' gestures beyond the marketing strategies of consumer culture to broader notions of American freedom that were of particular pertinence to the painting's Cold War context. Although Thiebaud rarely discussed his work in terms of social criticism, it is hard to separate this painting from contemporary notions of America as a torchbearer for liberty. Indeed, that January, President John F. Kennedy had made the concept of American freedom central to his inaugural presidential address, including in its famed closing aphorism: 'Ask not what America will do for you, but what together we can do for the freedom of man.' Certainly, Thiebaud's relationship to his work was inflected with patriotic notions of freedom: the decision to paint 'any kind of subject matter that tickles my fancy' was, for him, 'a kind of American independence'.[18] He believed there was 'some sort of American chauvinism' in his selection of homegrown subject matter.[19]

As in many of the still lifes that would make his name, Thiebaud moved in closer to his subject, placing it on a tabletop and eliminating extraneous detail. Reflecting in 1974 on this shift, he explained, 'I moved slowly toward more and more of an isolation of the object … an interest in the object as an object and objective painting.'[20] Further heightening this concentrated approach, Thiebaud radically lightened his colour palette, working with pale greys, whites, creams and blues to render space. While many compositional and chromatic elements of the present painting would remain signatures of Thiebaud's work, its evocation of a domestic setting remained highly unusual in an oeuvre that was focusing more fully on the public spaces of American consumption.

Depicting light was Thiebaud's principal concern at this time. It is boldly interrogated in *Cold Cereal*, which he described as 'one of my very favourites'.[21] Illuminated from the upper right, both cereal box and bowl cast emphatic purple shadows that stand out more starkly for the neutral surface on which they fall. The influence of the Italian painter Giorgio de Chirico, whose work Thiebaud thought 'indelible … like a tattoo', seems written into the distinctly theatrical organisation of object, light and diagonally cast shadow.[22] Another theatrical stimulus to Thiebaud's use of shadow came from student experience lighting college productions in the late 1930s – a memory evoked in *Cold Cereal*:

> he saw the stage floor as a flattened ground plane, often in an evenly lit condition and on which actors and props were distributed in organized configurations. His job was to track and isolate individual performers with the brilliant follow-spot. The light defined dramatically the focal points; it raked dense shadows colored by flaring footlights and the prismatic reflections from the prop's painted surfaces.[23] **CN**

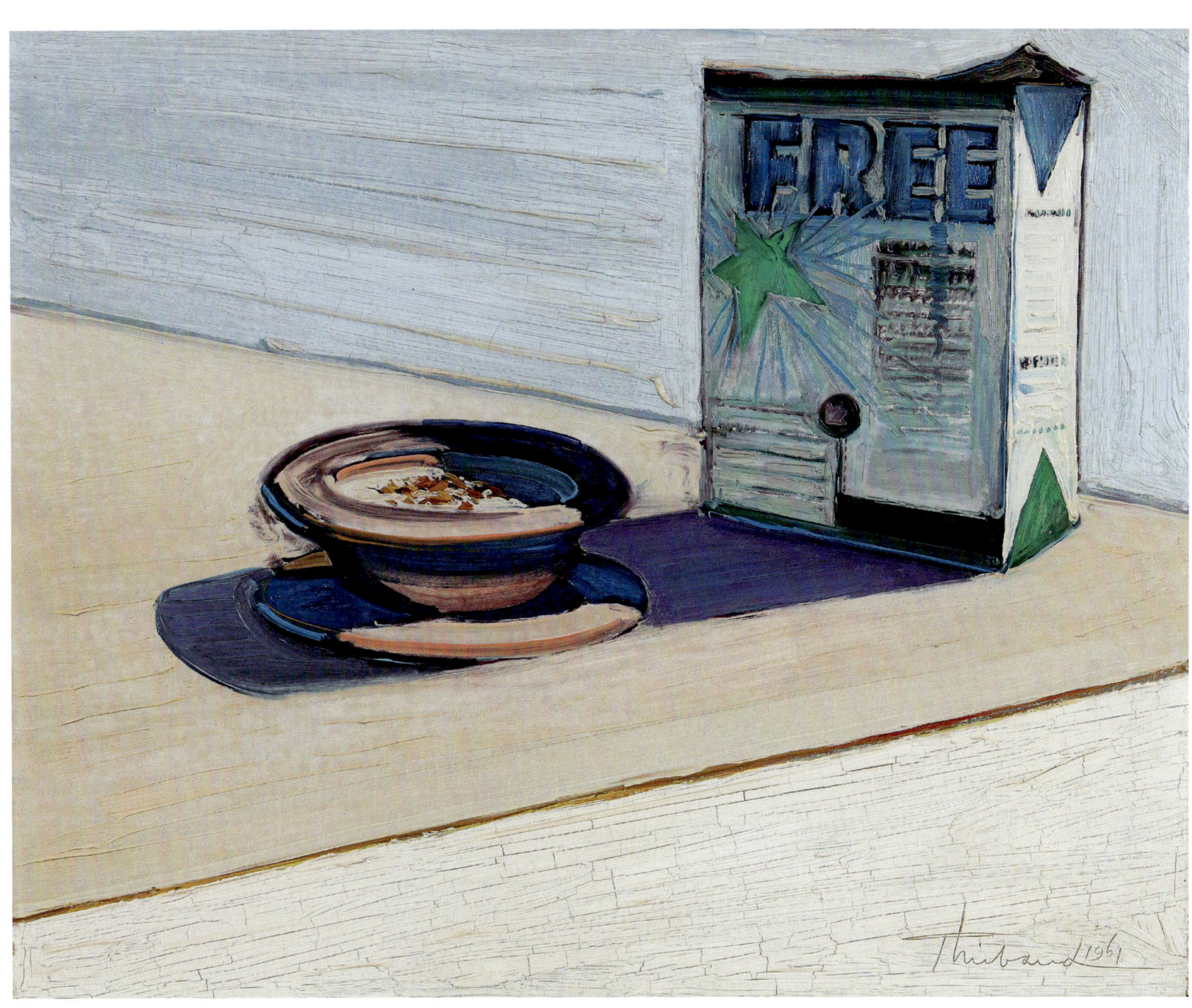
FREE

**5
Pie Rows**

1961
Oil on canvas
46 x 66 cm
Collection of the Wayne Thiebaud Foundation

Wayne Thiebaud often told the origin story of his pie paintings, which he credited with marking a decisive change in his practice. Following advice from Willem de Kooning to 'Find something you know something about, that you've experienced, and something you like or you love',[24] he began to search for a subject with personal resonance. He later recalled his thinking at that time:

> What has my life been? ... I worked in restaurants and helped cook hamburgers, washed dishes, was a busboy. What is that world? Is there anything in that world? So, I said, I'm going to just start as directly as I can. And I took the canvas and made some ovals, thinking about Cézanne – the cube, the cone, and the sphere – and put some triangles over them and thought, well, that maybe could represent a pie on a plate. I had seen them laid out in restaurants and I was always kind of interested in the way in which they formed these nice patterns. I said, alright, I'll go ahead with this and I'll make them into pies. I was really enjoying myself ... and as I finished, I looked at it, and said, my God, I just painted a bunch of pies.[25]

Thiebaud had come upon a subject of personal and formal integrity that would sustain rigorous painterly investigation for the rest of his long career. As he put it in a 2014 interview, 'there are still days that start with the thought: This morning, I'd like to paint a pie.'[26]

This breakthrough in subject matter and its treatment would come to define Thiebaud's career. In 1961, he was making his way around New York in the hope of finding a gallery interested in showing his work. His last stop was the Allan Stone Gallery, where it was his paintings of pies that won over an initially reluctant Stone.[27] As Thiebaud later recalled it, the gallerist explained his decision to give him an exhibition as one made almost by his unconscious: 'I went home and, for some reason, kept seeing these pies in front of my face as I was watching television. Well any image that can sustain itself like that I can't help but be interested in.'[28] The resulting exhibition, held in April 1962, was densely hung with around 46 works, including *Penny Machines* (cat. 3) and *Five Hot Dogs* (cat. 6).[29] Another version of the present painting, *Pies* (fig. 37), was also exhibited, and purchased by Stone himself. During the exhibition's run, Stone wrote to Thiebaud that it was the pie paintings that were the most in demand. Indeed, it was these that quickly became synonymous with the artist, bolstered in part by Stone's decision to place 'pie ads' in various art journals.[30]

The exhibition was a surprise and immediate sensation. Thiebaud would later reflect on it as 'so unreal and so strange that it is still one of those goofy experiences you can never quite reconcile ... one moment one thing, then another'.[31] Beside a number of high-profile collectors, institutional acquisitions were made by Alfred Barr for the Museum of Modern Art, New York (fig. 22), and by the Wadsworth Atheneum Museum of Art, Hartford (fig. 31). By August that year, Stone had sold around 65 works by Thiebaud – a remarkable number for a largely unknown artist who had never previously been shown on the East Coast. Reviews were published widely: *The New York Times* touted Thiebaud as the 'Edward Hopper of the dinette tabletop'.[32] Donald Judd, then writing art criticism, claimed that, 'in the protected circle of representational art he

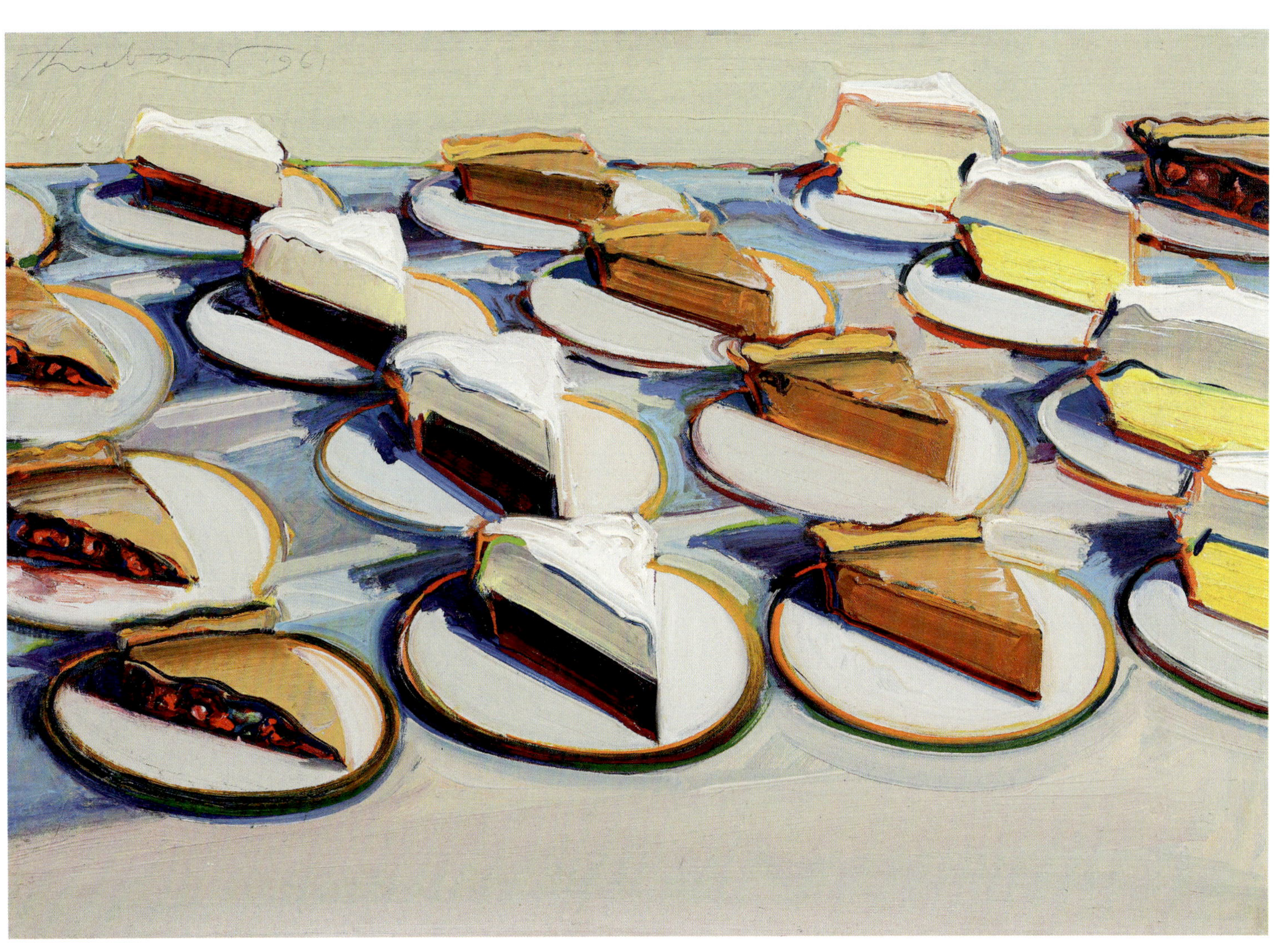

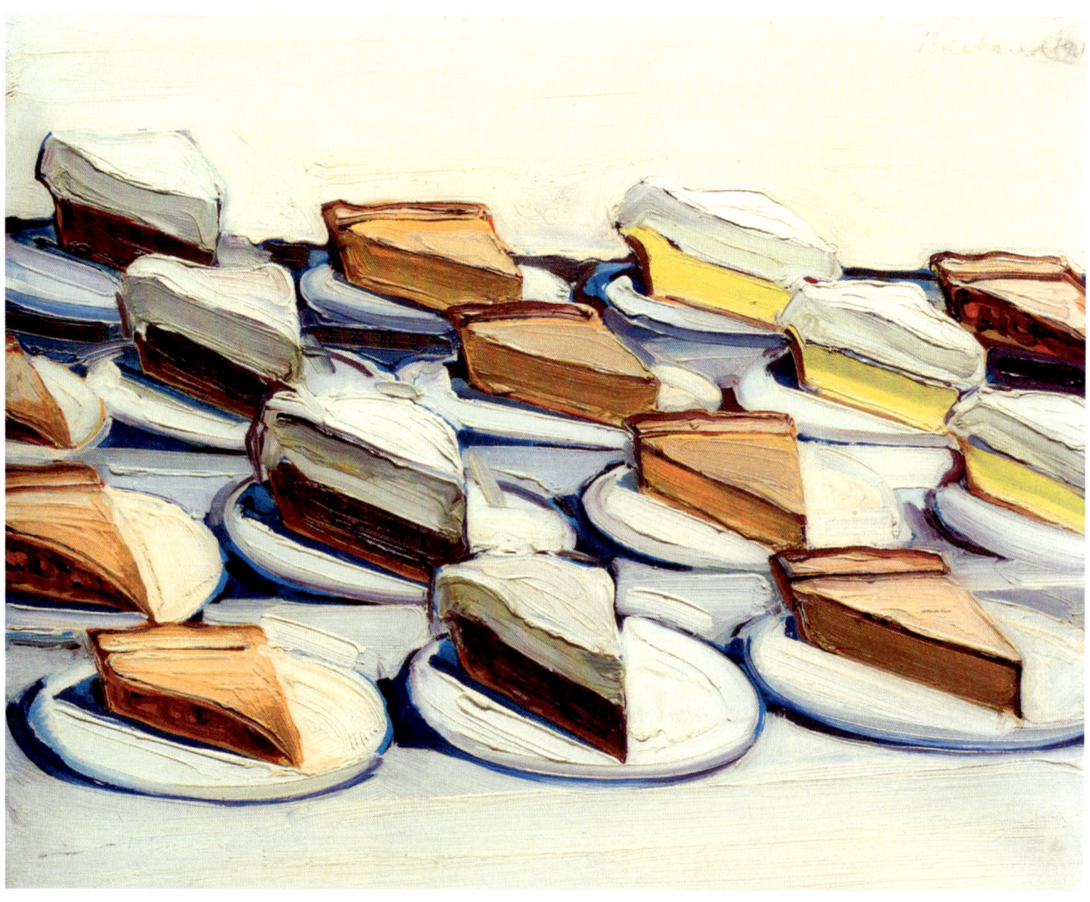

is one of the best. He is much better than his neighbors in the San Francisco area; he has done something rather than ape old art.'[33] Like many others, *Time* jumped at the chance of a gustatory pun: 'as his first Manhattan show closed … there was ample evidence that he had a number of connoisseurs drooling … sympathetically over the slice-of-cake school of art'.[34]

Widespread among the critical responses to the exhibition was the sense that Thiebaud's work was, in the words of Thomas Hess in *Art News*, 'social criticism made visual'.[35] Hess went on,

Looking at these pounds of slabby New Taste Sensation, one hears the artist screaming at us from behind the paintings, urging us to become hermits: to leave the new Gomorrah where layer cakes troop down air-conditioned shelving like chloresterol [sic] angels, to flee to the desert and eat locusts and pray for faith. [Thiebaud] preaches revulsion by isolating the American food habit.

Although, in 1962, Thiebaud would concede that his paintings offered 'some rather obvious notions about conformism, mechanized living, and mass produced culture', he would become increasingly averse to such readings of his work.[36] By 1980, he would proclaim, 'Conscious irony, or symbolism, or criticism of the American Dream, or celebration of American mass production – I'm very skeptical of all that sort of thing. That's why I always say that artists should not have ideas.'[37]

In the present painting, Thiebaud lays out diagonal rows of cherry, chocolate meringue, lemon meringue and pumpkin pie. At the right-hand edge, the appearance of another slice of cherry pie begins the sequence again, humorously suggesting that what we look on may be only a fraction of an infinite display. Such multiplication occurred beyond the canvas, with Thiebaud replicating this composition in four paintings made in 1961. He was encouraged in these repetitions by the example of Jean-Siméon Chardin, whom he described as 'one of the first multiple artists' in his repeated return to the same motifs.[38] Though Judd would claim the meaning of Thiebaud's work to lie in 'the existential nausea of innumerable things', his cakes 'neither good nor individual',[39] Thiebaud rather understood each piece of pie to possess 'a uniqueness and specialness in spite of its regimentation.'[40] In each iteration of the present composition, Thiebaud made various modifications to colour and arrangement and practised a different application, from the thinner, smoother strokes observable here to the thicker handling of other versions. **CN**

6
Five Hot Dogs

1961
Oil on canvas
45.7 x 61 cm
The Bransten Family Collection

Wayne Thiebaud's principal method when painting still-life subjects was to work from memory so as to capture what was 'most memorable about the subject'.[41] An important influence on this essentialising approach was cartooning, which had been Thiebaud's earliest introduction to draughtsmanship. By his teenage years, he was sending his own to magazines, a few of which were published, and in 1936 he worked briefly as an apprentice at Walt Disney Studios. For Thiebaud, the 'graphic energy' of cartoons stemmed from their 'method of reduction' – a principle to which *Five Hot Dogs* is visibly indebted in the recognisable simplicity of its forms, the bold blue outlines of the buns and the cartoonish streaks of red and yellow that indicate the obligatory ketchup and mustard.[42] Described by one food historian as 'America's chief iconic food item', the hot dog was already primed for such treatment; 'its mythic attributes might best be summed up in the phrase, "America's great democratic food"'.[43]

Thiebaud's procedure of distillation was further and perhaps more profoundly influenced by his experience working as an art director. This, he later said, had taught him 'a language of form – a kind of Esperanto of advertising art'.[44] The present painting calls upon strategies of commercial design in its organisation of the hot dogs on an unadorned white surface, a device that was typical of contemporary advertisements. However, more than mere allusion, Thiebaud's use of a white ground offered a painterly challenge with exciting potential for experimentation. Asked the reason for its appeal, he responded, 'Problem. It was a conscious problem in design and space … is there a way to make a transition from the very stark plane to a figure or an object in front of it?'[45]

Thiebaud's debut exhibition at the Allan Stone Gallery in 1962 quickly saw him associated with Pop Art due to a shared commitment to the depiction of everyday American subjects. In the same year that the present painting was exhibited there, it was also included in *New Painting of Common Objects* at the Pasadena Art Museum, widely credited with being the first museum survey of Pop. However, Thiebaud's status in the movement was never clear-cut. Reviewing the exhibition, the critic Jules Langsner wrote,

> It becomes quickly apparent at Pasadena that the Common Object painters are split with regard to literalness of presentation. It seems there are painterly commonists and meticulous copyists. Thus Warhol and Lichtenstein adhere strictly to accuracy of reproduction, while Dowd, Hefferton, and Thiebaud use the common object as a point of departure for painterly treatment. A hot dog or slice of cream pie by Thiebaud bursts with juicy pigment, a succulence that brings out the properties of paint more than it does the food he is obsessed with.[46]

As Langsner intuited, this full-bodied facture separated Thiebaud fundamentally from the chilly, detached style favoured by Pop artists. In contrast to their appropriation of mechanical means of reproduction in paint, Thiebaud passionately believed that the painter held a responsibility to 'ensure that each completed painting is not a repetitive manufactured product, but a unique and independent work.'[47] Nonetheless, Thiebaud was included in a number of further important Pop Art exhibitions in the first half of the 1960s.[48] **CN**

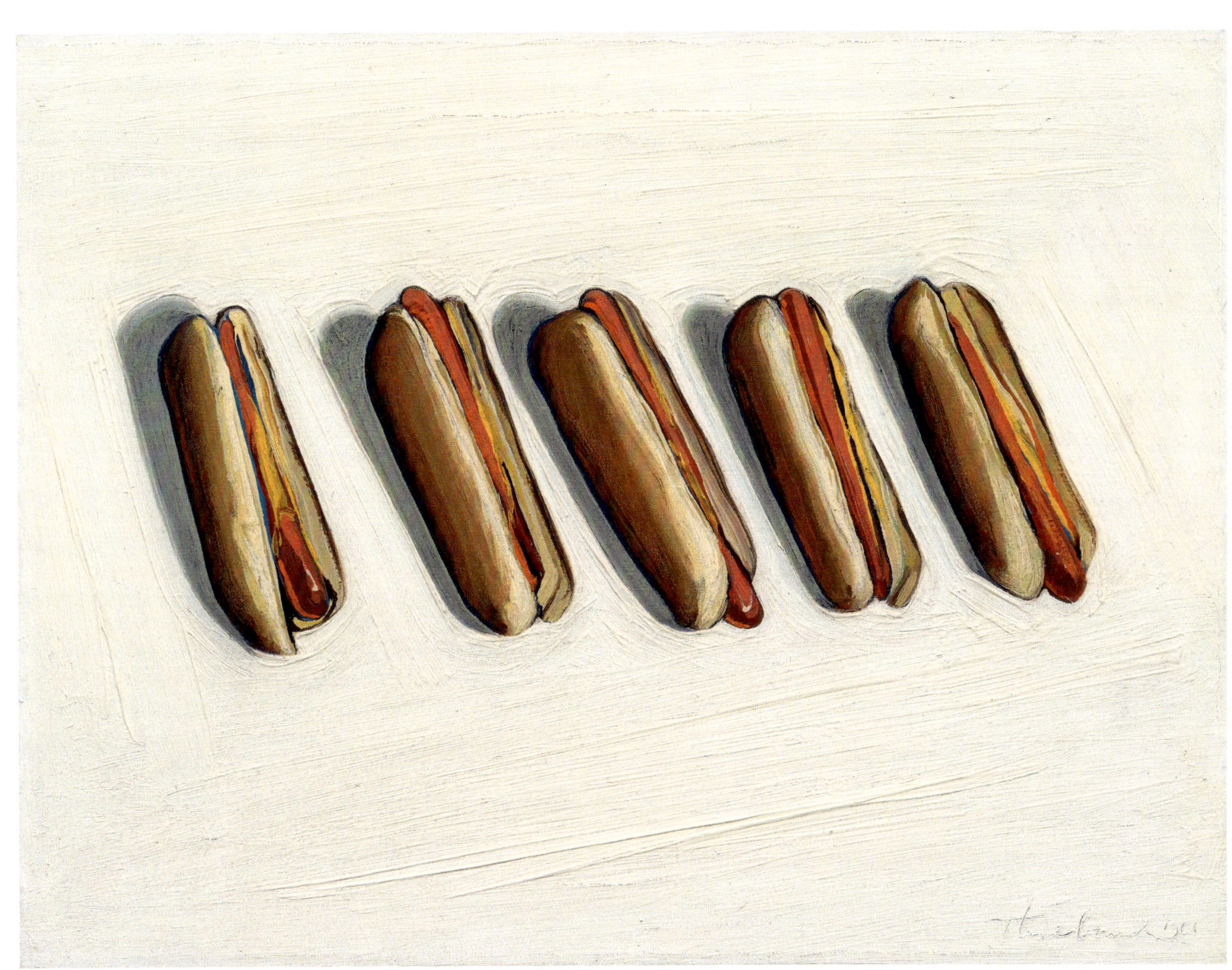

7
Cup of Coffee

1961
Oil on canvas
45.7 x 30.5 cm
The Fine Arts Collection, Jan Shrem and Maria
Manetti Shrem Museum of Art, University of
California, Davis
Gift of Fay Nelson

Cup of Coffee crystallised Wayne Thiebaud's new approach to still life during a crucial year for his development. Other paintings from 1961 show how he explored different types of expressive brushwork and compositional complexity (see, for example, cat. 3 and 4). However, this painting stands at the furthest edge of Thiebaud's moves to minimise extraneous detail and setting to focus intensely and exclusively on the painted object (see also cat. 5 and 6). Here, a plain white diner mug, placed on a white surface, is isolated save for the small shadow it casts. Its scale is modest and unassuming, akin to the actual size of the mug. This is a cup of coffee, simply served. Yet, as we stare into it – as we might a real mug of coffee at a diner counter – subtle complexities emerge, and it becomes a study in form and light. It is evident that Thiebaud began by defining the edges and contours in a variety of bright colours – blue, green, yellow and reddish orange. He then worked with broader brushstrokes of off-whites to form the cup and its background and with blues for the shadow. He paid exquisitely close attention to the mug's contours and the interactions of the coloured lines with the off-whites. Thiebaud spoke of how Californian light and shadow stimulated him: 'the longer one stares, the more differences one notices. One begins to see its color composition, that its edges have a different color than its inner part, that one can see the edges of the edges.'[49] He used Josef Albers's term 'halation' to describe the sensation of light and colour being set off at the edges of forms. In *Cup of Coffee*, these produce numerous glowing contours radiating from the brown oval and crescent of the coffee to the multiple encircling forms of the mug. The highly visible pushes and pulls of Thiebaud's brushwork further animate the cup, which in turn shapes and excites the lively strokes of the off-white background. His final flourish is a brushstroke across the bottom of the canvas ending with his signature. This does not so much define the edge of the counter or table as underscore Thiebaud's new language of painting.

Thiebaud's approach to his subject matter claimed everyday objects of quintessentially modern American life as worthy of deep painterly contemplation. Few objects from the period were more iconic than the diner mug. These thick-walled ceramic coffee mugs had first been produced by Victor Insulators Inc. during the Second World War as heavy-duty serviceware for the United States military but quickly became a ubiquitous feature of diners and restaurants, multiplying across the country in the post-war years. Thiebaud's way of working on his subjects accentuated their emblematic status, as he explained: 'they were painted from memory. I did not have the objects in front of me … this is perhaps what makes them seem like icons, in a sense; they're greatly conventionalized ….'[50]

Thiebaud's artistic breakthrough of 1961 occurred during his first year on the faculty at the University of California, Davis. He continued there for most of his long career, considering his teaching a vital part of his work as an artist. Thiebaud gave *Cup of Coffee* to Professor Richard Nelson, the founder of the art department at Davis, in gratitude for his support. The painting is also the one Thiebaud is photographed showing his former teacher, then colleague, Professor Paul Beckmann, in his Sacramento studio in 1962 (fig. 3).[51] It is fitting that the painting now forms part of the collection at UC Davis's university art museum, which Thiebaud helped to establish. **BW**

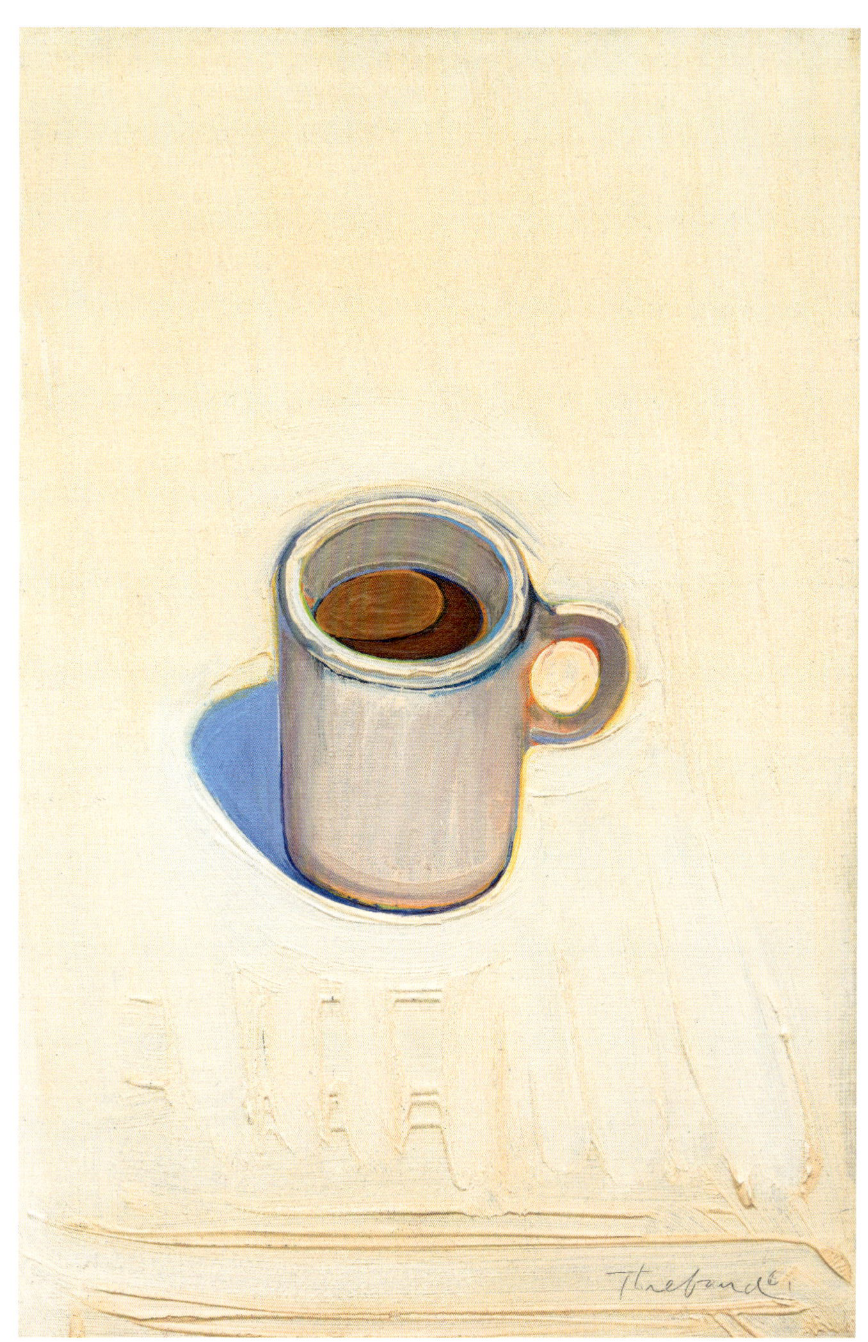

8

Jackpot Machine

1962
Oil on canvas
96.5 x 68.3 cm
Smithsonian American Art Museum,
Washington, D.C.
Museum purchase made possible by the American
Art Forum and gift of an anonymous donor

In the 1950s, Wayne Thiebaud became fascinated by the jackpot machines in the casinos at Lake Tahoe. He recalled that, 'at one point I was even making sketches of them and the great long lines of people playing them [until] two security men came and told me I had to leave.'[52] Suspected of trying to game the casino's system, Thiebaud abandoned his sketching but went on to produce a number of depictions of jackpot machines in the 1950s, including prints and a painting in his then expressionistic style (*Jackpot Machine*, 1955, private collection). Once he had established his new painterly approach at the beginning of the 1960s, he returned to the subject, most notably with this major canvas, included in his second solo exhibition at the Allan Stone Gallery in New York in 1963.

As with many of Thiebaud's still-life subjects, the gambling machine was an icon of modern American consumer culture. The first three-reel slot machine was the 'Liberty Bell', invented in California by Charles Fey of San Francisco and first sold in 1898. It paid out a jackpot of 50 cents if all three bell symbols aligned, with other prizes for matching fruits. Spurred by its success, various companies made their own versions, and they proliferated rapidly across the country in the first half of the new century with bigger, more colourful and enticing machines rolling out of the factories. These mechanical, lever-operated machines reached their zenith in the 1950s and early 1960s when electronic versions started to take over. Rather than being a specific model, Thiebaud's *Jackpot Machine* is his own idealised version, the lever arm of this painted 'one-armed bandit' raised even higher than most actual examples, ready to hold you up and take your money, the central line tantalisingly just one lemon away from a win. The clarity of his design and the lushness of his paint make Thiebaud's slot machine appear perhaps even more arresting than the real thing.

Thiebaud explained that part of his interest in painting *Jackpot Machine* was its strangely anthropomorphic qualities: 'I think they do represent an odd extension of the human configuration in that they have arms and sort of eyes. And the kind of icons of decorations … involving things that we eat and things that we play with like cherries and stars …. I don't pretend to have any answers to the questions that they raise but certainly something was very compelling about it in terms of some sort of tattle-tale evidence that they have about us as a human species.'[53] He also recalled the artist Barnett Newman seeing this painting at his Allan Stone exhibition and calling it 'a very surreal object', adding that it represented a distinctly American type of surrealism.[54] With these remarks in mind we might indeed see it as a portrait of a human-machine hybrid; its coin-slot eye, raised lever-arm and the open mouth of its payout chute embodying a hectoring demand for money on the promise of big wins, redolent of the economic boom years of the post-war period in the United States. Indeed, *Jackpot Machine* wears its American identity to excess with its array of stars, bold stripes and palette of red, white and blue. Yet, as the art historian Jonathan P. Binstock has argued, whereas Thiebaud's lush brushwork often brings us within tasting distance of his food subjects such as cakes and pies, here it serves to render the machine illusory and out of reach.[55] With its untouchable, blurred line-up of coins at the top, the schematic deadness of its fruit symbols and Thiebaud's decision to paint over some of the details on the side panels, *Jackpot Machine* also carries a strange sense of loss.[56] **BW**

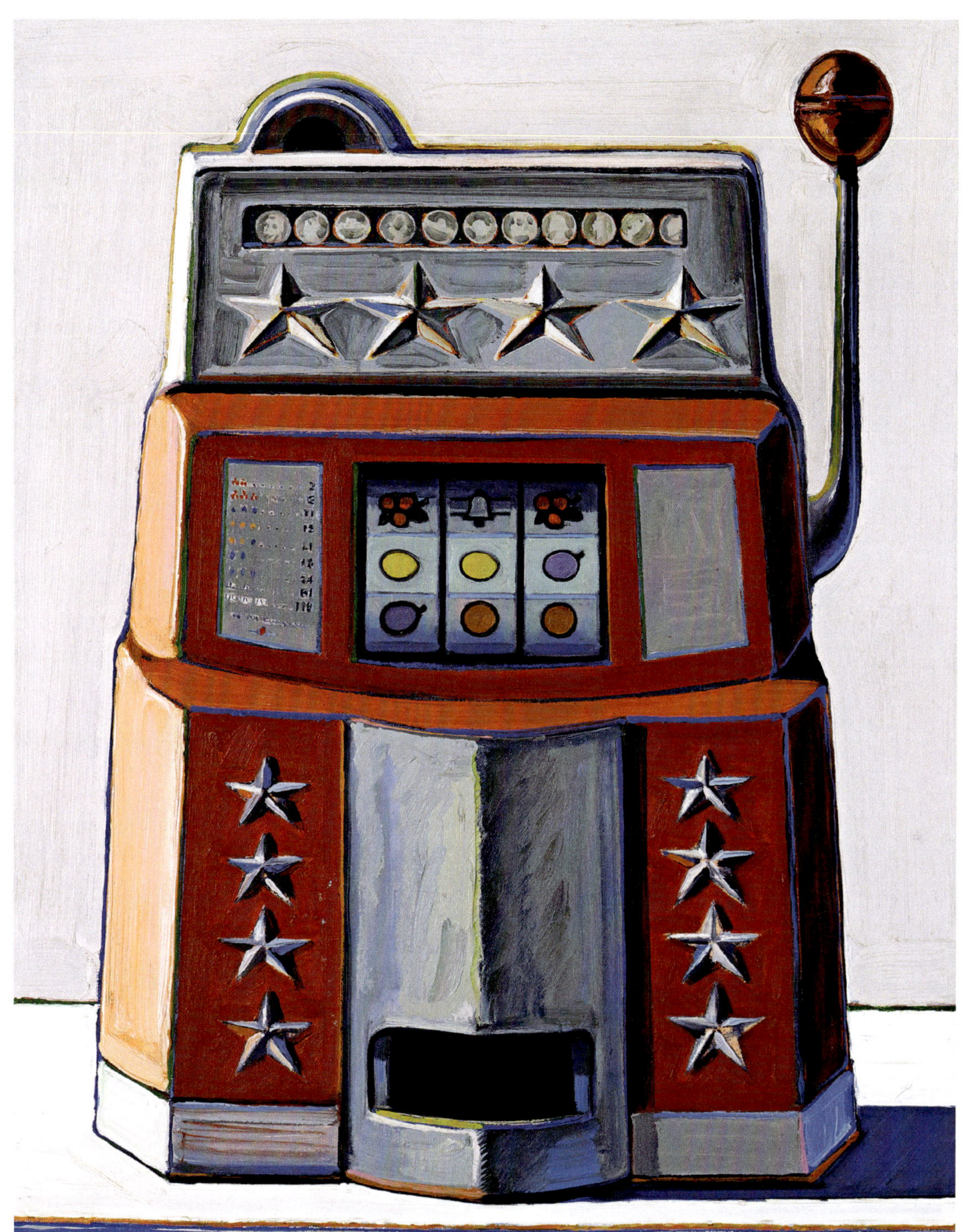

9

Four Pinball Machines

1962
Oil on canvas
172.7 x 182.8 cm
Private collection
Courtesy Acquavella Galleries

One of Wayne Thiebaud's largest and most ambitious canvases from this period, *Four Pinball Machines* was painted and exhibited the year he first came to prominence as a significant contemporary artist. His breakthrough solo exhibition at the Allan Stone Gallery in New York in April 1962 announced him as a highly original painter of modern American still-life subjects. In September of that year, Thiebaud's inclusion in the influential *New Painting of Common Objects* exhibition at the Pasadena Art Museum saw him grouped with artists including Roy Lichtenstein and Andy Warhol as part of a new tendency in art concerned with the depiction of everyday objects and imagery, which would soon become more widely known as 'Pop Art' (see cat. 6). In the summer between these shows, Thiebaud had his first museum exhibition devoted to this new work at the M.H. de Young Memorial Museum, San Francisco, where *Four Pinball Machines* was shown (see fig. 11).[57] Although it was Thiebaud's depictions of cakes and pies that initially caught the imagination of early reviewers and collectors, it is this painting that engages most explicitly with the entwinement of art and popular culture that was such a defining new feature of contemporary art during these years.

At first glance, the painting seems to be a straightforward depiction of the modern phenomenon of pinball machines, decorated in bright colours and with illuminated backglasses, lined up as one might find them in penny arcades across America. Pinball machines took shape in their modern form during Thiebaud's childhood in the 1930s but the 1950s and 1960s are considered their golden age, ushered in by the invention of machines with button-operated flippers to keep the ball in play, introduced by the Chicago manufacturer D. Gottlieb & Co. in 1947. Although hugely popular, pinball machines were also divisive, associated with moral corruption in youth culture, gambling and organised crime. Lawmakers campaigned against them and, during this period, they were even outlawed in major cities, including Chicago, Los Angeles and New York. Painting his imagined pinball machines on a grand scale, Thiebaud elevated these controversial icons of popular culture to monumental subjects, worthy of contemplation – the three graces of the penny arcade. Except there are two further machines extending beyond the edges of the canvas, a reminder of the seriality of modern mass-produced culture. Thiebaud counts four, not five, in his title, perhaps a play on the idea of the production line; the two partial machines ready to be bolted together to make a fourth. In fact, he originally planned the composition in an oil study with four machines depicted (fig. 38) but the move to a larger format prompted the addition of another.[58] It also inspired a further major change that sets running a more complex interplay between the realms of art and popular culture than is first apparent.

The backglasses in the oil study have numbers and symbols that are simplified versions of those found on the actual games – indeed, they are closer to the more rudimentary pinball machines Thiebaud remembered from childhood in the 1930s than to the loud and elaborate graphics of the post-war flipper machines.[59] In the large painting, he reduces them even further; the backglasses of the three central machines are sparely decorated with squares, circles and grids respectively. In contrast to the bright colours

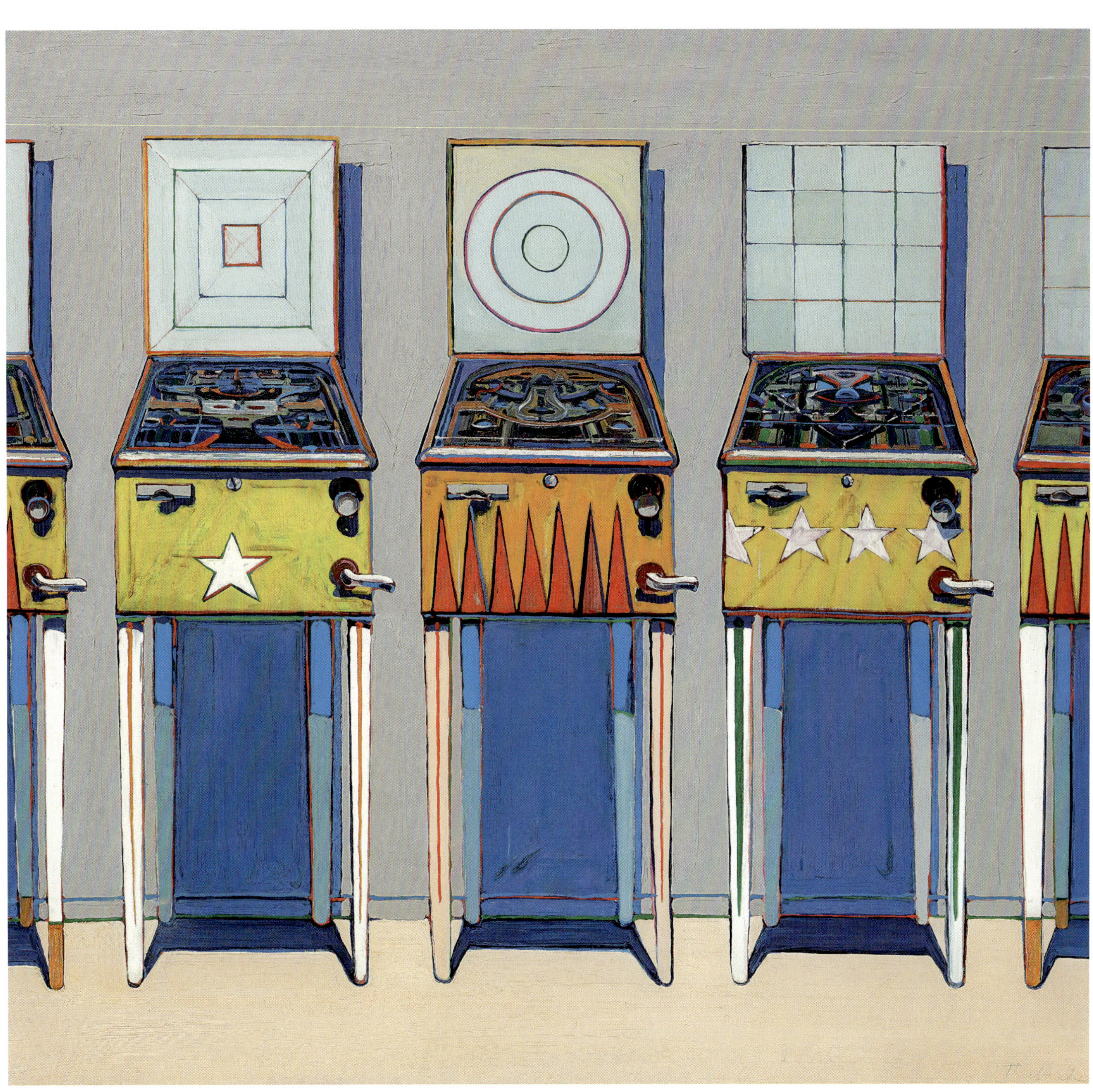

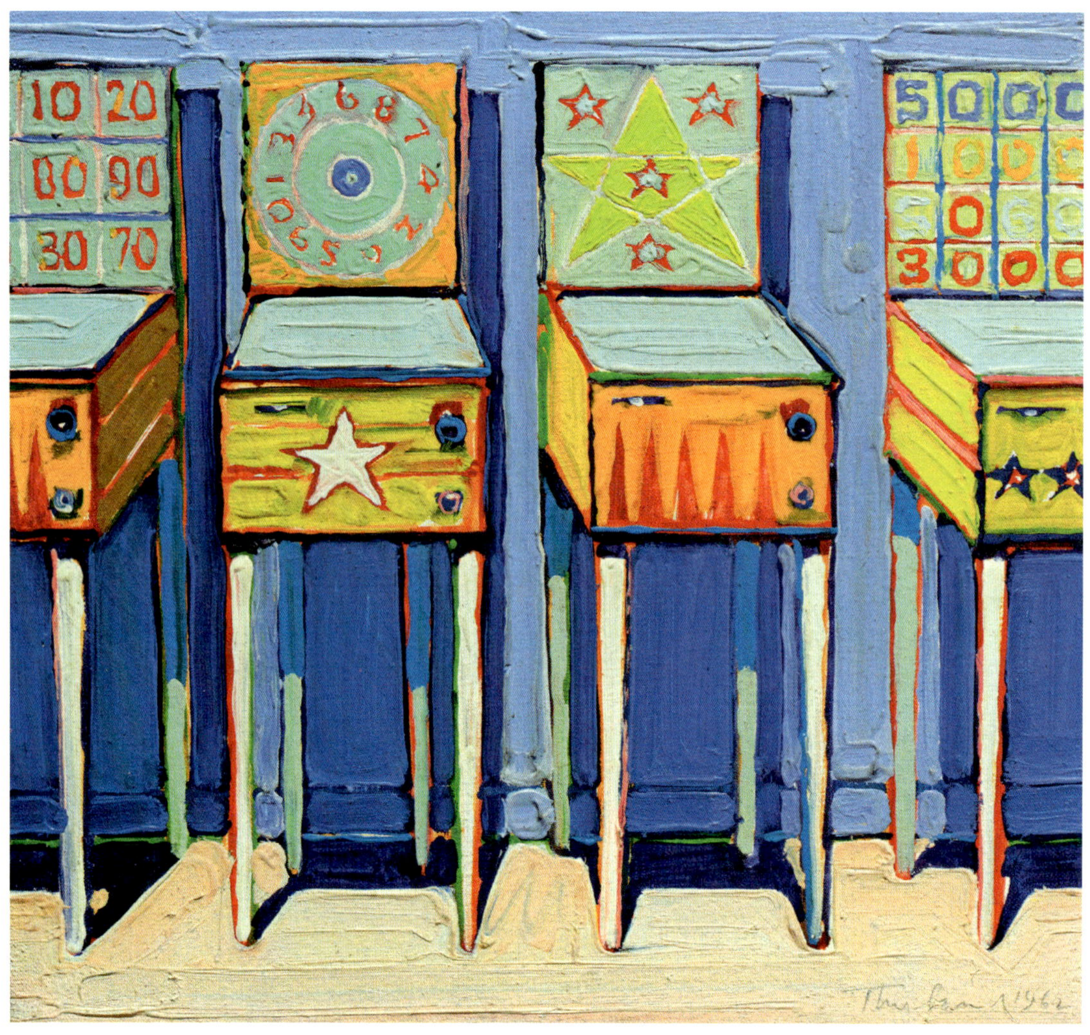

38 Wayne Thiebaud, *Four Pinball Machines (Study)*, 1962, oil on canvas, 28.3 x 30.8 cm, private collection

elsewhere, they are painted in distinctly muted tones, gently dislocating them from the rest of the machine so that we might imagine them as pictures on a wall. In a playful act of juxtaposition, Thiebaud turns these pinball machine backglasses into a line-up of abstract paintings that resemble the recent work of some of the leading figures of contemporary art, including Frank Stella's concentric squares, Kenneth Noland's targets and Ellsworth Kelly's coloured square grids.[60] A year before Thiebaud's painting, Robert Indiana painted his major satirical work *The American Dream, I* (1961, Museum of Modern Art, New York), a composition based on the backglasses of pinball machines. Thiebaud reverses the more familiar process whereby artists appropriated aspects of popular culture for their art by instead taking art itself into the realm of 'low end' entertainment. Cued to the fact that *Four Pinball Machines* is explicitly a painting about painting, we might extend this further and read Thiebaud's machines as an amalgam of styles. If the backglasses are forms of recent geometric abstraction then Thiebaud's more frenetic depiction of the playfields themselves appears to be a callback to his own earlier abstract expressionist style, used for his major pinball machine painting of 1956 (cat. 1). The fronts of the cabinets, with their bold stars and chevrons, foreground an aesthetic of commercial graphics that was becoming synonymous with Pop Art. Finally, the play of light and shadow under the machines has the appearance of a colour field painting not unlike Barnett Newman's recent work.

Thiebaud's painterly facture, which was a defining feature of his own successful new style in 1962, is especially evident in *Four Pinball Machines* because his thick and creamy brushstrokes are at odds with the hard surfaces and flatly applied colours of the actual machines being depicted. In the year he finally found a voice amongst the array of styles jostling for position within the contemporary art world at the time, this painting stands as a witty and profound exploration of contemporary art and American popular culture. **BW**

10
Boston Cremes

1962
Oil on canvas
35.6 x 45.7 cm
Crocker Art Museum, Sacramento

For Wayne Thiebaud, the decision to depict the same object multiple times on a single canvas was a challenge to the superficial glance and a paean to the rewards of deep, close looking. He explained,

> In spite of the fact that every pie appears to be similar, it was interesting to take all the spaces in between and make each shape dissimilar … all the pies are painted at a slightly different angles and they vary in size and area displacement. It is a play on the closeness of similarities and dissimilarities. At first glance, the pies look mechanical and have a sameness. At least, most people will think they do until they study them closely.[61]

Boston Cremes exemplifies this absorbing exercise of creating difference among the seemingly uniform. Arranged in three rows are fifteen slices of the same variety of cake.[62] Yet, each slice is chromatically singular and positioned variously, forming its own shape and producing subtle variations in the space around it. As the critic Robert Hughes put it, 'differences of color and shape … save the serried ranks of piedom from monotony … you are drawn into the small but clear discriminations that make an interesting painting'.[63]

That these objects were individual and manmade rather than 'mechanical' was related to Thiebaud's manner of painting them. For his dealer, Allan Stone, it was the artist's sensuous handling of paint that separated him from contemporary artists exploring similar subject matter in a less painterly register – Andy Warhol's work was 'a little flat' for Stone's taste.[64] In the rich brushwork of the present painting, Thiebaud delights in producing thick, creamy swathes of oil paint in his depiction of cake slices. But more than just a result of his stated enjoyment of working with the medium in this way, such application was also an act of what he termed 'object transference': 'working the paint to look like the substance of the image and playing that idea back and forth'.[65] Here, the relationship between subject and medium reaches its zenith, as flounces and swirls of white paint create an almost *trompe-l'œil* effect in imitation of the icing they describe. As the critic Max Kozloff noted in 1962, 'By some alchemy … Thiebaud does not seem to be working with oil paint at all, but with a substance composed of flour, albumen, butter and sugar.'[66]

Looking back on his work from this period, Thiebaud would later remark that 'the color is coincidental to the value structure'.[67] His observation is pertinent to the present painting, which, with its various tilts and angles, seems a direct enquiry into the play of light on multiple, proximate surfaces. Indeed, a monochrome ink drawing of the same title made in 1964 demonstrates the degree to which he conceived of the related painting as an exploration of light and shadow (cat. 28). Thick, unbroken horizontal and diagonal lines of yellow paint construct the sponge, each slice of which is topped with bright white frosting and a red cherry of sufficient sheen to reflect the light. Applied wet-on-wet, pale green and blue paints combine with white; yellows deepen to ochre, all working to render light and shadow.

The painting was purchased in 1964 by Sacramento's E.B. Crocker Art Gallery, which had first exhibited Thiebaud's work in 1951.[68] Thiebaud wrote to Stone at the time, 'Nice to be "OKd" in your own home town'.[69] **CN**

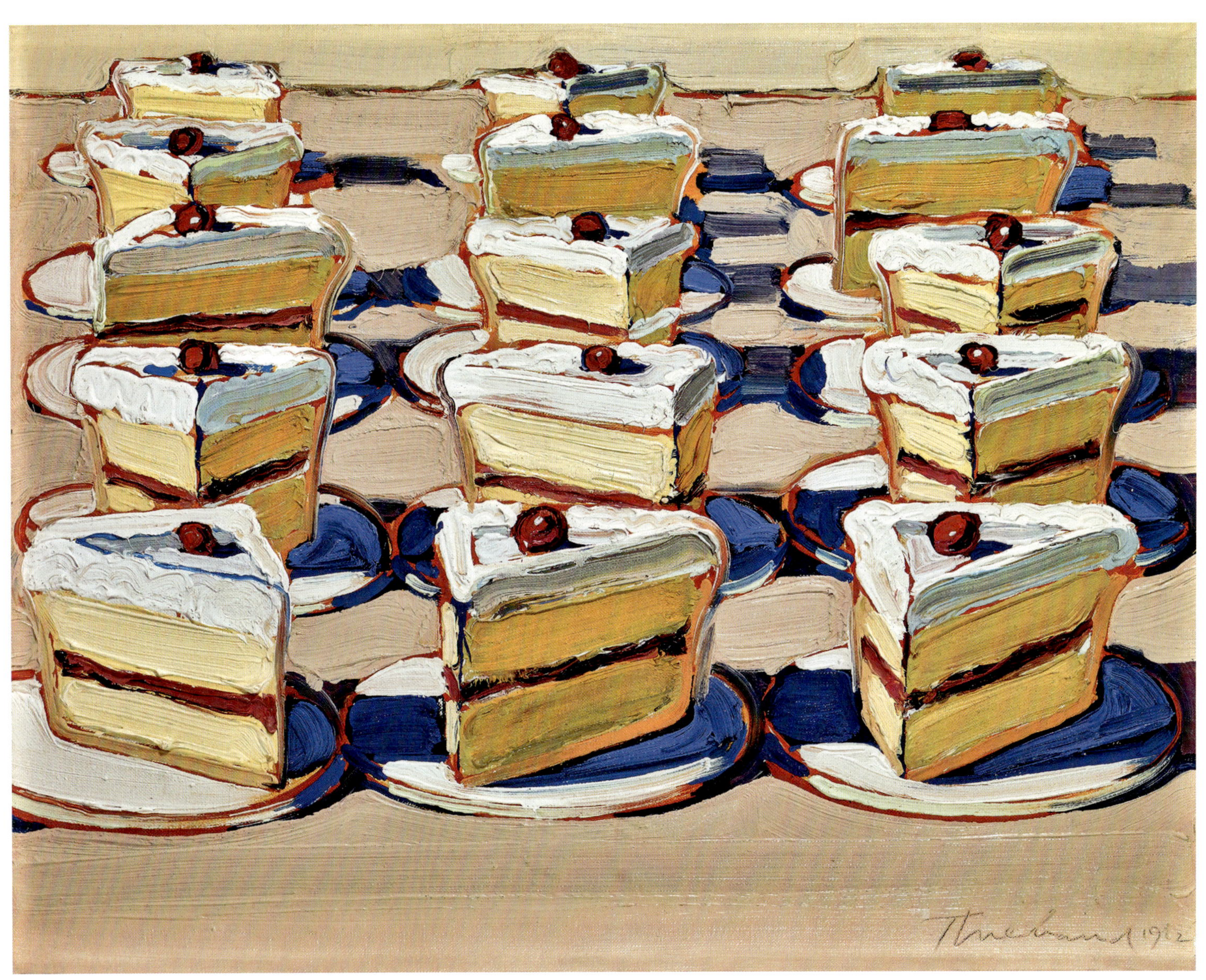

11
Caged Pie

1962
Oil on canvas
51.1 x 71.4 cm
San Diego Museum of Art
Purchased through the Earle W. Grant
Acquisition Fund, 1977

Reflecting on his work of the early 1960s and his habit of painting still-life subjects from memory, Wayne Thiebaud recalled,

> Most are fragments of actual experience. For instance, I would really think of the bakery counter, of the way the counter was lit, where the pies were placed, but I wanted just a piece of the experience. From when I worked in restaurants, I can remember seeing rows of pies, or a tin of pie with one piece out of it and one pie sitting beside it. Those little *vedute* in fragmented circumstances were always poetic to me.[70]

His comments resonate with his still-life paintings more broadly but are especially pertinent to *Caged Pie*, one of the sparest of his compositions from this period. A single slice of cherry pie is left over in a glass display case on a countertop. The poetry that Thiebaud evokes in this fragment of painted memory seems akin to elegy. His tactile, almost caressing brushstrokes draw the viewer in close. But even the seductive smear of cherry juice on the white plate turns out to be so obviously wet-in-wet paint that we are held back, as we are by another illusion – our sense of the glass display case keeping the last remaining piece of pie just out of reach. Thiebaud described it as 'caged', which draws attention to his conjuring of glass from only the bars of the box and their shadow. He had long been fascinated with the sensation of looking at objects behind glass, from shop windows to display counters. He explained to his friend the artist Gregory Kondos, 'What I want is to get the dimension between the viewer and the glass and the object',[71] and in another statement, 'It's the exclusionary aspect that gets me – there's a lot of yearning, there'.[72] It was an interest shared by the artist Claes Oldenburg whose contemporaneous sculpture *Four Pies in a Glass Case* (fig. 34) makes a compelling comparison with Thiebaud's painting.

Caged Pie was among the paintings included in Thiebaud's first European exhibition at the Galleria Schwarz in Milan in 1963. His New York dealer, Allan Stone, writing under a pseudonym in the accompanying catalogue, was clear to position the artist and his work as deriving 'entirely from American culture'.[73] The subject of cherry pie was a slice of quintessential Americana for the exhibition but Stone maintained that Thiebaud's work was far from being simple nostalgia:

> He revels in the fluorescent lit staples of the American roadside diner, cafeteria and five-and-ten cent store .... His richly painted canvases reveal what the wealthiest culture on earth offers the cult of mass-produced happiness .... Thiebaud has drawn on the history of still-life painting, yet his work is disturbingly topical.

This emphasis on biting social critique may have been intended to situate Thiebaud more prominently within the contemporary avant-garde of what was becoming known as Pop Art but seems somewhat overstated in relation to a work such as *Caged Pie*. Thiebaud's painterly vision of his modern American subject matter reveals itself here to be a meditation on themes of desire, longing and isolation. **BW**

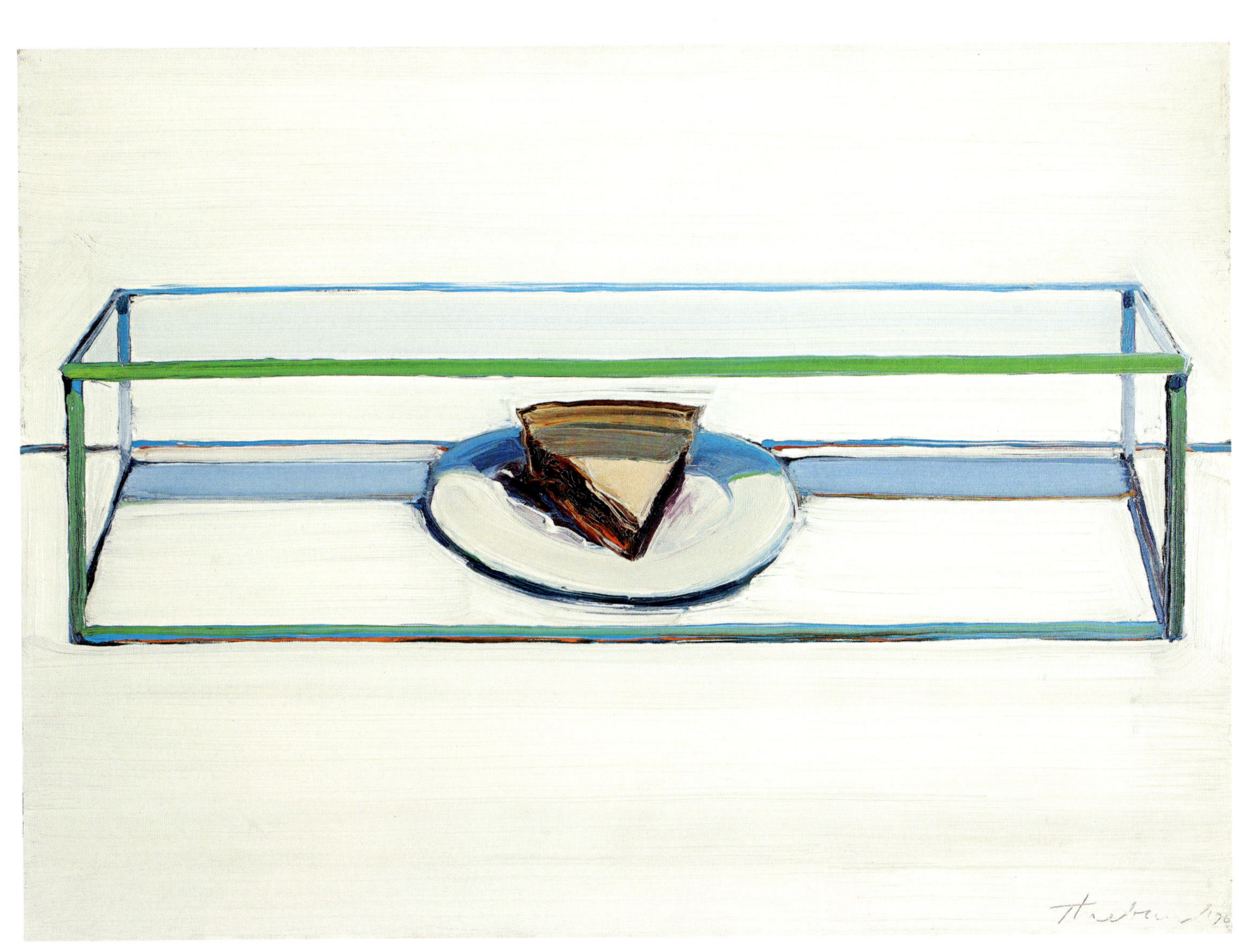

12
Candy Counter

1962
Oil on canvas
140 x 182.8 cm
Anderson Collection at Stanford University, Palo Alto
Gift of Harry W. and Mary Margaret Anderson, and
Mary Patricia Anderson Pence

Candy Counter is one of a small group of ambitious, large-scale canvases painted by Wayne Thiebaud in the early 1960s, alongside *Four Pinball Machines* (cat. 9), *Delicatessen Counter* (cat. 14) and *Cakes* (cat. 17). The painting epitomises the approach he described in his artist's statement that same year: 'I depend upon a line a great deal. The lines are painted and drawn in several intense hues one over the other to make them as lively and as strong as possible. Later on in the painting I may obliterate them in part or repaint them as needed.'[74] In *Candy Counter*, Thiebaud first set out his composition with a few lines of bold colour, using a lime green to establish the vertical of the glass case and a darker green to mark the horizontal edges. Elsewhere, a thin stripe of red peeks out from under the cobalt blue lines. Interestingly, Thiebaud did not cover the coloured lines once the elements of his composition were fixed but painted thickly around them, creating a physical contrast between the linear structure and coloured planes, which reinforce each other. Thiebaud noted his use of hues and brushmarks in a pencil drawing that is most likely a working sketch or perhaps made as a record of *Candy Counter* (fig. 39). The annotations in pen, added later and which give details about the type of paint used and his compositional approach, demonstrate how Thiebaud returned to his early work for inspiration and in his teaching.

The use of colour was also crucial in Thiebaud's mind for the rendering of light and, in particular, the new type of bright, fluorescent light used to make items for sale more desirable. As he described in 1962,

> Today the idea of light is tremendously variable. Strong display lights have been developed which can do all kinds of goofey and wonderful things … make an object cast colored shadows, change its local color before your eyes, glow and develop a halo or imbue it with a pulsating effect. Often these things have ten, twenty, or more light sources to heighten them … used cars, diamonds, and candied apples are displayed and sold to us in this way. Foods, costume jewelry in cafes and stores are visual feasts for the eyes if they can be captured. The problem of catching some of this keeps me going.[75]

The multicoloured outlines were meant to capture this 'pulsating effect' around the objects, as were Thiebaud's thick brushmarks that followed its outline: 'When I stroke around the object with a loaded paintbrush it is calculated to echo the presence of that object.'[76] This is particularly visible in how the thick application of the blue background helps shape the lollipops, askew in their stand, and heightens the contours of the scale on the other side of the counter.

The coldness of the blue light enveloping Thiebaud's candy counter sets it apart from his other works of that period, as does the spareness of the offerings on display. The trays in the glass case present candy under different guises – candied apples, individual cubes and sticks, large lumps of nougat ready to be cut and weighed – but absent is the sense of abundance and excess found in works such as *Peppermint Counter* (cat. 15), *Pie Counter* (cat. 16) and *Cakes* (cat. 17). This slight eeriness enhances the feeling of wistful nostalgia

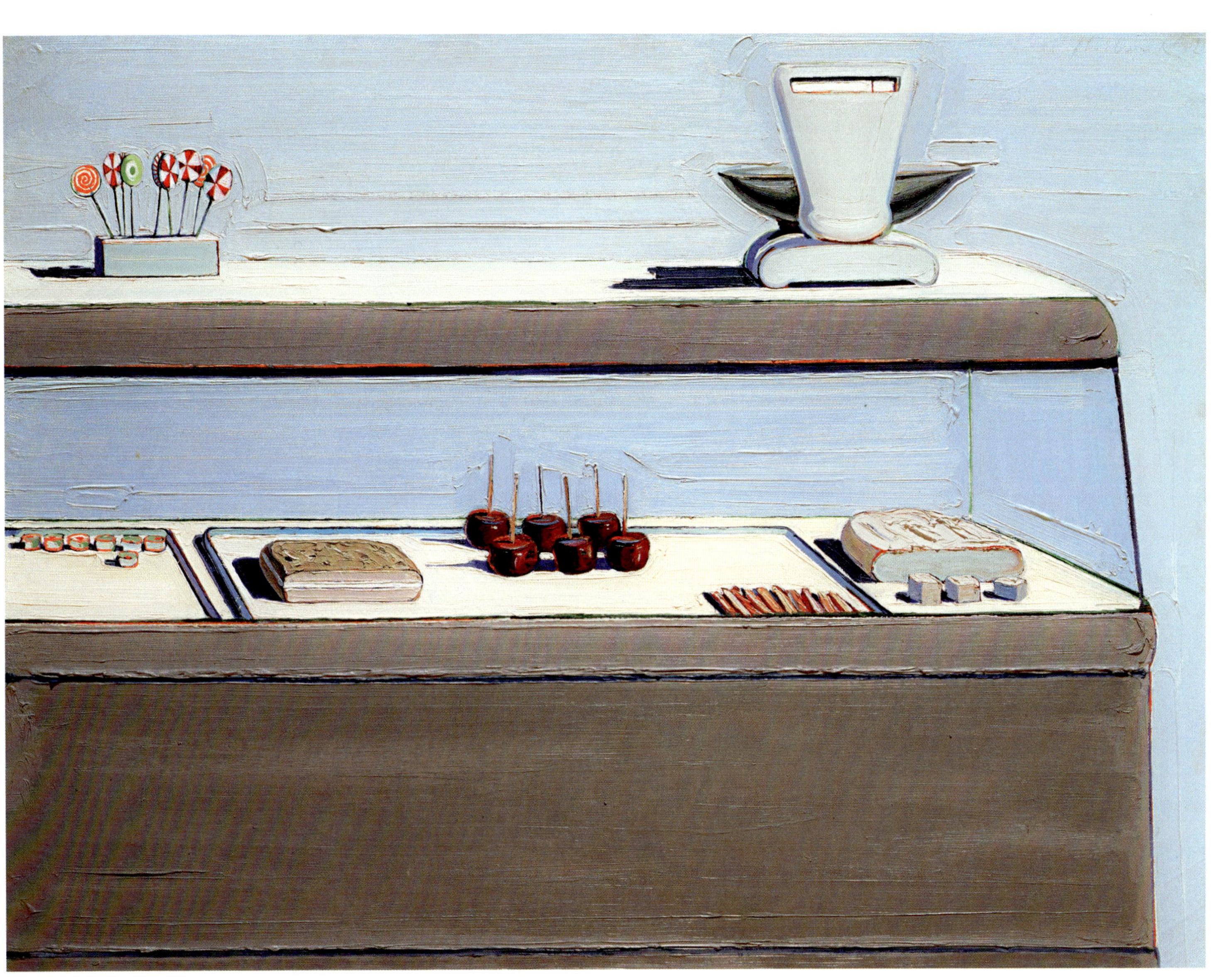

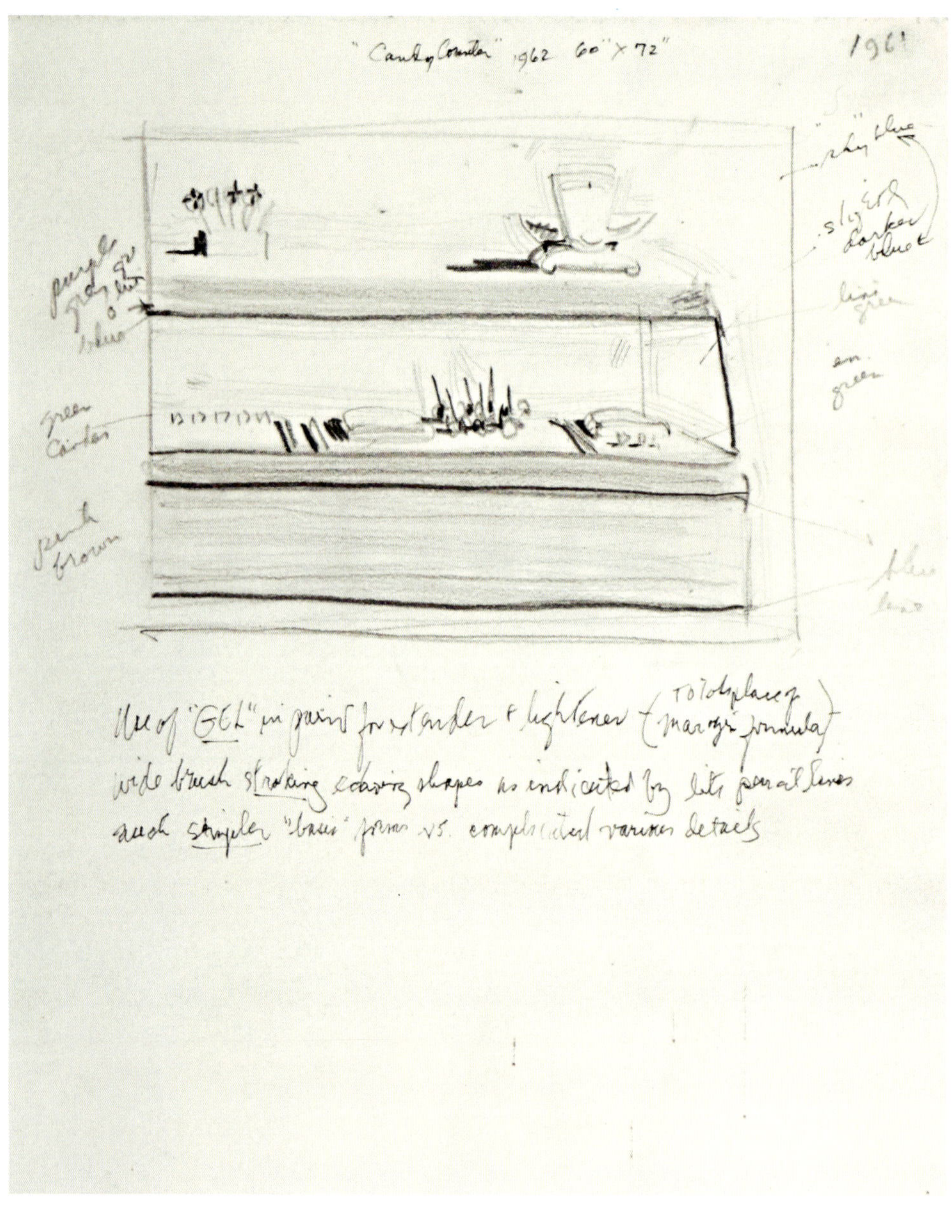

39 Wayne Thiebaud, Drawing after *Candy Counter*, c. 1961–62 with later inscriptions, pencil and ink on paper, Collection of the Wayne Thiebaud Foundation

sometimes ascribed to Thiebaud's works. By the 1960s, candy counters such as this one were slowly disappearing, as handmade sweets sold by weight were superseded by individually wrapped, pre-packaged candy bars. As one of Thiebaud's colleagues, the artist and professor Seymour Howard, noted, 'Despite their sweet and infectious child-like pleasure in vernacular Americana, paintings by Thiebaud reveal a bitter pang of isolation and melancholy in pop culture. Beneath the bright paint is a dark after-image of nostalgia for the wonders of lost innocence – and a glimpse of mortality.'[77] **KS**

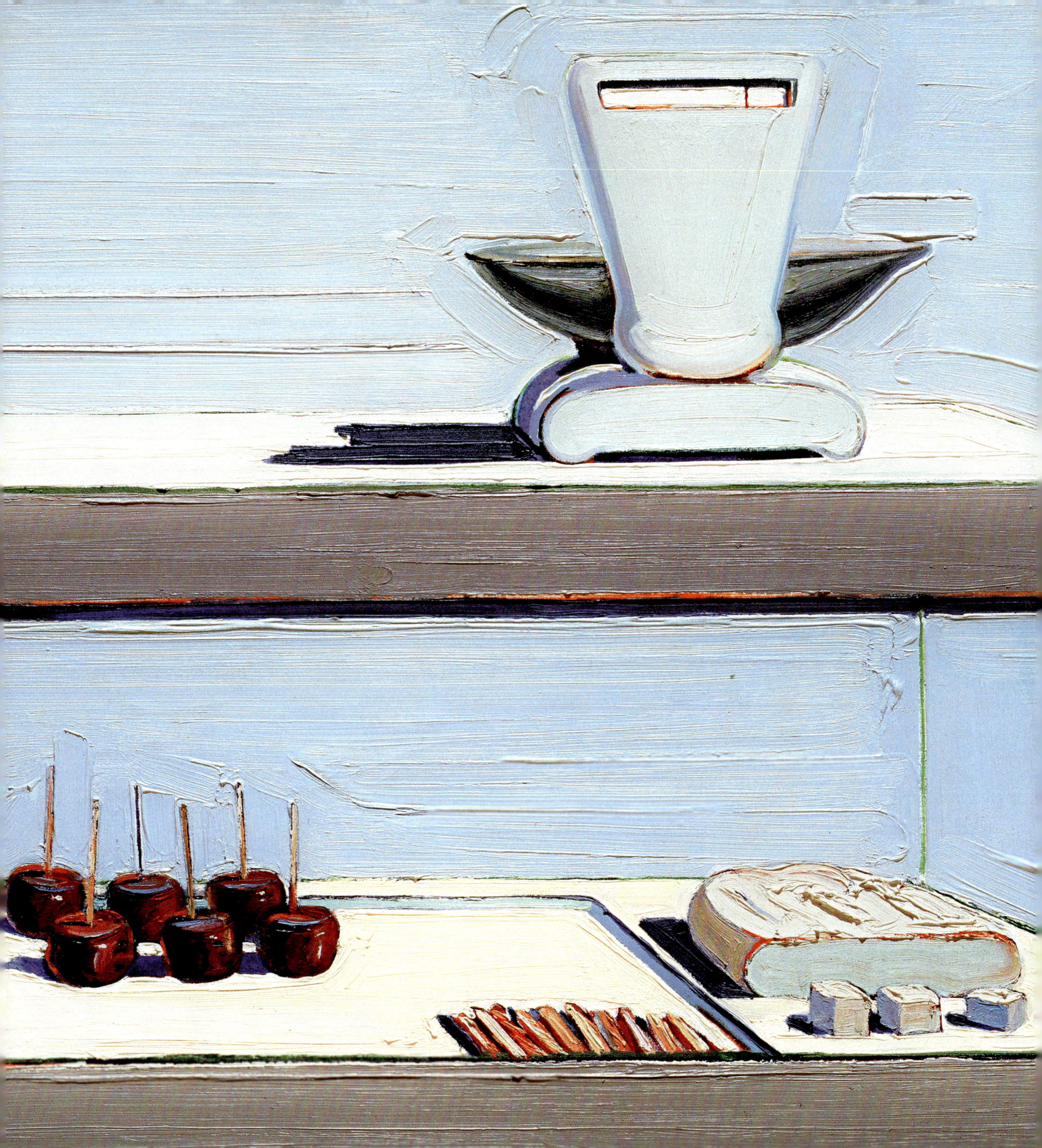

13
Delicatessen Counter

1962
Oil on canvas
76.8 × 92.1 cm
The Menil Collection, Houston

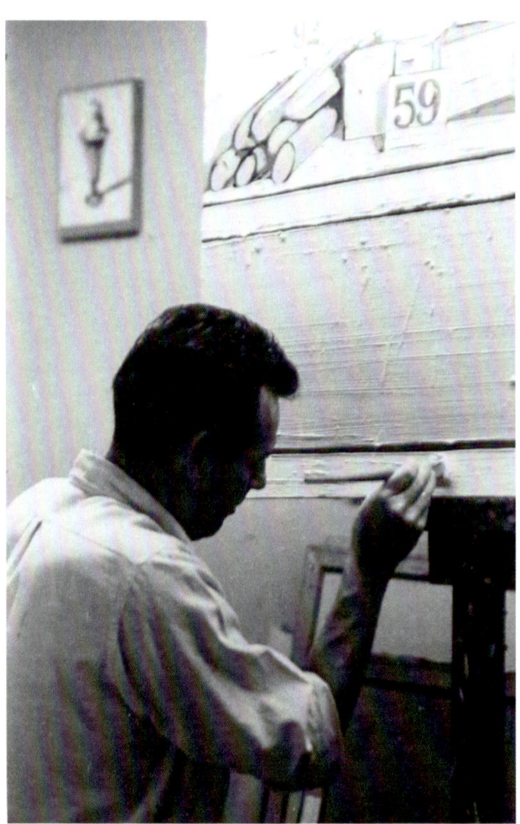

40 Wayne Thiebaud working on
Delicatessen Counter (cat. 13), Collection
of the Wayne Thiebaud Foundation

In the 1950s, Wayne Thiebaud became fascinated with shop windows and counters as a subject of his art (see cat. 2). As he developed his new style of still-life painting in the early 1960s, counters displaying various types of manufactured sweet and savoury foods became a major preoccupation for him. This painting is one of several variations on the theme of delicatessen counters that Thiebaud produced between 1961 and 1963 (see cat. 14). They share a common aesthetic but, in each, he explores different approaches to composition and the handling of paint. In this work, he pulls the viewer in close to the counter, so that one section of the display completely fills the canvas. He focuses on the assortment of cheeses and baloney sausage above and empty enamel trays below, which were a late addition to the painting (see fig. 40). More than in some other works, Thiebaud greatly emphasises the impasto, making every ridge and furrow of his brushstrokes visible; it is as if we are also getting up close to the painting itself and looking at it with a magnifying glass. At this time, Thiebaud began using an additive to alter the levels of viscosity, drying time and matte qualities of his oil paint to achieve a variety of different surface effects in his works.[78] In an artist's statement he wrote in 1962, Thiebaud explained that his varied use of impasto 'is done for a specific purpose. It alludes to the tradition of illusionistic painting. In my case an experiment with what happens when the relationship between paint and subject matter comes as close together as I can possibly get them .... And while it is clearly in the line of "trick-of-the-eye" painting where the artist is like a magician, I would like to show my hand and expose the trick ... allowing the thrill of self discovery and the ability to see oneself having the illusion.'[79]

In this painting, Thiebaud takes his experimentation and play with illusionism, what he also called 'actualism', to an extreme. His painted display – as with a real delicatessen counter – entices the viewer with its array of different surfaces and textures. We follow the movements of Thiebaud's brushstrokes as we also imagine the cuts of the delicatessen owner's knife through the soft and hard cheeses and the smooth processed meat of the sausages. Yet, the directional pulls of Thiebaud's brush often go against the grain of the cut surfaces depicted, such as the white and orange cheeses, or, in the case of the empty trays, seem at odds with the actual feel of the hard and flat enamel surfaces. This oscillating sensual experience of *Delicatessen Counter* is as much about the process and reality of painting as it is about the depiction of the food on display – itself of the processed kind that Thiebaud favoured for his still lifes.

Thiebaud emphasises another type of painting in the form of the price cards, beautifully and vividly delineated with red numbers in a striking serif font. He had great respect for the art of commercial sign painting and described his own early experience working in a 'little sign shop', trying to master 'one-stroke' letters and numbers: 'You have to practice a lot to give these strokes, so it has a nice roundness, doesn't look crammed, doesn't look studied.'[80] By 1962, the hand painting of show cards was a slowly vanishing art but, for Thiebaud, attending to the often overlooked skills of commercial artists held a profound relevance for modern painting in the age of machine process. **BW**

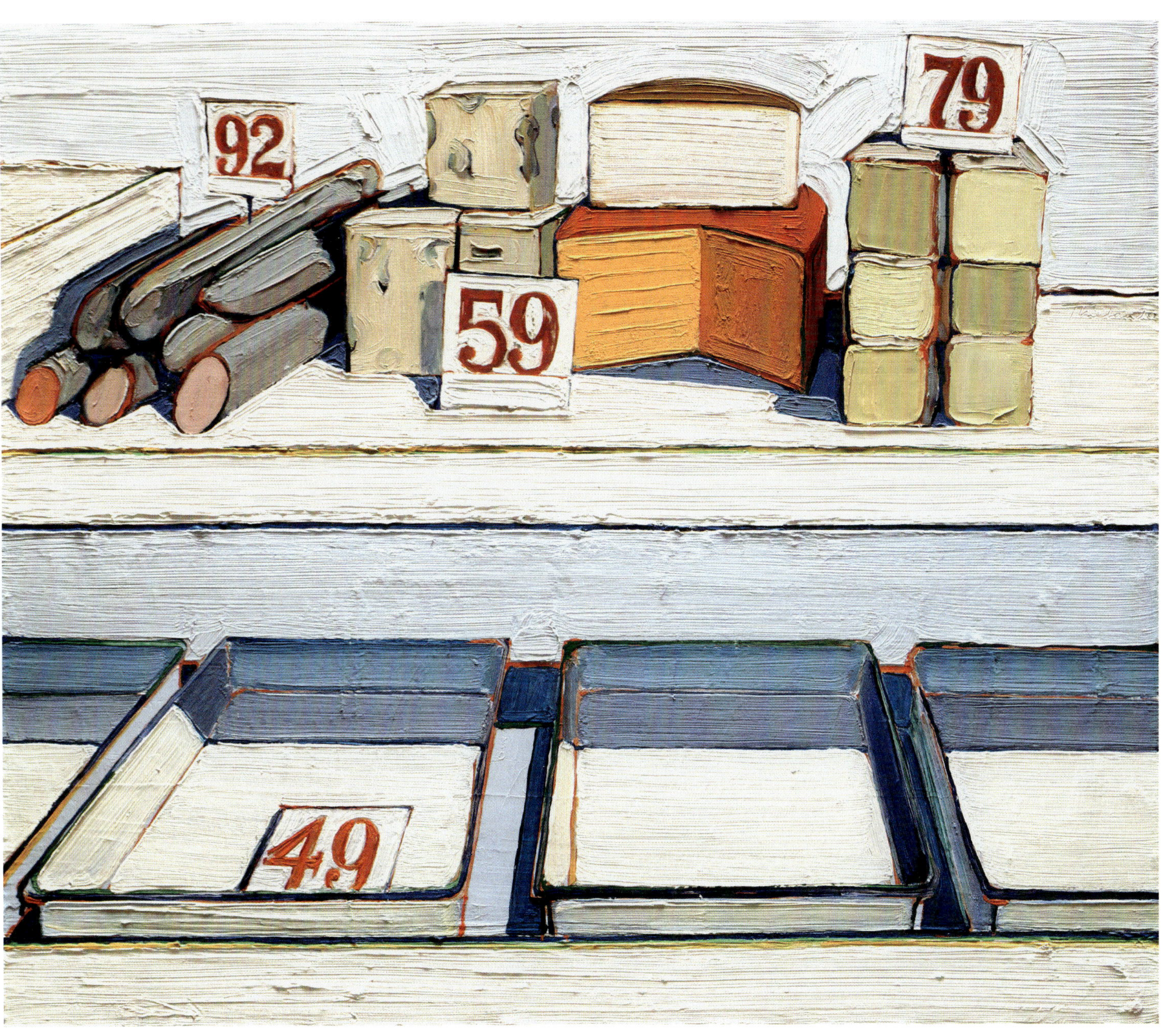

92
59
79
49

This is the largest and most expansive of the closely related delicatessen counter paintings that Wayne Thiebaud produced during the early 1960s (see cat. 13). It is also part of a wider group of paintings of shop counters that preoccupied the artist at this time, including bakeries and candy stores (see cat. 12 and 17). These imagined compositions were as much drawn from Thiebaud's memories of shopping trips of his youth as they were from contemporary stores of the 1960s. Thiebaud was especially interested in the modernity of American processed foods, as seen here in the array of clean-cut, smooth-faced cheeses and processed meats. Accordingly, the delicatessen, since the nineteenth century in America the home of processed meats and dairy products, was favoured by him over butchers or grocery stores. Also, Thiebaud did not focus on the advent of supermarket shelves filled with pre-packaged goods that was so characteristic of modern consumerism at this period. For him, the direct and carefully arranged depiction of the displayed product, rather than the overlay of its packaging, was key to his attempt to create still lifes that might reveal something essential about his time and, as he put it, 'allow us to see ourselves looking at ourselves'.[81]

Delicatessen Counter was one of seven paintings by Thiebaud included in the influential exhibition *Six More* at the Los Angeles County Museum of Art in 1963. The 'six more' were all West Coast artists, including Mel Ramos and Ed Ruscha, who were shown alongside a parallel exhibition of East Coast artists, entitled *Six Artists and the Object*, which included Jasper Johns and Andy Warhol. These exhibitions were an attempt by their curator, Lawrence Alloway, to explore a range of different contemporary approaches to depicting objects of popular culture and everyday life. Alloway introduced Thiebaud as being a 'laureate of lunch counters and diners' and a contemporary still-life painter but in the tradition of Jean-Siméon Chardin and Paul Cézanne who had extended the genre into the modern era.[82] *Delicatessen Counter* underscored this description, its ambition and visual intensity redolent of the radical table-top still-life paintings of both artists as well as other touchpoints in the history of the genre. Thiebaud's preference for commercial counters, as opposed to domestic tables, prompts an interesting comparison with Édouard Manet's famous *A Bar at the Folies-Bergère* (fig. 28). Manet's similarly stark and frontal depiction of a bar counter, with its display of consumables like so many still-life vignettes, is a vision of contemporary French life and the birth of consumer society that prefigures Thiebaud's use of similar devices to convey something that was quintessentially modern American. Both works share a sense of austerity and melancholy amidst the apparent abundance of consumer goods on offer. In Manet's case, the detached expression of the bar worker carries this theme. In Thiebaud's *Delicatessen Counter*, it is the lack of a human presence, despite a space seemingly left for a shop keeper in the centre of the composition, that partly creates this atmosphere of absence and austerity. It is also inherent in Thiebaud's handling of paint itself and his ability to delineate each object to such a degree that they feel strangely isolated from one another and somehow abstracted from us, regardless of our proximity to the counter and implied role as customers. **BW**

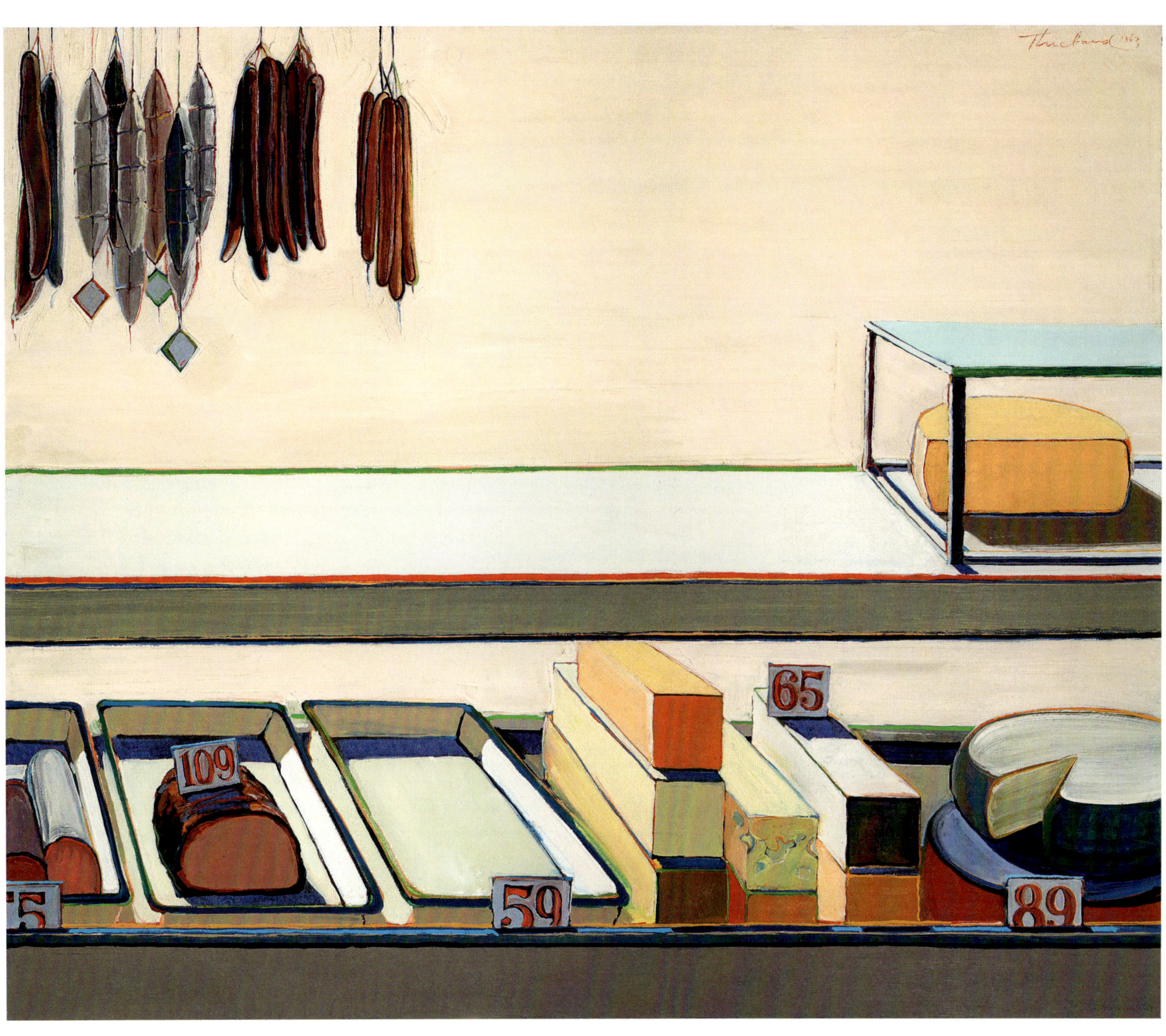

15
Peppermint Counter

1963
Oil on canvas
71.5 x 96.6 cm
Collection of the Wayne Thiebaud Foundation

Peppermint Counter presents the viewer with an abundant array of sugary sweets. The display is neatly arranged and untouched: the red-and-white striped peppermint sticks that give the painting its name are perfectly stacked on either side of a group of fifteen luscious candied apples. The bins below have been restocked to the brim, pressing and flattening the gumballs and pieces of candy against the glass. The two large openings are represented frontally, albeit with a slight tilt backwards that hints at the slopping front of the counter. This viewpoint seems at odds with the angled perspective of the objects on the upper shelf, emphasising the deliberate artificiality of the arrangement. A striking feature of the composition are the five triangular, hand-painted signs giving the prices (in cents) of the items on display. Those on the top shelf are priced individually while the candy in the bins is priced by weight. Wayne Thiebaud had a particular admiration for hand-painted signs (see cat. 13) and even took a course to master this particular technique. The skills required of sign-painters certainly find an echo in his work: control and precision in the application of paint, as well as a sense of balance in the composition.

As with Thiebaud's other paintings from that period, his elements are placed against a neutral background and lack any wider context. The spareness of the background, however, is counterbalanced by the rich texture imparted by the thick strokes of white paint dragged across the canvas and around the various objects. By using the impasto to frame and contour his objects, Thiebaud gives them a greater sense of modelling and uses the natural light hitting the edges of his raised paint to animate his surface. As he noted in his 1962 artist's statement for the Museum of Modern Art in New York, 'My surfaces are activated and brushed heavily to try and keep them visually available. The heavy linear activity formed by ridges of paint helps to "lock in" the planes and make them "flatter." This is one practical reason for the impasto.'[83] Thiebaud also occasionally used his thick brushstrokes to add a certain playfulness to his work, as with the dash of thick white paint that tops each colourful stick planted in the candied apples.

The configuration of *Peppermint Counter* – with goods stored in bins seen through large windows that occupy two-thirds of the composition while objects line a long shelf above – recurs in several guises in Thiebaud's work and for a variety of wares. One of the earliest is *Meat Counter* (cat. 2), which adopts the same composition, followed by a series of toy counters, brimming with teddy bears, dolls and beach balls (see fig. 4). Such counters, however, were already quaint by the early 1960s, having been partly superseded by self-service supermarket shelves. In Thiebaud's mind, they were closely linked to childhood memories: 'I remember when I was a kid selling papers on the street in Long Beach when I was 11 or 12 years old. We didn't have a lot of money and I loved sweets and I'd go in the store and look at those bins full of candy with scoops in them. I'd even pick up candy off the floor which had dropped out of the weighing box.'[84] **KS**

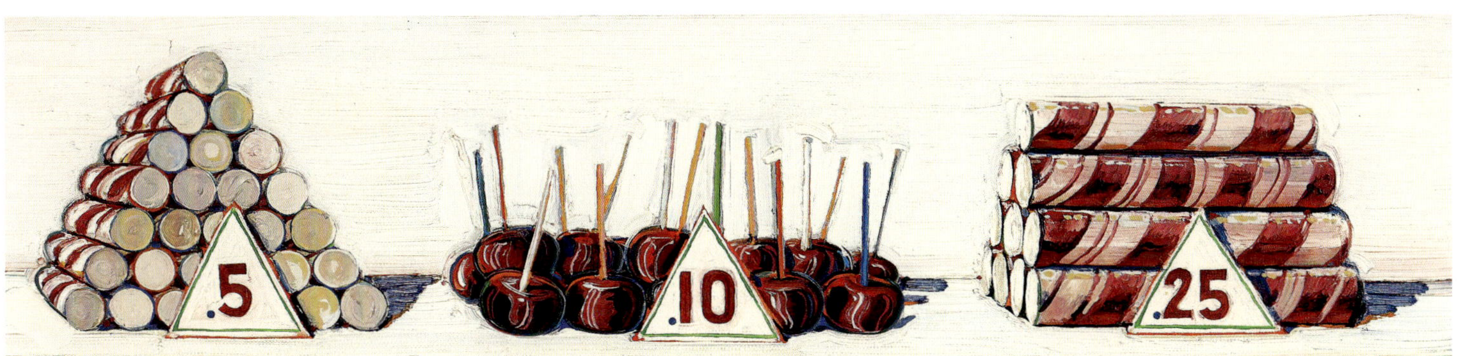

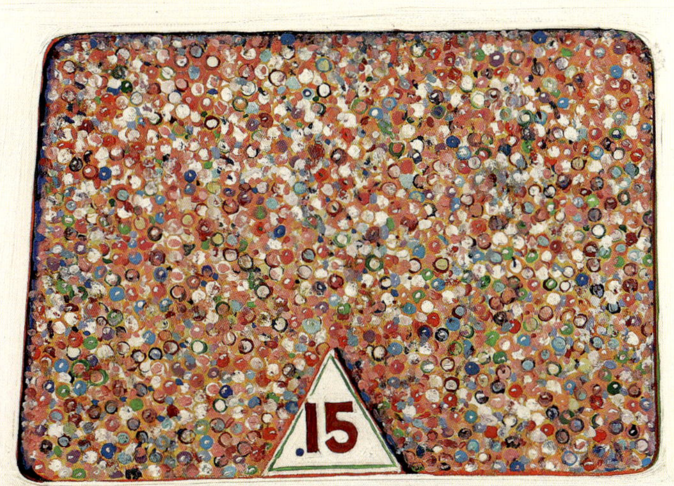

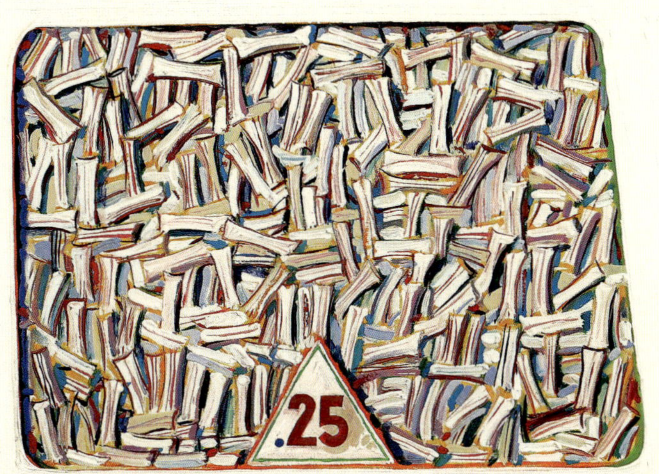

A few years on from his first experiments with painting pies (see cat. 5), Wayne Thiebaud continued to interrogate the subject. Divided from a stark white wall by a high, green horizon line, a buff-coloured countertop is bedecked with 28 slices of pie and cake in five varieties. The painting speaks strongly of mass production, its sense of infinitude further animated by the increase in the canvas size from the earlier pie paintings. By this time, Thiebaud's application had become greatly finessed, with the outlines of the pies and plates now unequivocally handled. Light is more brilliant, deployed in the manner of the photoflood lightbulbs that Thiebaud used in his studio and which 'illuminated a subject, in some ways, like the sun'.[85] He also further experimented with the introduction of unexpected colours into his renderings of the same varieties of pie – here, bright green stripes run along the right side of ochre pumpkin pie filling while lines of pink, blue and green intrude into the white of his meringue. Thiebaud's increasing interest in colour had seen him move from an initial position ('pumpkin pie color is one color, damn it, and it is an ochre with some orange in it') to the realisation that

> When you place [that] mixture next to a slab of pumpkin pie, it seems to match in color but on a canvas it definitely does not – why? It lacks life, vitality – one must add patches of orange, of blue, of other colors, in fact, a mosaic of colors to give it some semblance of the pumpkin color one sees in reality.[86]

As such, colour could blur the distinction between realism and abstraction – something that was fundamental to Thiebaud's endeavours in painting. Although often categorised as a realist, Thiebaud felt that, by adding 'any number of manipulations and additions to what one sees', it was possible 'for representational painting to be both abstract and real simultaneously'.[87]

Although Thiebaud increasingly sought to emphasise a formalist approach to his work, he continued to offer illuminating analysis of its cultural resonances. In a 1969 interview, he delved into the symbolic aspects of his by-now signature subject, the pie:

> As I started painting these very simple triangles on platters, I got more and more intrigued with pies. A pie has all kinds of marvelous complex associations. The whiteness of meringue became for me of great poetic preoccupation; it's like snow, like frost, like the concept of purity and, from a painter's standpoint white both absorbs light and reflects light, it's composed of all colors, like Chardin's tablecloths. But then … why a pie instead of a snow bank. Well, pie has a long history and it has other implications: the idea of "Pie in the Sky", the old American preoccupation with Mom and Apple Pie, pie throwing contests, pie eating contests, pie throwing in Chaplin films.[88]

In this extended meditation, Thiebaud weaves a lyrical landscape out of art historical references and sentimental Americana that elucidates some of the reason for the impact of these works on both the American public and critical establishment. The purchase of the painting in 1964 by the Whitney Museum of American Art signalled the cultural significance of Thiebaud's depiction of contemporary American life at the time. **CN**

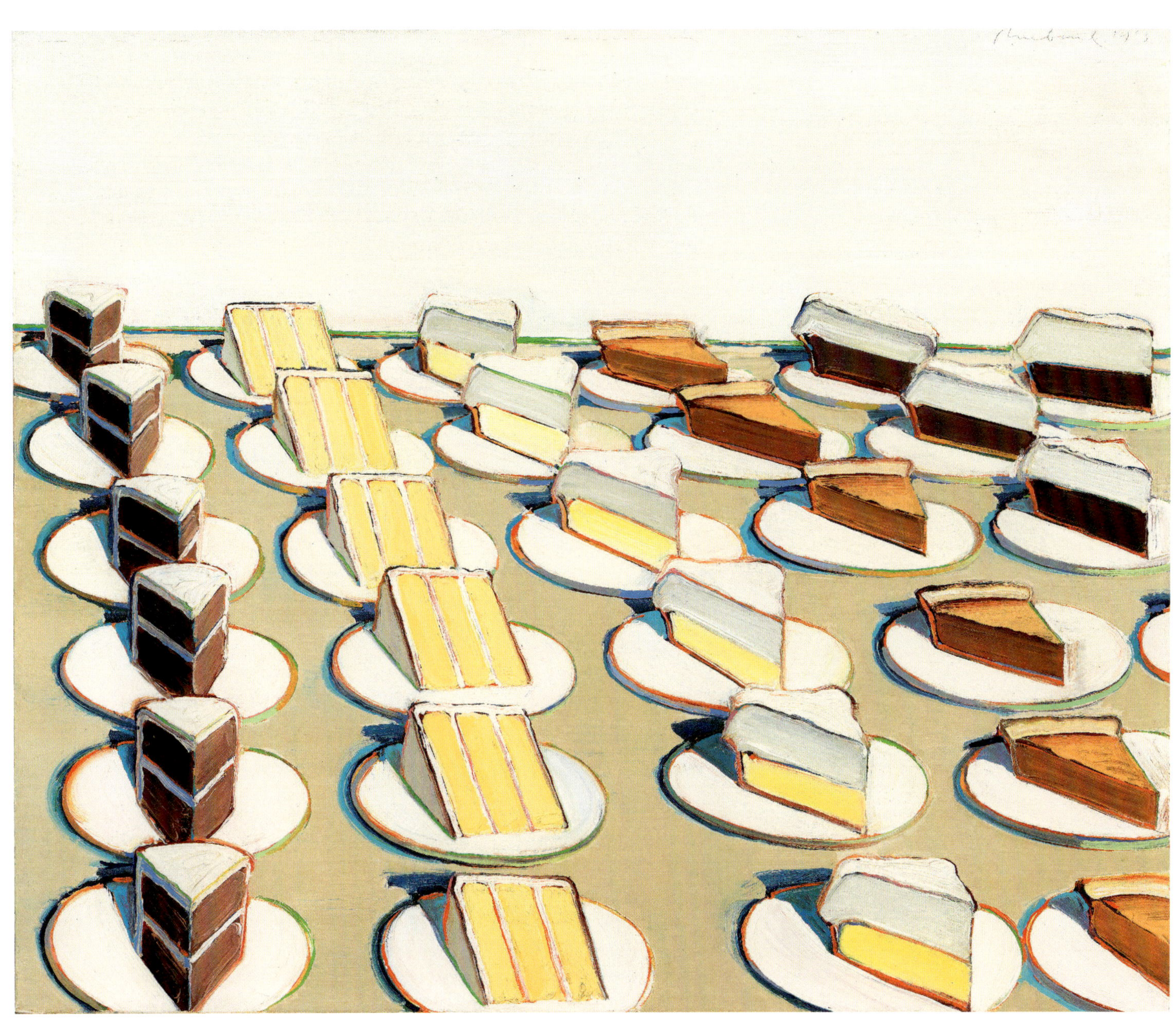

17
Cakes

1963
Oil on canvas
152.4 x 182.9 cm
National Gallery of Art, Washington, D.C.
Gift in Honor of the 50th Anniversary of the
National Gallery of Art from the Collectors
Committee, the 50th Anniversary Gift Committee,
and The Circle, with additional support from the
Abrams Family in memory of Harry N. Abrams, 1991

Cakes is one of Wayne Thiebaud's most significant paintings of the early 1960s, depicting on an epic scale the subject matter that made his name. Unlike his rows of pie slices, the cakes here are presented whole, save for the cake in the upper right, which has been cut in half, revealing the chocolate layers within. This allowed Thiebaud to focus on their decoration, whose exuberance he perceived as uniquely American:

> The decoration in Europe, particularly of cakes, seems more delicate. Here they are full of big gobs of material such as chocolate or cream. The materials are used as a kind of metaphor of plentitude [sic]. Americans always put on much more frosting, etc. than is needed.[89]

It was that very excess that attracted him, fuelling his interest in 'what happens when the relationship between paint and subject matter comes as close together as I can possibly get them … white, gooey, shiny, sticky oil paint spread out on the top of a painted cake "becomes" frosting.'[90] For him, the thick application of paint became a way of 'playing with reality … making an illusion which grows out of an exploration of the propensities of materials'. Dosing his ingredients like a baker, Thiebaud varied the thickness and viscosity of his oil paint by adding Liquin, damar, linseed oil and turpentine.[91]

The allure of Thiebaud's cakes is enhanced by their life-size scale and the sense that the display expands beyond the picture plane – a device adopted in other works of the period, including *Pie Rows* (cat. 5) and *Pie Counter* (cat. 16). The viewer is immersed in their reality, almost overwhelmed by it. Also present, however, is a slight feeling of revulsion at their overabundance and artificiality, amplified by his excessively thick paint. Thiebaud emphasises the manipulated appearance of the confections, sealed in their sheets of icing and marzipan. As he explained,

> I'm interested in foods generally which have been fooled with ritualistically, displays centered and arranged in certain ways to tempt us or to seduce us or to religiously transcend us.[92]

The transformation of the cakes' frosting into oil paint is the last step in their overprocessing. While early writers perceived a veiled criticism of American food culture in works like *Cakes*, Thiebaud rejected such a reading. For him, 'Only when food is used obscenely is it banal. But cakes, they are glorious, they are like toys.'[93] Their allure, then, resided principally in their ornamentation. In it, Thiebaud found a 'common surface decoration'[94] with other equally colourful – but non-edible – items such as pinball machines and yo-yos, with their swirls and sunray motifs (see the discussion in cat. 19).

The presentation of Thiebaud's weighty cakes, thickly frosted with 'gobs of materials', on tiny stands, teetering on impossibly thin spindles, creates a disconcerting element in the composition, something Thiebaud carefully constructed to add 'a little bit of shock or sense of awe or question or maybe even awkwardness, something that builds some

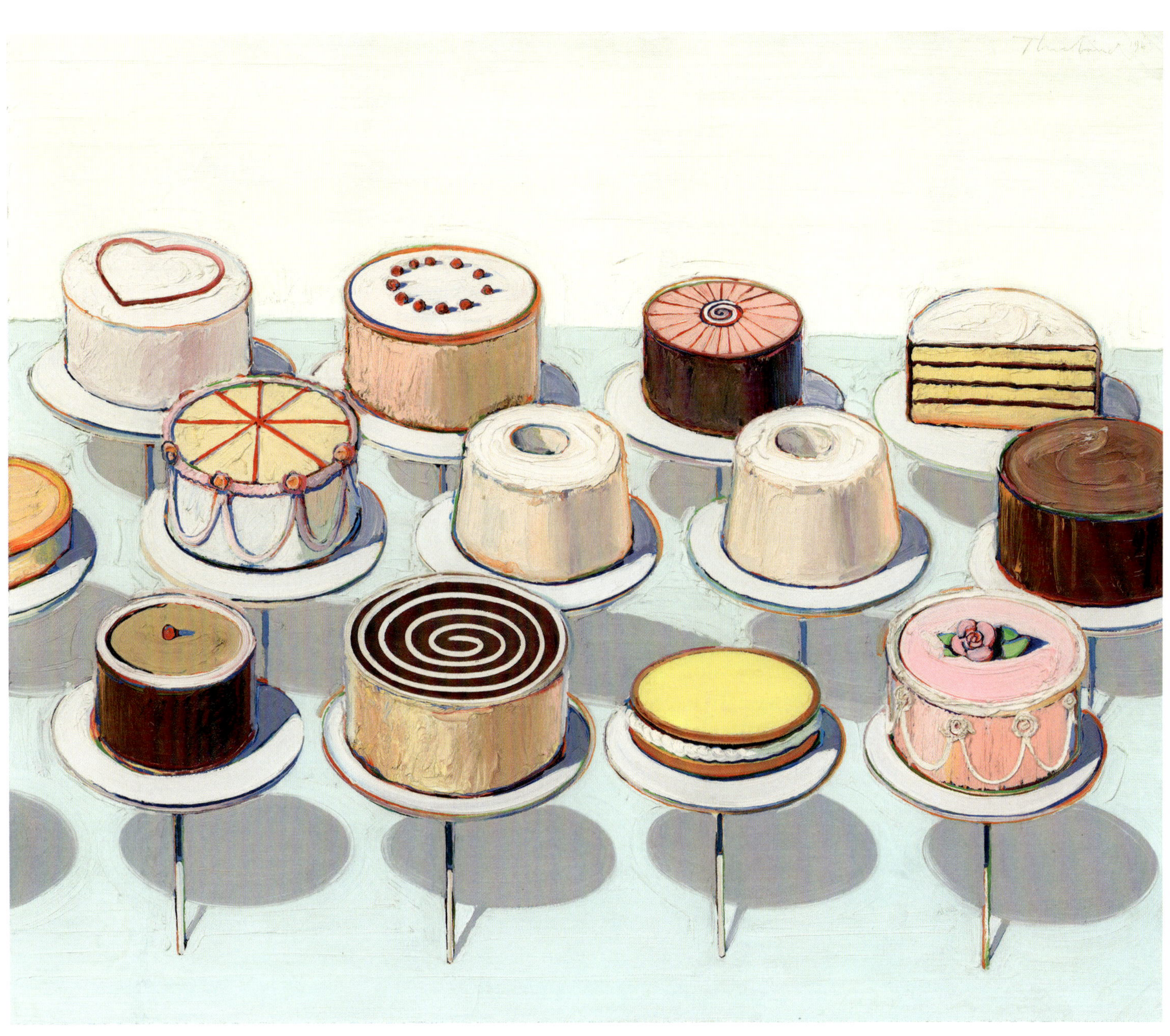

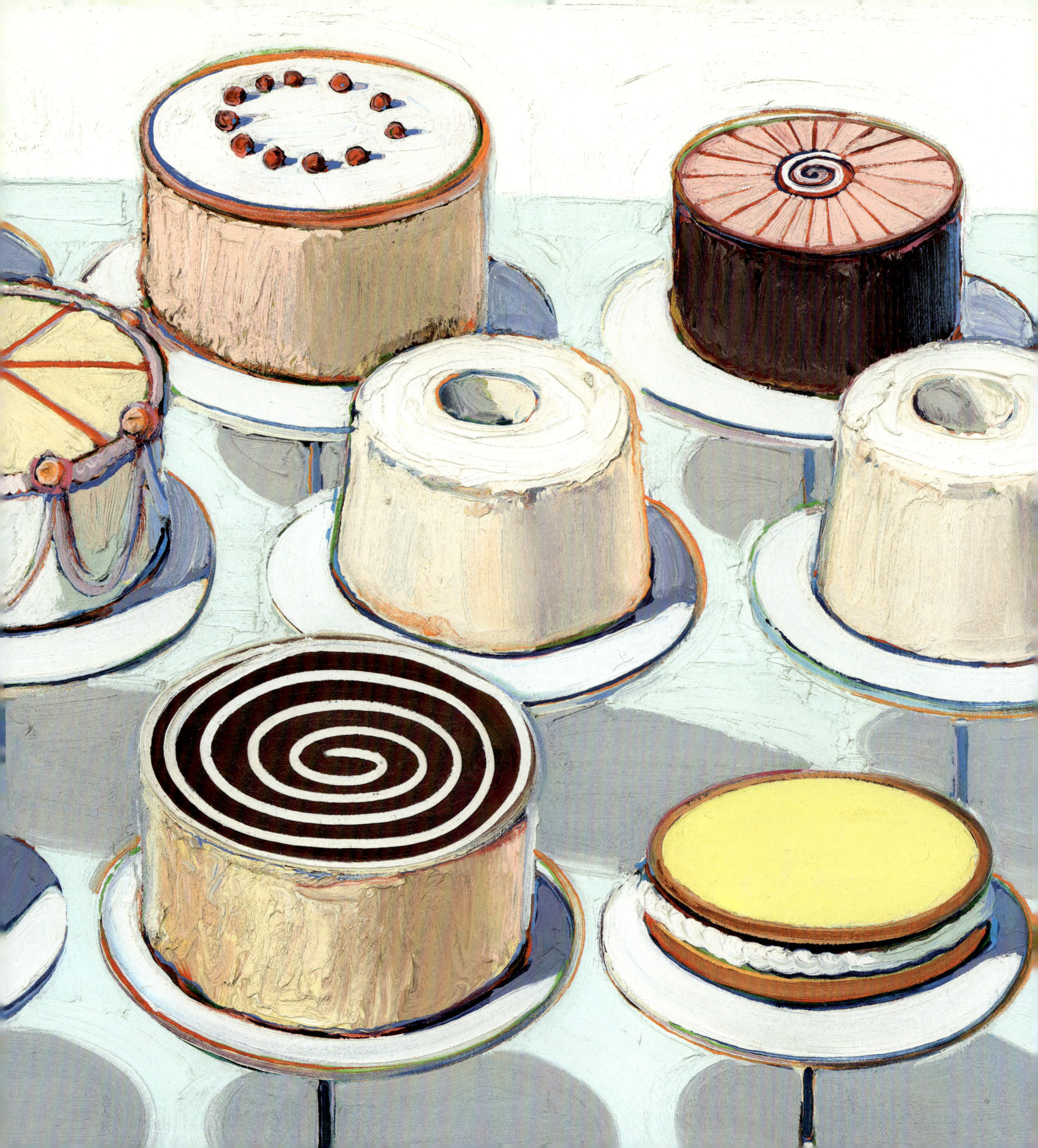

41 Wayne Thiebaud, *Display Cakes*, 1963, oil on canvas, 71.1 × 96.5 cm, Collection SFMOMA

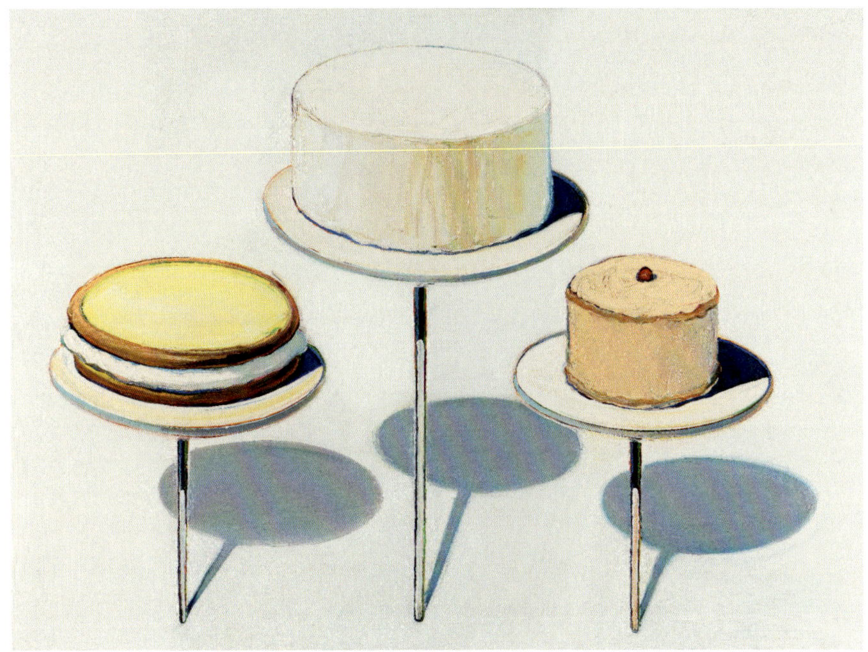

tension in the painting.'[95] A related painting (fig. 41), showing only three cakes, exaggerates this feature even further. In these arrangements, the art historian Timothy Burgard has noted the influence of Edgar Degas's millinery paintings, in which high-fashion hats, adorned with colourful ribbons and feathers, are similarly presented on stands.[96]

One of the standout works in Thiebaud's second solo exhibition at the Allan Stone Gallery in New York in April 1963, *Cakes* was acquired there by the famed art book publisher Harry N. Abrams. A few months later, it was one of seven paintings by Thiebaud included in the landmark exhibition *Six More* at the Los Angeles County Museum of Art, under the title *Cake Counter*. **KS**

18
Three Machines

1963
Oil on canvas
76.2 x 92.7 cm
Fine Arts Museums of San Francisco
Museum purchase, Walter H. and Phyllis J.
Shorenstein Foundation Fund, the Roscoe and
Margaret Oakes Income Fund, with additional funds
from Claire E. Flagg, the Museum Society Auxiliary,
Mr. and Mrs. George R. Roberts, Mr. and Mrs. John N.
Rosekrans, Jr., Mr. and Mrs. Robert Bransten, Mr. and
Mrs. Steven MacGregor Read, and Bobbie and Mike
Wilsey, from the Morgan Flagg Collection

In her 1971 film about her husband's work, Betty Jean Thiebaud described how Wayne Thiebaud 'spends a great deal of time looking at objects which offer interesting painting possibilities. Most of these images are uniquely common to the American environment.'[97] Gumball machines were one such object that had preoccupied Thiebaud's painterly imagination since the 1950s (see cat. 1). From the early 1960s, he produced several paintings, drawings and prints of these machines, usually singly but also, as in this celebrated canvas, in groups of three. Along with pies and cakes, gumball machines soon became identified as an iconic Thiebaud still-life subject. An American invention of the 1880s, the gumball machine acquired its characteristic bubble-topped form in the early twentieth century and soon became an ubiquitous feature of everyday American life. They were positioned on stands on the sidewalk outside shops or inside stores, diners, barbershops, movie theatres or anywhere a passing child or youth might be tempted by the lure of their globes full of brightly coloured candy, usually dispensed for a single cent. By depicting his three machines out of any context, strongly lit against a plain white background and on an abstracted shelf or counter, Thiebaud changes the nature of the viewer's conventional encounter with them. Rather than stimulating a swift impulse for a sweet treat, we are slowed down by his carefully crafted brushwork, compelled to devote maximum attention to the machines themselves and the subtle differences between them, scrutinising their forms as objects of desire.

At the end of the 1960s, Thiebaud reflected on his choice of this subject, asking, 'How does one ever figure out how one was responsible for choosing a gumball machine? On the one hand, one can say it was a common object that has a parallel with those of Chardin … but then again what about the psychological implications of a gumball machine?'[98] Like the once everyday objects of Chardin's still lifes, Thiebaud chose to depict items that he thought might be seen as pertinent to the essence of his own time. He recalled how the artist Barnett Newman had been struck by his gumball paintings in the early 1960s, quoting him as saying, 'You know the gumball machine is in a way the most surreal object in the world, it promises things inside, it's like gift-wrapped elegance. All it supplies is something to chew on, but look at it with its brightest kind of colors plus the fact you put in the dirtiest, grimiest kind of copper money and out comes a beautiful magenta or yellow ball full of sweet promise.'[99] Later writers have extended this reading of *Three Machines*, considering its gumballs 'a sort of atomic particle of American consumer culture … almost every American child's first experience of longing for a non-essential commodity', with the operation of the machine itself encapsulating the cycle of desire, consumption, brief satisfaction, leading to a sense of loss and longing again.[100]

Thiebaud's painterly preoccupations when working on *Three Machines* from memory led to him omitting the release lever on each device and their one-cent price signs that are supposed to be on the chrome coin plates. The basic function of the machines is deactivated. These decisions were taken in the interests of visual impact but nonetheless add a further twist to our reflections on this quintessentially modern American still life. As Thiebaud put it, 'when you think about a gumball machine, it is both a most elementary mechanism and a gadget for stimulating the grandest sort of associations and references.'[101] **BW**

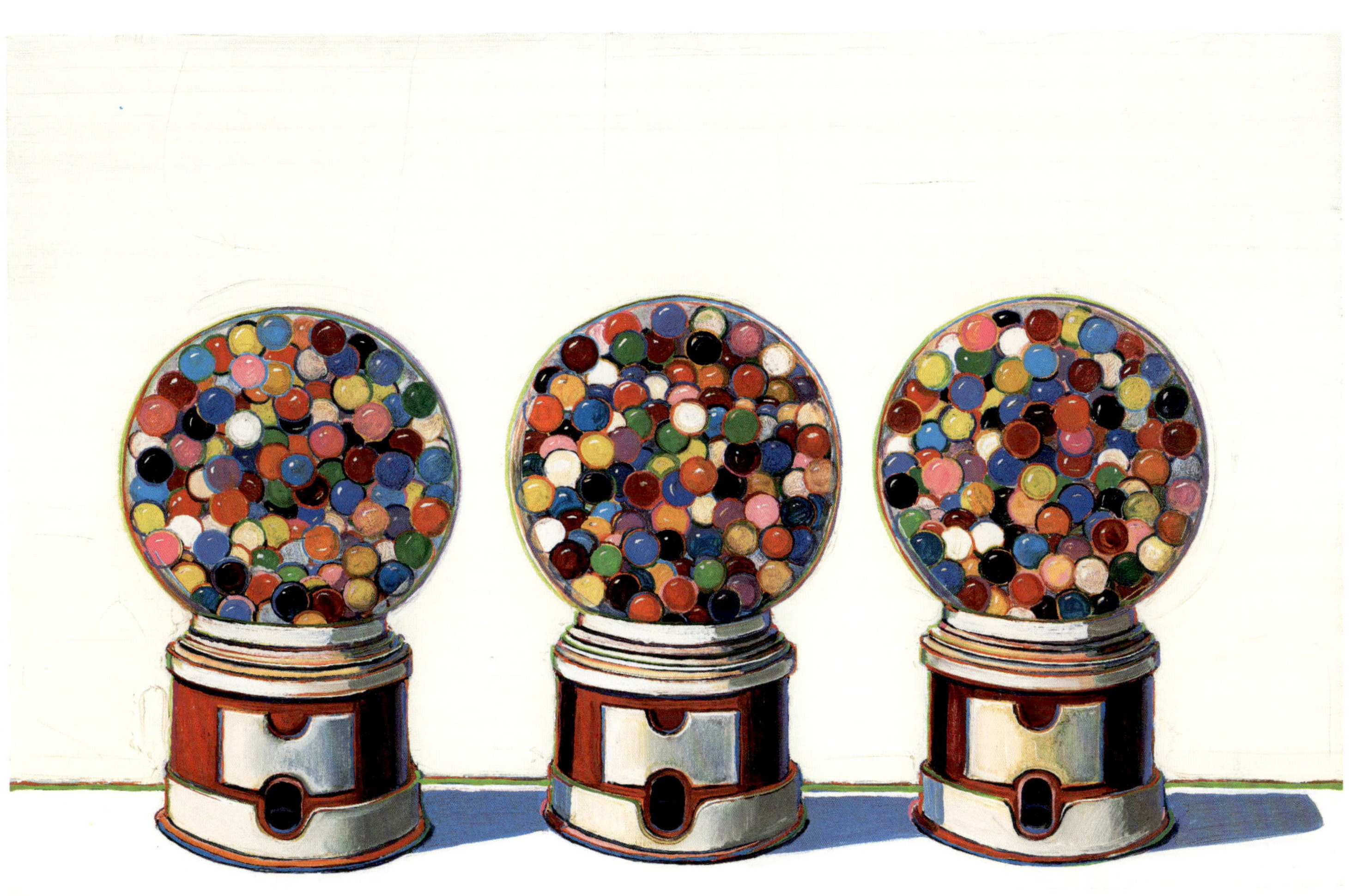

19
Yo-Yos

1963
Oil on canvas
61 x 61 cm
Buffalo AKG Art Museum
Gift of Seymour H. Knox, Jr., 1963

This painting formed part of Wayne Thiebaud's first comprehensive travelling exhibition at five museums across the United States in 1968, originating at the Pasadena Art Museum. Less than ten years after his breakthrough show at the Allan Stone Gallery in New York, this touring exhibition further established Thiebaud's reputation as one of the country's leading modern painters. It was an opportunity to see the developing connections and continuities between his chosen subjects. An artist's interview in the catalogue with the exhibition's curator, John Coplans, allowed Thiebaud to give insights into his recent practice. He spoke about his fascination with still lifes comprised of repetitions of the same foods or objects, as exemplified by his pies and cakes and this painting of yo-yos:

> The cakes, the hors d'oeuvres and the yoyos all relate to one another because of the common surface decoration. The pinwheels, bars, crosses, stars and other geometric and heraldic devices are shared in common. I have no idea why they are used, but they are fascinating nonetheless. I got tired of painting cakes, and yoyos have a different look … they are split in the middle and flatter in shape. They posed some different formal problems.[102]

Thiebaud rejected the suggestion that mass-produced foodstuffs and objects were banal or monotonous subjects, describing his paintings as 'a play on the closeness of similarities and dissimilarities'.[103] With *Yo-Yos*, that play is particularly evocative: it depicts a display of rows of the ubiquitous child's toy, which conforms to a uniform design but whose different, brightly coloured decorations provide variations on a common theme, offering a degree of consumer choice. Thiebaud's attentive and thickly applied brushwork gives a strange sense of the factory-made yo-yos being remade by hand, undercutting our expectation of industrial uniformity. In her film about her husband's work, Betty Jean Thiebaud described how 'in his mind while working is a conviction that he is actually carving, modelling and building the object rather than rendering it'.[104] Accordingly, every yo-yo depicted has an idiosyncrasy of one sort or another – the changeable fall of a shadow, an unexpected shift in scale, a slightly distorted ellipse or a mismatched centre join. On one level, in *Yo-Yos* Thiebaud's painterly craft expresses beauty and love in these common objects of childhood joy, perhaps even a longing or nostalgia for simple pleasures. On another level, the painting suggests bigger issues regarding one's consciousness of individuality and conformity. In the interview with Coplans, Thiebaud shared his conviction that the subtleties of close looking at things that were usually overlooked might hold profound significance: 'It is one of the ways I think about art. It has the capacity to build alternatives in a peculiar way – it is full of little discriminations and insights which are terribly important and only a very few individuals ever think about them.'[105] **BW**

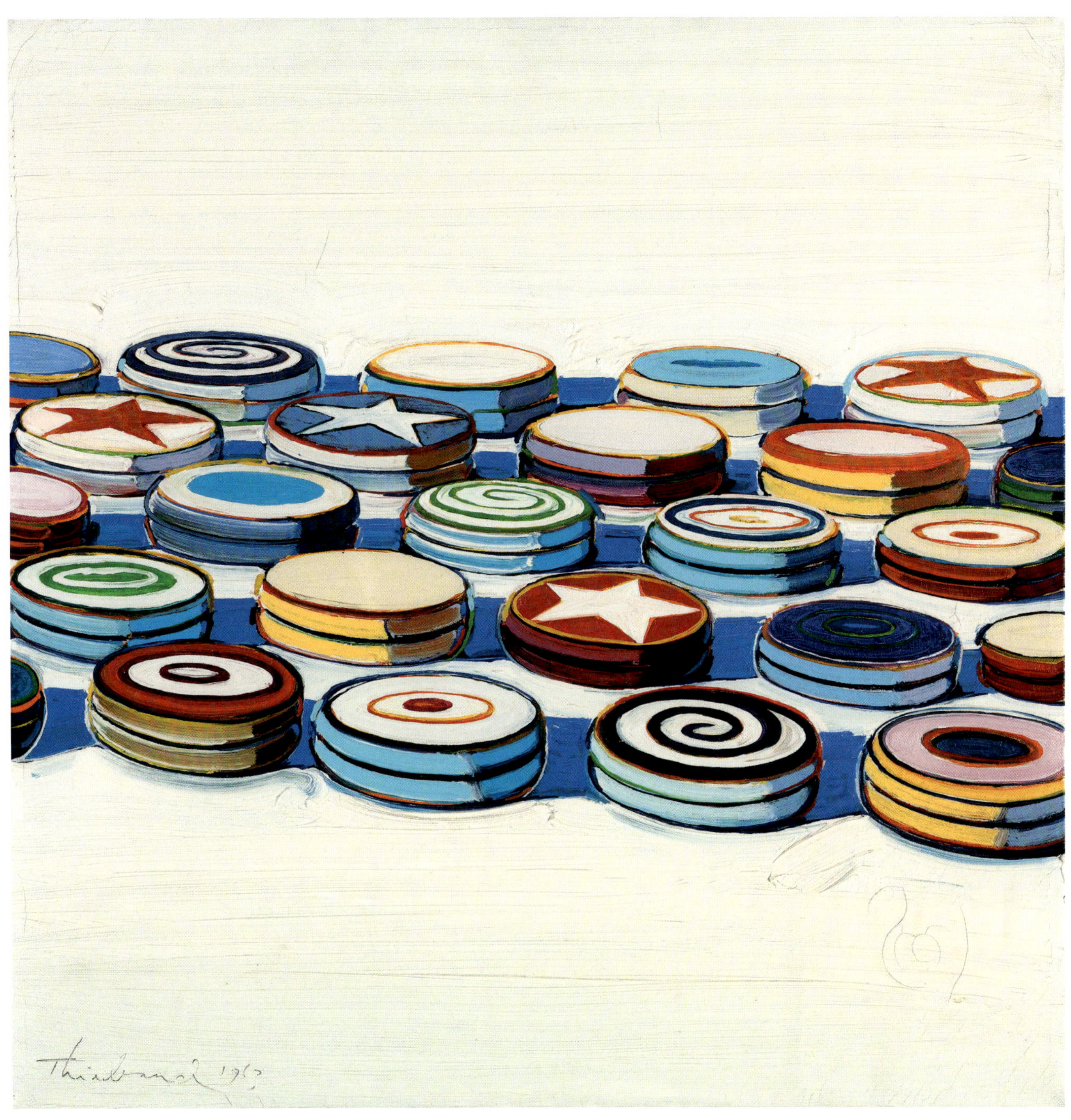

1964
Oil on canvasboard
33 × 37.5 cm
Acquavella

With *Three Cones*, Wayne Thiebaud offers the ubiquitous summer treat: ice cream cones in the classic flavours of strawberry, chocolate and vanilla, just waiting to be picked up from their stand. The painting's small scale adds to the sense of intimacy and private pleasure. One can almost feel the weight of the scoops pressed upon the lower ridges, soon to start melting and dripping. As Thiebaud noted, 'The ice cream cone, for me, represents a kind of joy, the sort of temporariness. It's here and very fresh, firm. That very bright spirit that it once had, that kind of colour, light, liveliness, soon will be gone.'[106] *Three Cones* can thus be seen as the transposition into a modern American idiom of the long European tradition of still life as *memento mori*, using the representation of fresh food and its inevitable decay as a meditation of the fleeting nature of life.

Beyond its associations with short-lived pleasure and American leisure, the ice cream cone undoubtedly appealed to Thiebaud because of the formal possibilities offered by its deceptively simple shape – a circle atop an inverted triangle. These basic shapes inevitably evoke the advice given to a young painter by Paul Cézanne, a greatly influential artist for Thiebaud, to approach nature through its most fundamental forms, 'the cylinder, the sphere, the cone', using horizontal parallel lines to create breadth. Thiebaud often talked about seeking the essence of the object, and the instantly recognisable form of the ice cream cone was a favourite motif. He returned to it often, in different media and configurations, varying the number of cones and scoops. One of the plates of the *Delights* portfolio depicts three so-called 'double-deckers', cones with two large scoops of ice cream one on top of the other, in a precarious balance (cat. 36).

Three Cones is one of the compositions that demonstrates most clearly Thiebaud's debt to commercial art and cartoons. As he explained in 1962, 'My time spent as an advertising art director, cartoonist, and illustrator some years ago is partly responsible for the look of some of the things.'[107] The clear arrangement of the present painting, the rhythm of the cones and the spare background all echo advertising posters. One senses Thiebaud the art director in the bright light coming from the left of the composition and the resulting strong shadows cast by the cones. Thiebaud's use of colour and thick application of paint are, however, specific to him as painter. Three short, diagonal brushmarks on each cone create highlights that add volume to their form, all the while evoking their waffle-like texture. Shadows are rendered in blue, enhanced by a subtle line of red on the cones themselves, in an effort to create 'a little bit of vibration' on the edges of things, 'so the eye will accept the form as not being pasted on'.[108] Thiebaud borrowed the term 'halation' from the artist and professor Josef Albers to describe his approach, although it stemmed just as firmly from his observation of the use of complementary colours by artists from previous centuries. One of these was Vincent van Gogh who, Thiebaud noted, used 'a different colored line around a form to heighten the color.'[109] With a few basic shapes and lines of colour, Thiebaud has conjured up a striking representation, albeit one whose effectiveness and evocative power rely on shared experience. Indeed, as the art historian Isabelle Dervaux has noted, 'His pictures look real not because they are realistic but because they match everyone's conception of the perfect hamburger or ice cream cone'.[110] **KS**

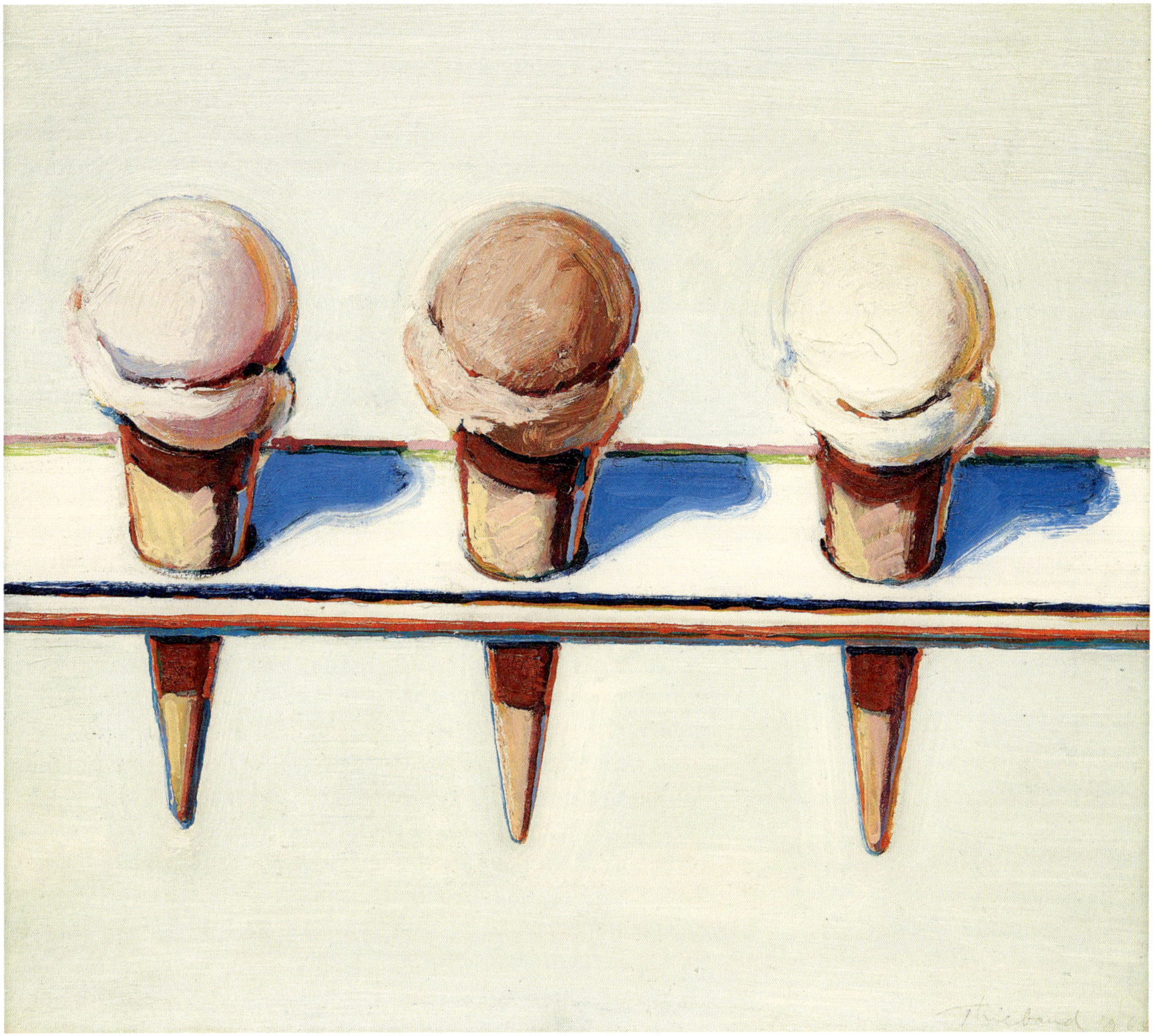

21
Candy Counter

1969
Oil on canvas
120.7 x 91.8 cm
Private collection

In *Candy Counter*, Wayne Thiebaud revisits, seven years later, a subject matter first treated in one of his large-scale canvases of the early 1960s (cat. 12). The present painting, however, shows a different approach to the candy counter, with a tighter composition and warmer, brighter colours. On the lower shelf, multicoloured peppermint sticks are stacked against an enamel tray containing candied apples. To the right sits a large slab of nougat, its white substance enlivened with bits of candied fruit. On the long upper shelf, a lidded glass jar holds peppermint pillows and a scale awaits customers. The bright lines of lime green, yellow, red and cobalt that Thiebaud had used in the early 1960s to first set out his composition are now amplified, enhancing the luminosity of the painting and the structure of the stacked display.

The painting's vertical, portrait format is unusual in Thiebaud's still-life painting and may reflect his most recent interest in the depiction of figures. Following the successful exhibitions of his still lifes that saw him burst onto the art scene, Thiebaud decided, in late 1963, to shift his focus, for a time, to representing the human figure (see fig. 29). His approach to his new subject, however, echoed his earlier work as he isolated his figures against a white background. As the art historian Steven Nash noted, 'In both cases, Thiebaud attempted to objectify as fully as possible the basic subject. He situated figures in the same abstract, open spaces that engulfed the still lifes, flooding them with the same intense illumination, and constructing them with a similar materiality of paint.'[111] In the latter part of the 1960s, he also experimented with landscape, something that fed into his return to still life: 'The objects are for me like small landscapes, buildings or characters in a play with costumes; they have all of these images for me.'[112] Ever the art director, Thiebaud has created, in *Candy Counter*, a balanced but varied composition, with peaks and troughs as the eye travels from the low peppermint sticks up to the verticality of the apples' sticks and back down to the nougat slab.

Thiebaud signed and dated the painting along the upper edge of the canvas, in the centre. After the date, he added a heart, which he would continue to do over the next decades. While this is an early example of this form of signature, the heart motif is already present, in the same position and angle, in the decoration of one of the confections in *Cakes* from 1963 (cat. 17). *Candy Counter* closes Thiebaud's breakthrough decade of the 1960s by looking back to his earlier still lifes and hinting at new directions. **KS**

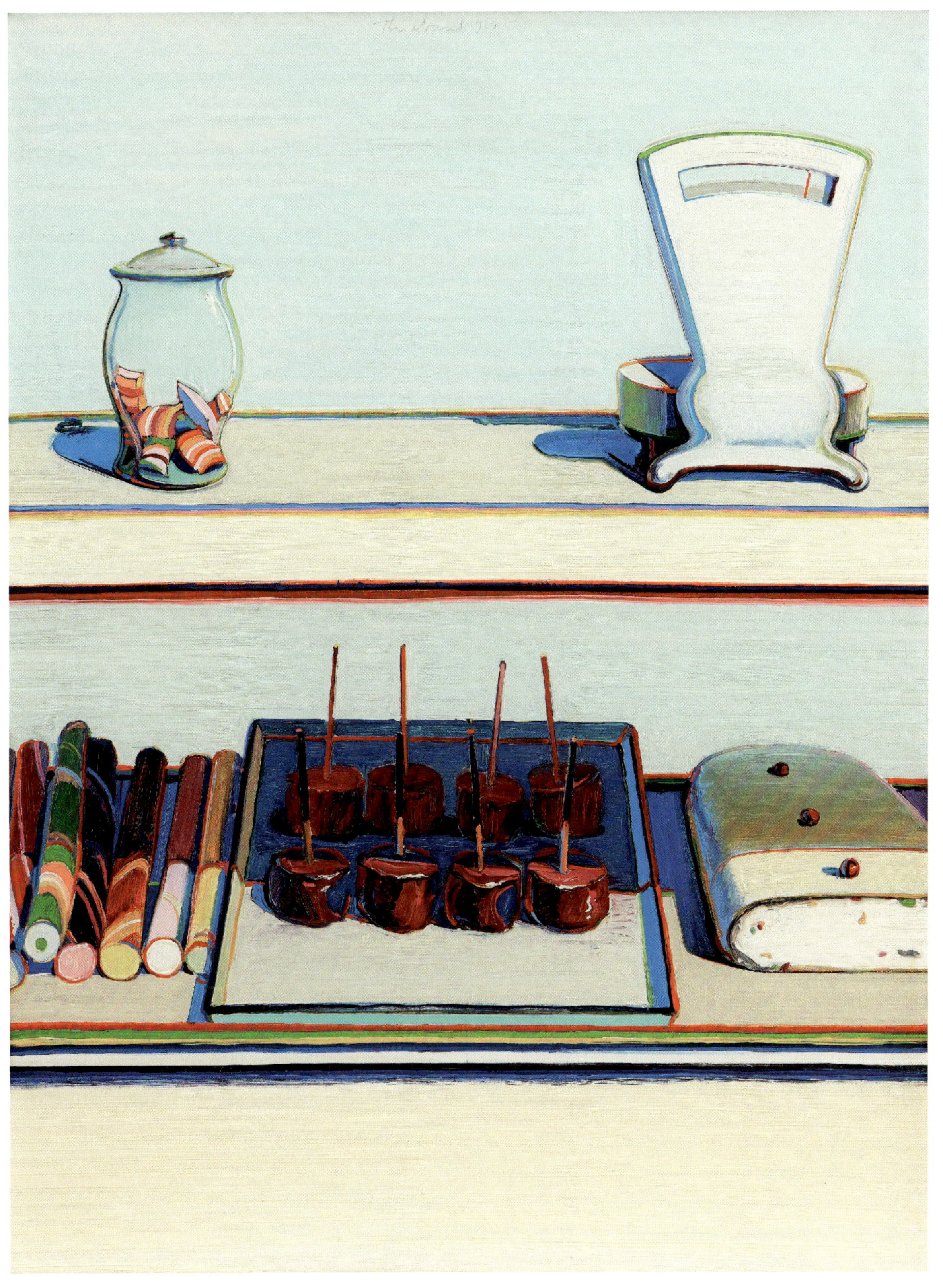

Wayne Thiebaud traced his lifelong interest in drawing to his teenage years when, recovering from a broken back in hospital, he started to draw cartoons. From then on, he drew on a daily basis and advocated for it as a vital, life-enriching skill that could teach its students how to 'see a lot better and a lot deeper.'[113] Finished standalone drawings, often virtuosic in their concision, formed a fundamental aspect of his practice, while sketchbooks made for study and research constituted another. He thought of the sketchbook as 'a kind of visual journey, diary, and research plan, a place for problem and shorthand notations, developmental sketches, teaching aids, and museum notes'.[114] Thiebaud carried these sketchbooks with him everywhere, conjuring a picture of twentieth-century American life in his enumeration of 'hospitals, churches, ships, airplanes, even to the tennis courts … walking in museums, viewing athletic events, riding in the car, listening to concerts, watching television, and attending lectures'.[115] Also significant to Thiebaud was the copying of master drawings by artists such as Honoré Daumier and Giorgio Morandi. Ever eager to learn from the 'bureau of standards'[116] that was the work of other artists, he encouraged his students to do the same, praising copying as an exercise that allowed you to 'realize more intimately what it [the copied work] is'.[117]

While Thiebaud's own method of teaching drawing to his students was in the academic tradition, his own art training had been very different.[118] As he explained it, 'I didn't go to art school. I had these wonderful people in commercial art and sign painting and old cartoonists and lettering men. They are the ones who showed me how to do things.'[119] Elsewhere, he elaborated, describing learning to draw

> Sunglasses … rings, bowties, straight ties. There's a certain way to do crystal; there's a certain way to do a glass of water; certain way to do something that looks like a bottle of milk; a way to identify all these – you could call them cliches or decorative structural manifestations of a kind of essentialization.[120]

The idea of crystallising the depicted object, learnt from commercial art, remained central to Thiebaud's fine art method. As he would put it in 2011, 'I'm still working as if an old art director's looking over my shoulder, trying to get a thumbnail that might be possible to then project or to graphically transfer'.[121] Such an approach is evident in the stunning clarity of *Cake Slices* (cat. 23), which seems to scale up an art director's thumbnail, the graphite lines that squarely border the ink drawing summoning such graphically oriented ways of working.

Despite an abiding association of Thiebaud's lushly painted surfaces with their subject matter ('You can pretend you are actually icing the cake', as he put it in 2001), he worked across many media in the early 1960s and throughout his career, including watercolour, brush and ink, woodblock printing, etching and pastel, as demonstrated by the selection of works on paper included here.[122] He would often replicate compositions across diverse media to understand what of the image remained or shifted between them, always asking himself whether 'a more legitimate medium' could be found.[123] Speaking specifically

about the relationship between painting and printmaking, he explained
his interest in the process of transposing an image between media: 'It's …
fascinating to see what happens when you make what I would call translations
or transpositions; take a highly colored form, like a gumball machine, and
reduce it in size and color … it's like … translating language'.[124] Elsewhere, he
compared it to the transposition of music.[125] Exemplary is *Boston Cremes* (cat.
28), which does away with the chromatic extravagance of the earlier painting
of the same name (cat. 10), exchanging thick, creamy impasto for the sharp, flat
definition of black ink. Other changes accompany this shift: the horizon line is
lowered, allowing for a larger area of the white paper to remain visible, while
the sense of recession so central to the painting is substituted in the drawing
for a looser, horizontal sprawl of plates and cake slices.

Such experimentation was rooted in his experience of 'five or six art
directors, all with the problem of redesigning [a logo]. And they all come up
with solutions or possible solutions, put them up on a blackboard, and then
everybody argues about which one has the best graphic power, or the strongest
image for the corporation.'[126] Thiebaud continued to work in this way, testing
ideas across numerous sheets, often reworking a composition in the same
medium. Across two versions of *Suckers*, we watch as he revises an image of
four patterned lollipops fanning out from a semi-circular stand. In one
(cat. 24), he utilises the unmarked white sheet to provide sharp contrast with
the black patterns and shadows, creating the illusion of glaring light. In the
other (cat. 25), he introduces a beige wash, producing a mid-tone that softens
the transition between surface and object. Which, we might imagine him
asking himself, has the best graphic power?

Thiebaud exploited the visual force of monochrome in many works of this
period, such as the large-scale drawing *Delicatessen* (cat. 22). Almost half of the
sheet is daringly blocked out with the black ink that constructs the counter,
while silhouettes of hanging salamis pattern the upper part, recalling his love
of cartoon imagery. From the mid 1960s, the increasing appeal for Thiebaud of
colour for its own sake rather than as a conduit to the representation of light
is demonstrated in the chromatic variety of a work such as *Seven Candy Sticks*
(cat. 27), which uses the bright white centres of the sticks to heighten the lavish
exuberance of the synthetic food dyes depicted.[127] **CN**

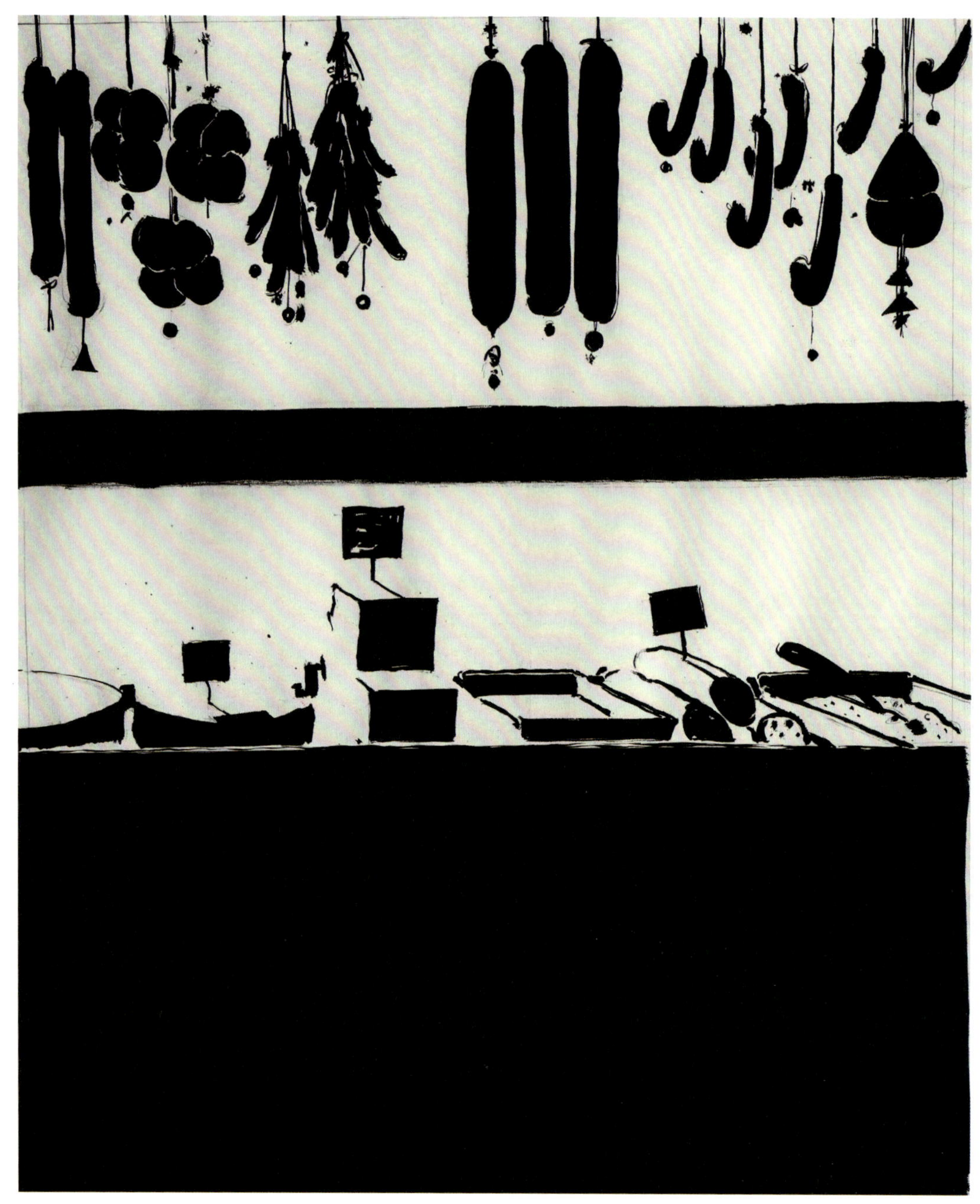

22

Delicatessen

1963–64
Ink on paper
62.5 x 53 cm
Collection of the Wayne Thiebaud Foundation

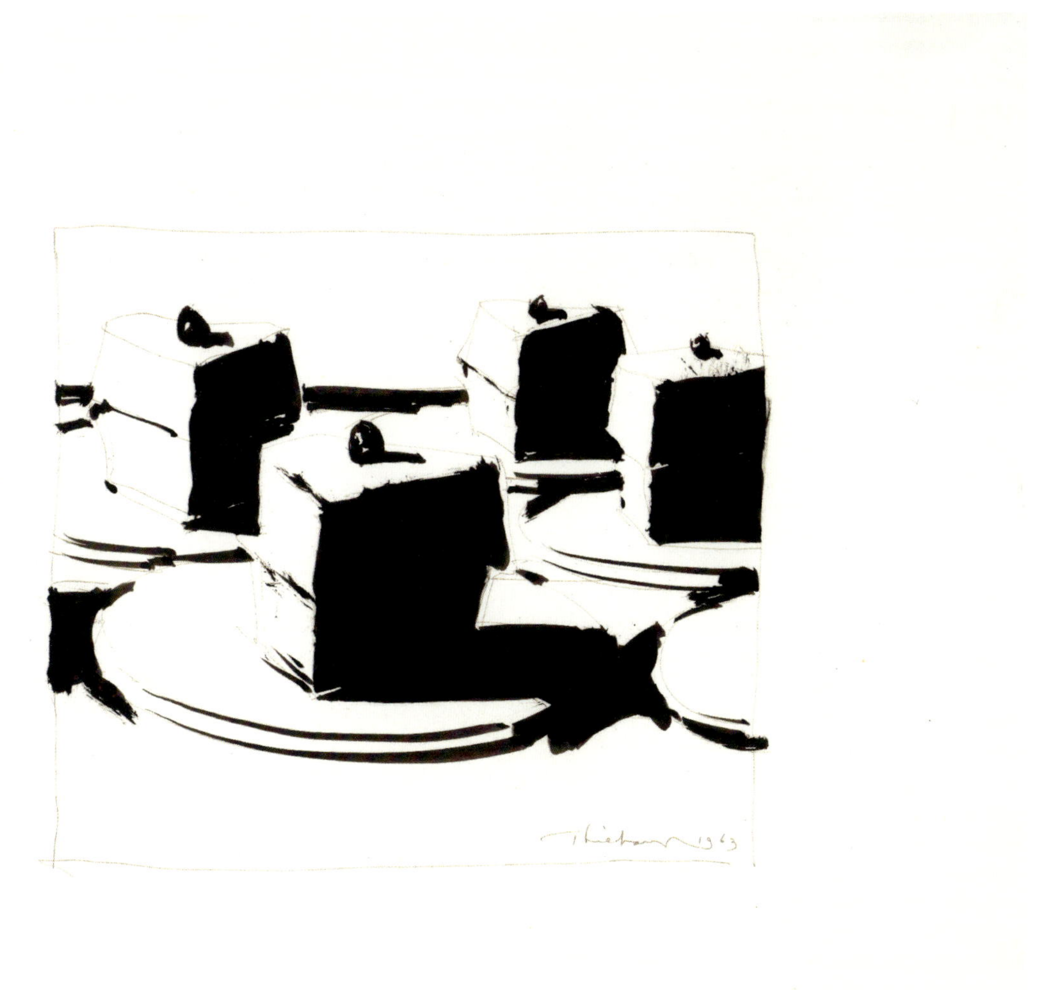

23
Cake Slices

1963
Graphite and ink on paper
29.5 x 37.2 cm
Promised gift by Linda Karshan in memory of her
husband, Howard Karshan. On long-term loan
to the Courtauld Gallery, London

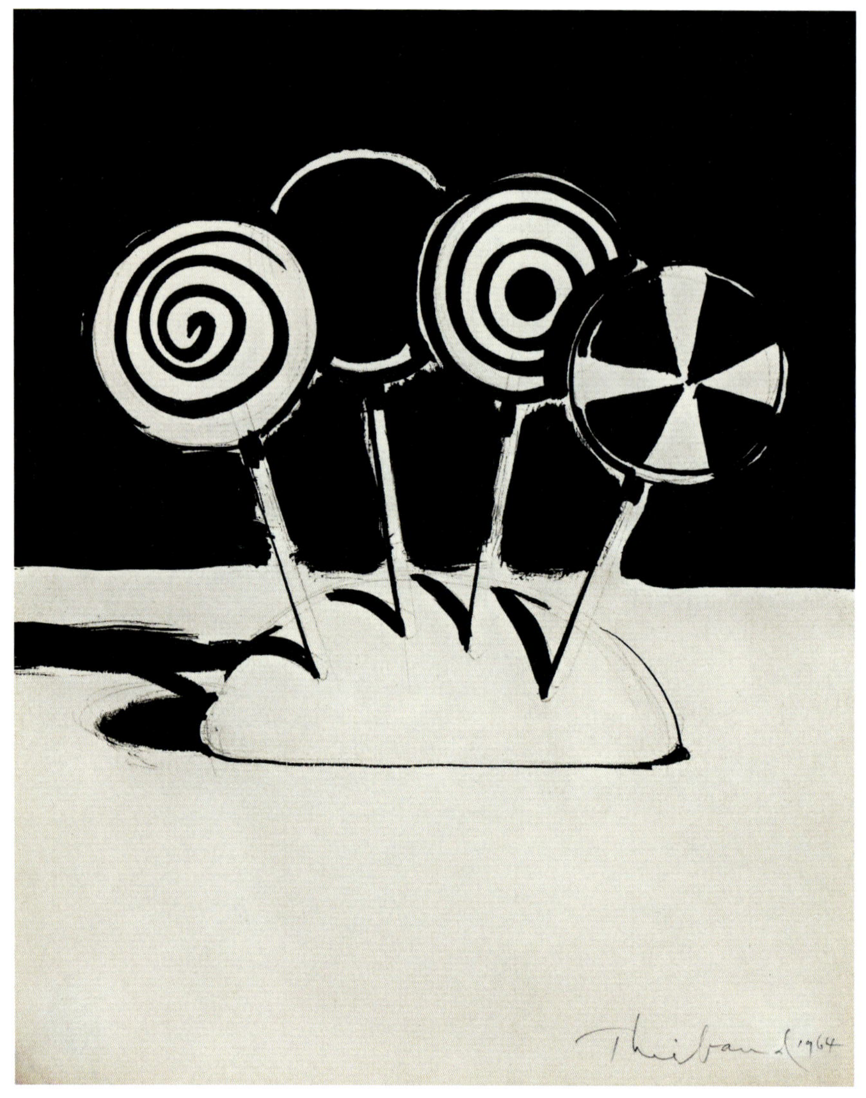

24

Suckers

1964
Ink and graphite on paper
24.2 x 19.5 cm
Collection of the Wayne Thiebaud Foundation

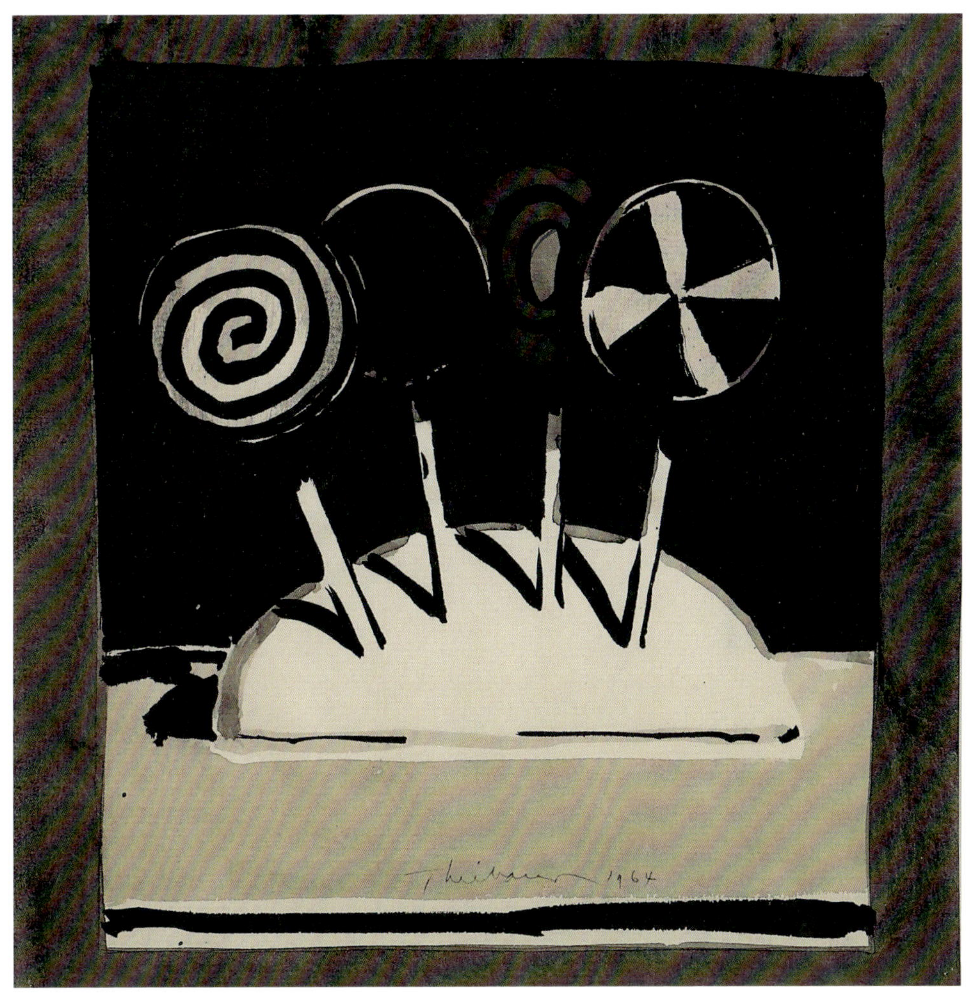

25
Suckers

1964
Ink and wash on paper
21 x 21.5 cm
Collection of the Wayne Thiebaud Foundation

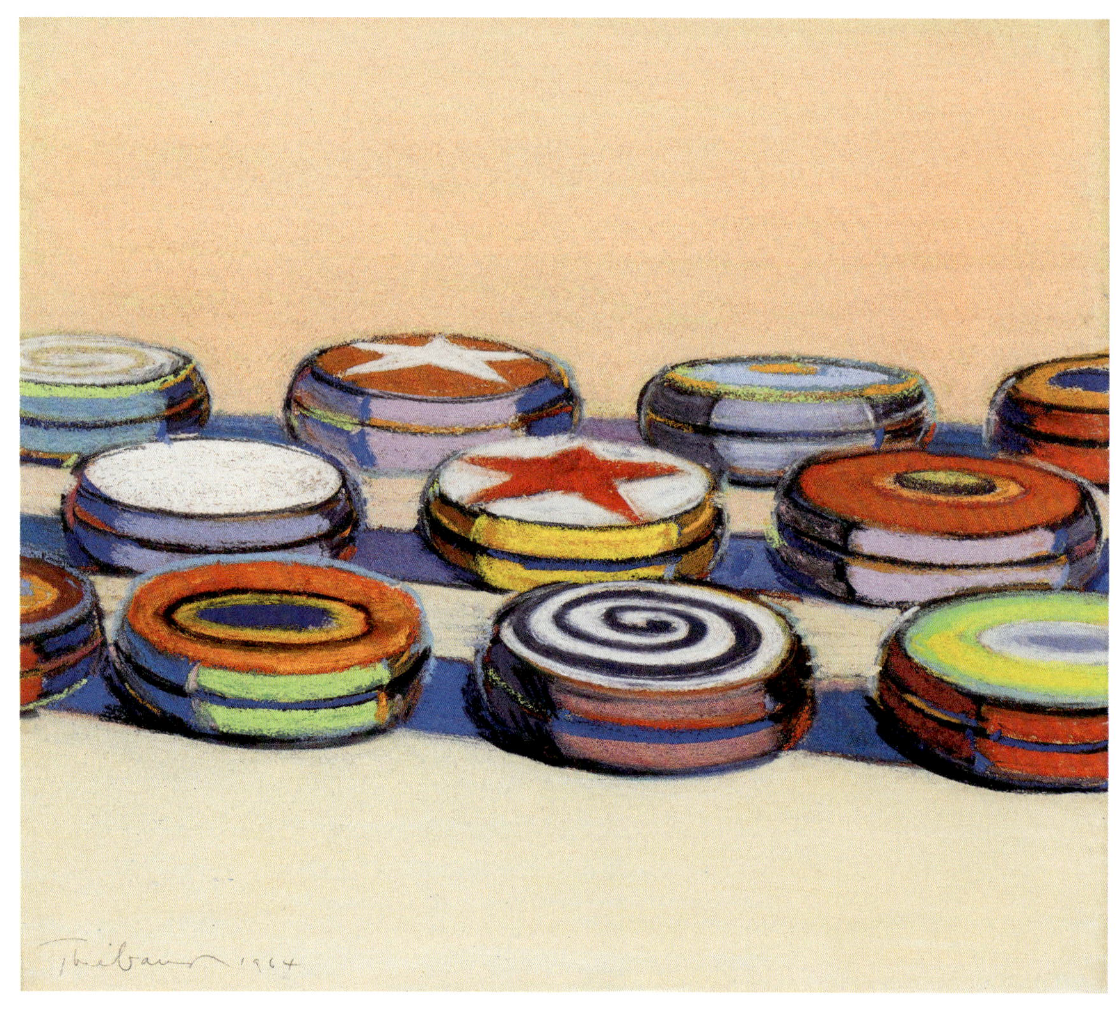

26

Yo-Yos

1964
Pastel on paper
21.6 x 25.4 cm
Collection of John Berggruen

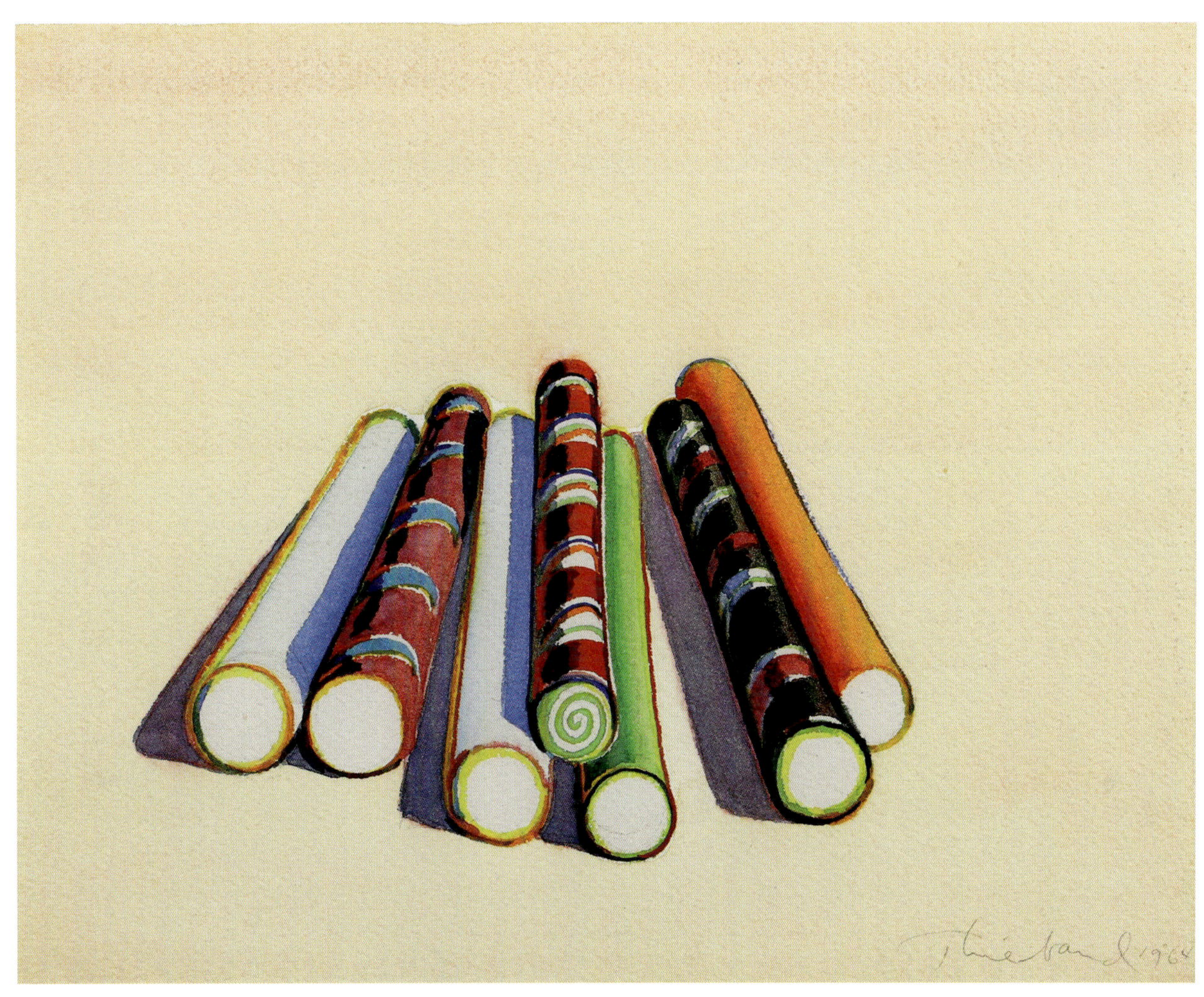

27
Seven Candy Sticks

1964
Watercolour and gouache on prepared paper
21.4 x 27 cm
Collection of Matt and Maria Bult

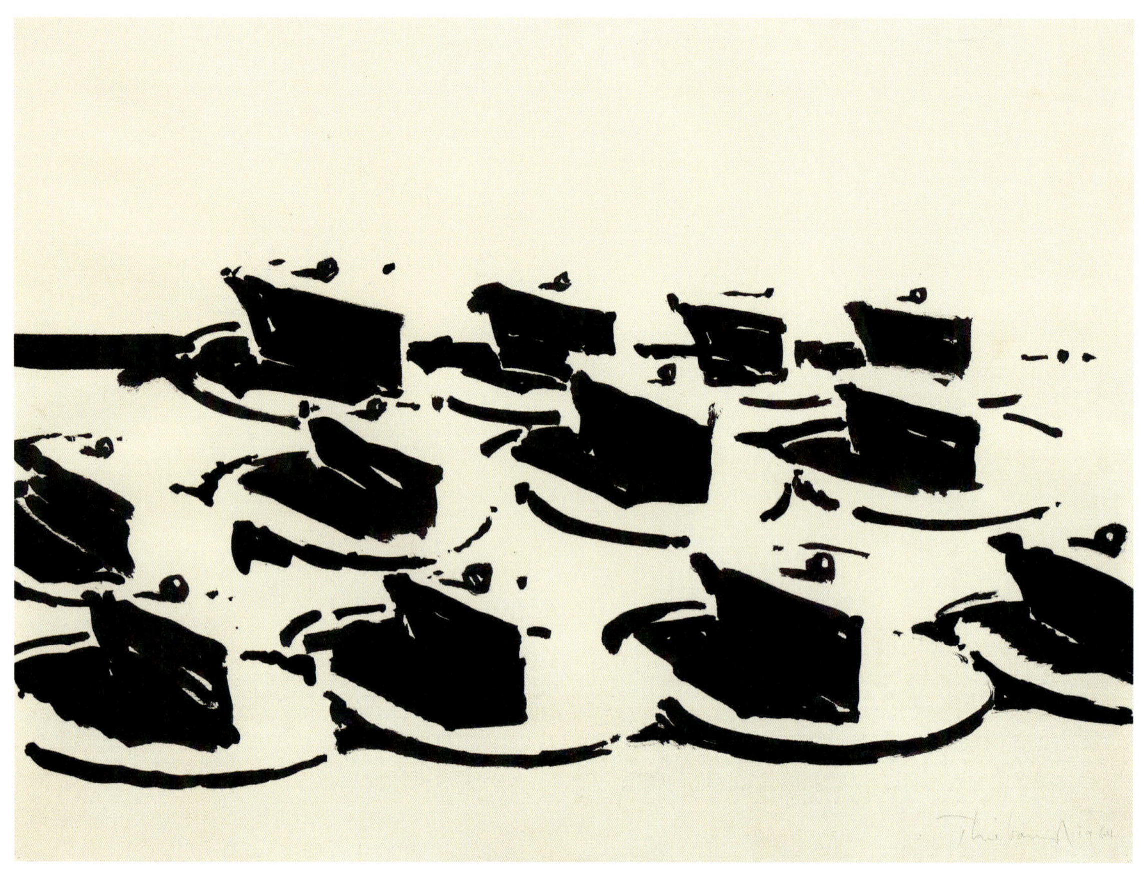

28
Boston Cremes

1964
Ink on paper
33 x 45.5 cm
Collection of the Wayne Thiebaud Foundation

29
Four Pies

1964
Woodcut
State 1, no. 2
Edition of 8 + 3 artist's proofs
21.3 x 29.5 cm
Collection of the Wayne Thiebaud Foundation

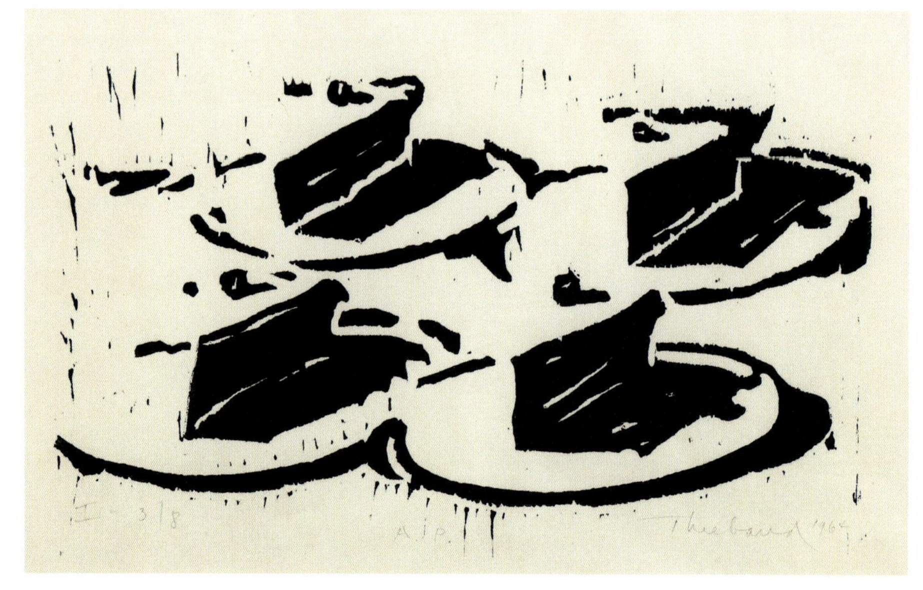

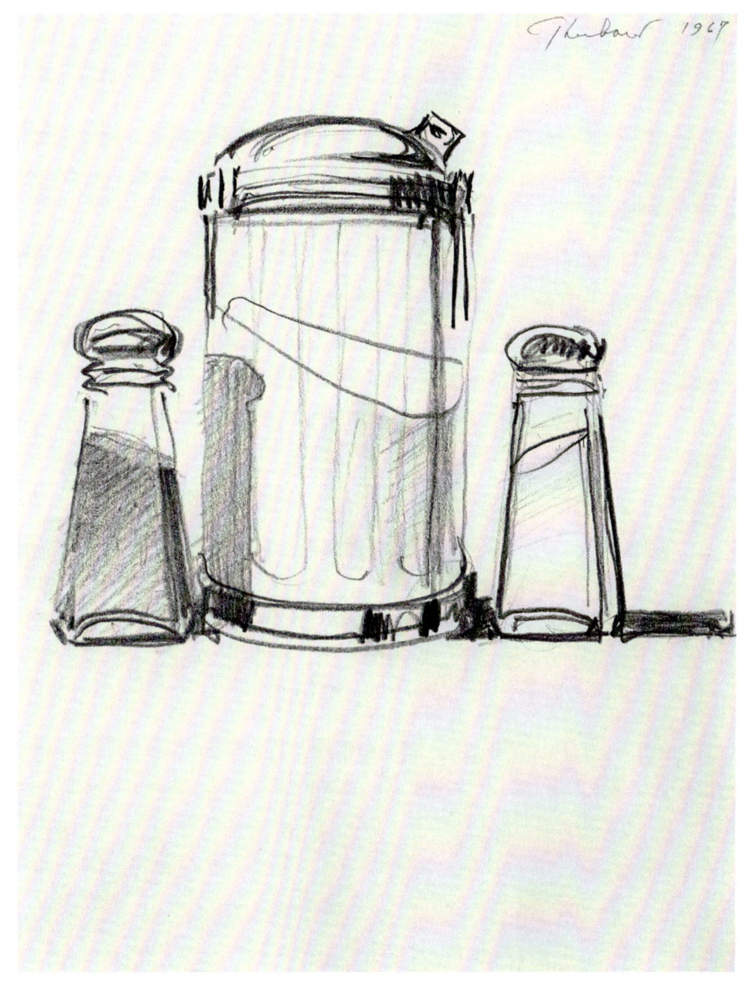

30
Untitled [Sugar, Salt and Pepper Shakers]

1967
Graphite on paper
27.5 x 21 cm
Collection of the Wayne Thiebaud Foundation

Delights

1964 (published 1965)
Seventeen etchings on Rives BFK paper,
sheet size 32.8 x 27.4 cm, individual plate sizes vary
Printed by Kathan Brown and published by her
Crown Point Press, Berkeley, California
Edition of 100 (50 as portfolios, 50 as bound books)
This edition from the portfolio edition, numbered
100/100
Collection of the Wayne Thiebaud Foundation

In 1964, Wayne Thiebaud worked extensively on a group of etchings that would result in his now celebrated series *Delights*. He had been invited to make a print series by Kathan Brown (1935–2025), who had set up her printmaking studio, Crown Point Press, just two years previously. He was the first artist Brown had formally approached to work on a project with her and it was the first time Thiebaud had worked with a printer on a series of this kind. Both Thiebaud and Brown recalled the first day he began in her studio, which was then in the above-ground basement of her house in North Berkeley, California. She had prepared several small, hard-ground copper etching plates for him, and he began working on them from photographs of his recent paintings of still-life subjects. Brown, committed to the idea of printmaking as a unique creative act, was dismayed and told him, 'Printmaking should be original. What is the point of copying yourself or redoing something that has already been done?'[128] Thiebaud responded by taking out a fresh etching plate and drawing the lunch on the table before him that they were about to share – avocados, sandwiches and two cans of beer. This etching, *Lunch*, would become the first plate of his *Delights* series (cat. 31). However, it would be the only print in the group worked on from life, as opposed to from images of his recent compositions. In his discussion with Brown, Thiebaud maintained that working in this way was not mere copying or reproduction but a complete transformation and fresh exploration of his images and subjects in the unique language of printmaking, be it, in the case of *Delights*, etching, aquatint or drypoint. As he put it to her, 'When you change anything, you change everything.'[129]

Following this significant first printmaking session, Thiebaud began travelling often between Sacramento and Brown's studio in Berkeley, working for up to ten hours a day on the prints before returning home in the evening (fig. 42). Although he had made individual screenprints and lithographs during the 1950s, Thiebaud had not worked much with etching techniques. As he recalled, 'it was a chance to learn about etching and all the things it could do. I had no notion for instance of aquatints or sugar lift or soft ground. And Kathan was very patient. She let me make a lot of mistakes, a lot of trial and error which is the only way I know how to work, and that's why it's comfortable working with her.'[130] These sessions throughout 1964 resulted in Thiebaud producing 47 etching plates of compositions, which, apart from *Lunch*, were based on his recent paintings and drawings. He selected seventeen of them to comprise his *Delights* series, which were printed on high-quality Rives paper. Brown, inspired by the tradition of artist's books, had from the outset planned with Thiebaud for it to be published as a bound edition. Accordingly, half of the edition of 100 was made as a handsomely produced book in a leather binding with gilded lettering, bound by the San Francisco bindery Schuberth, and with a letterpress printed dedication (to Betty Jean Thiebaud), title and contents pages by the specialist Bay Area printer Lawton Kennedy (1900–1980). The other half of the edition was published as loose sheets in a boxed set. Although the printing project was at its outset experimental for Thiebaud, the result, published in 1965, was an edition of high quality with an emphasis on the practice of traditional arts and crafts.

Delights is an anthology of Thiebaud's American still-life subject matter with which he had had made his name as an artist over the previous three

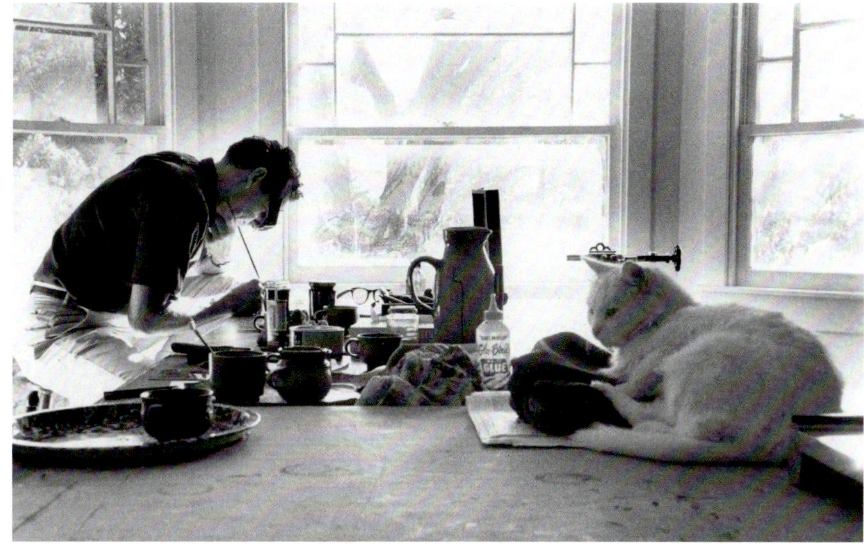

years. Many of his notable motifs appear in the prints, from cakes and pies to a deli counter and gumball machine. Also included is a rare composition of an entire roadside stall, *Cherry Stand* (cat. 34), based on his painting *Fruit Stand* (1963, private collection). It helps to stage the sense of Thiebaud as a painter (or printmaker) of modern America, seeking out common subjects of everyday life. Most importantly, the etchings were a way for Thiebaud to explore the transformative effects of working in another medium, in black and white, and on a very different, much smaller scale. A comparison of his epically proportioned painting *Cakes* (cat. 17) and its etched counterpart, *Cake Window* (cat. 43), makes the point. Both achieve a monumentality that is at odds with their ephemeral and commonplace subject matter but engage us in very different ways. The painting is a sensual and almost overwhelming whipping-up of oil paint and frosting, while the etching is an intimate and sensitive exploration of line and form. Thiebaud later reflected that, 'There's nothing really that I've ever found in other lines that is like an etched line – its fidelity, the richness of it, the density. You just don't get that any other way.'[131]

Thiebaud's experience working on the *Delights* series with Brown ushered in a commitment to printmaking that would last for the rest of his long career. He would return to Crown Point Press throughout his life to work on print projects with Brown. It also led to Thiebaud valuing printmaking as an essential creative practice that informed his painting and drawing; as he put it, 'It is hard to think of printmaking separate from painting, or painting separate from printmaking.'[132] Over the decades, Thiebaud returned periodically to some of the *Delights* prints that he had retained as proofs (see cat. 48 and 49), as well as prints made in 1964 but not included as part of the series (see cat. 50 and 51), and hand-coloured them, using watercolour and other media.[133] With these works, existing somewhere between painting and printmaking, Thiebaud created yet another transposition and new expression of his motifs. **BW**

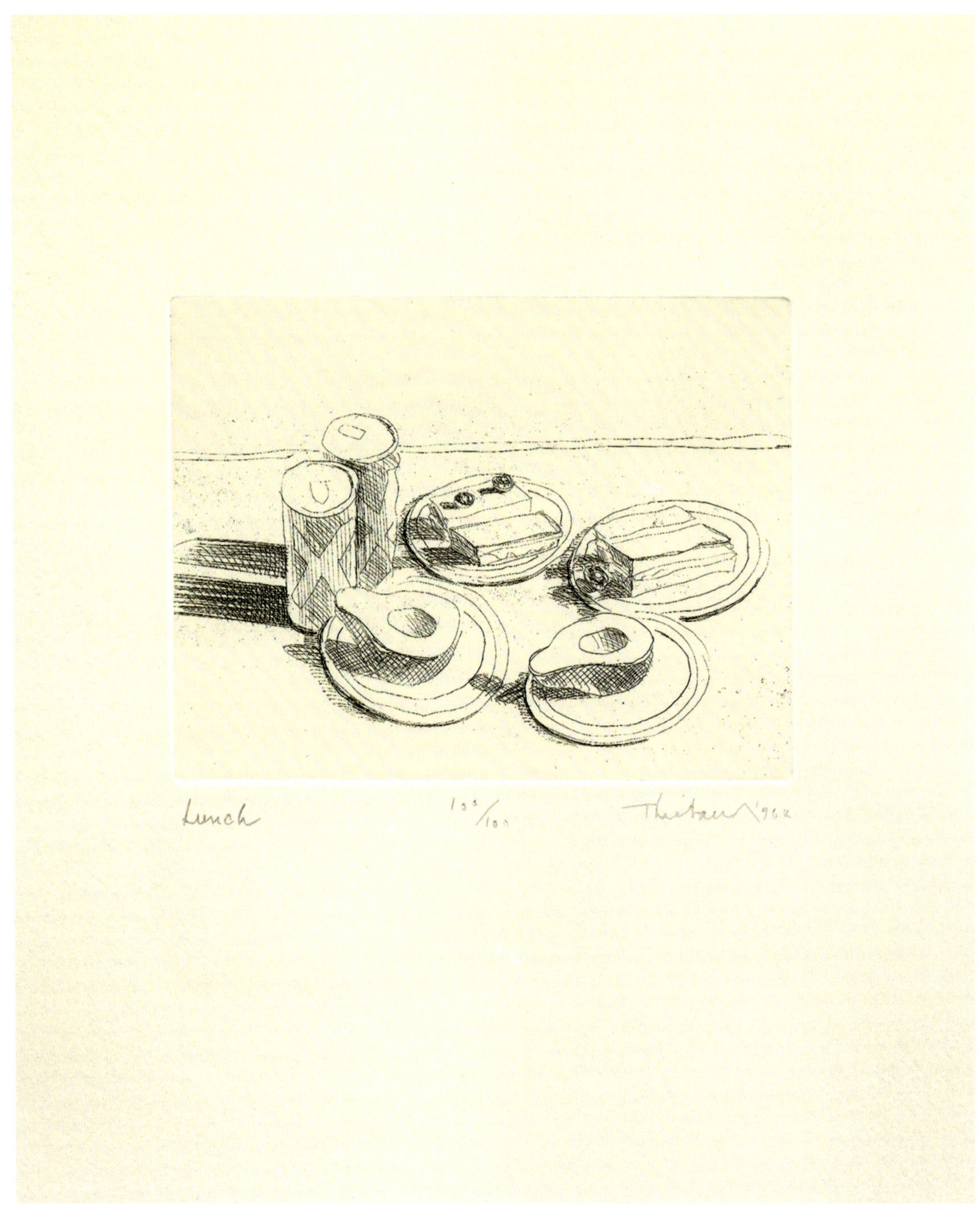

31
Lunch

First plate
Etching
Plate size: 12.7 x 17 cm

144

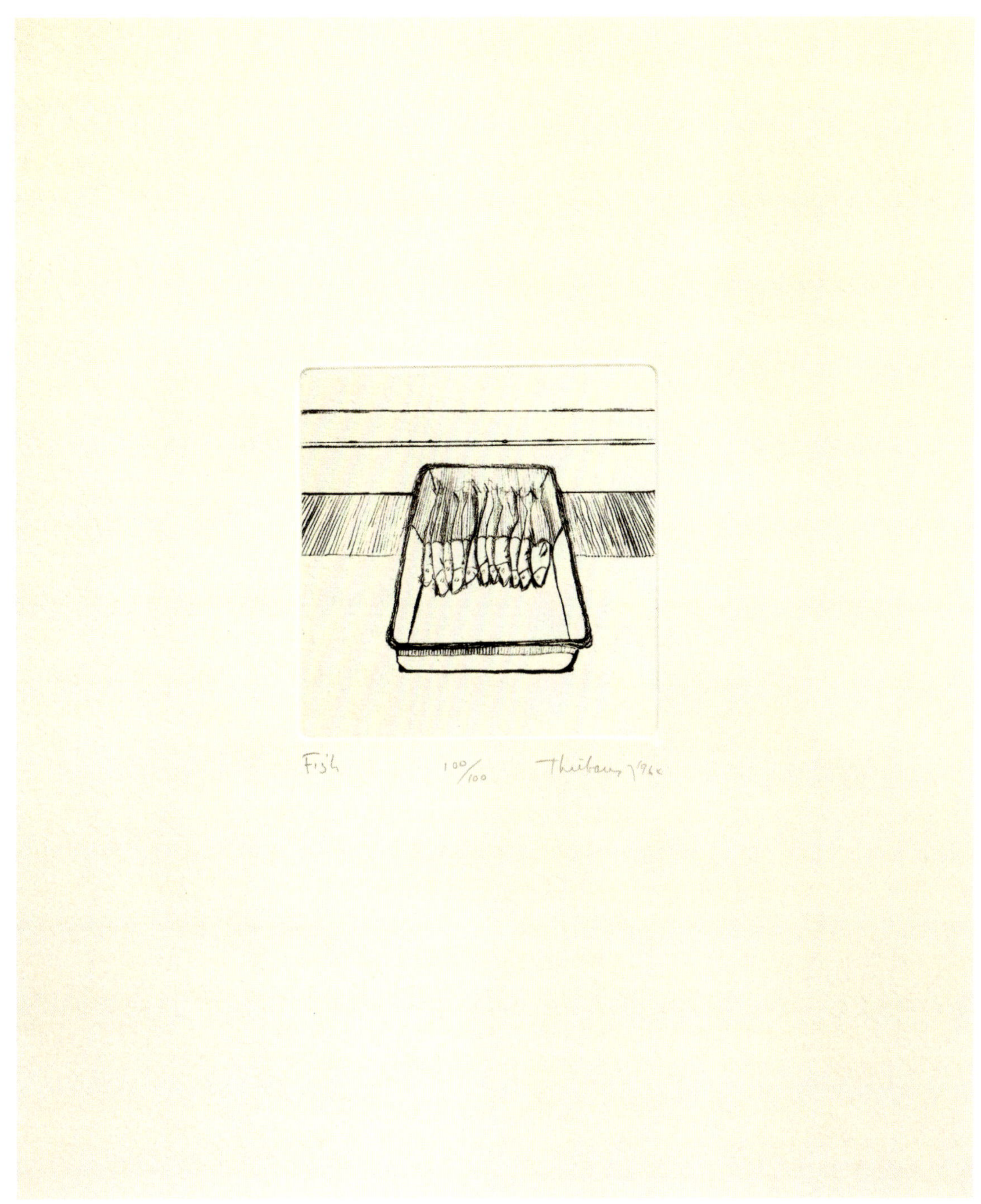

32
Fish

Second plate
Drypoint
Plate size: 10 x 10 cm

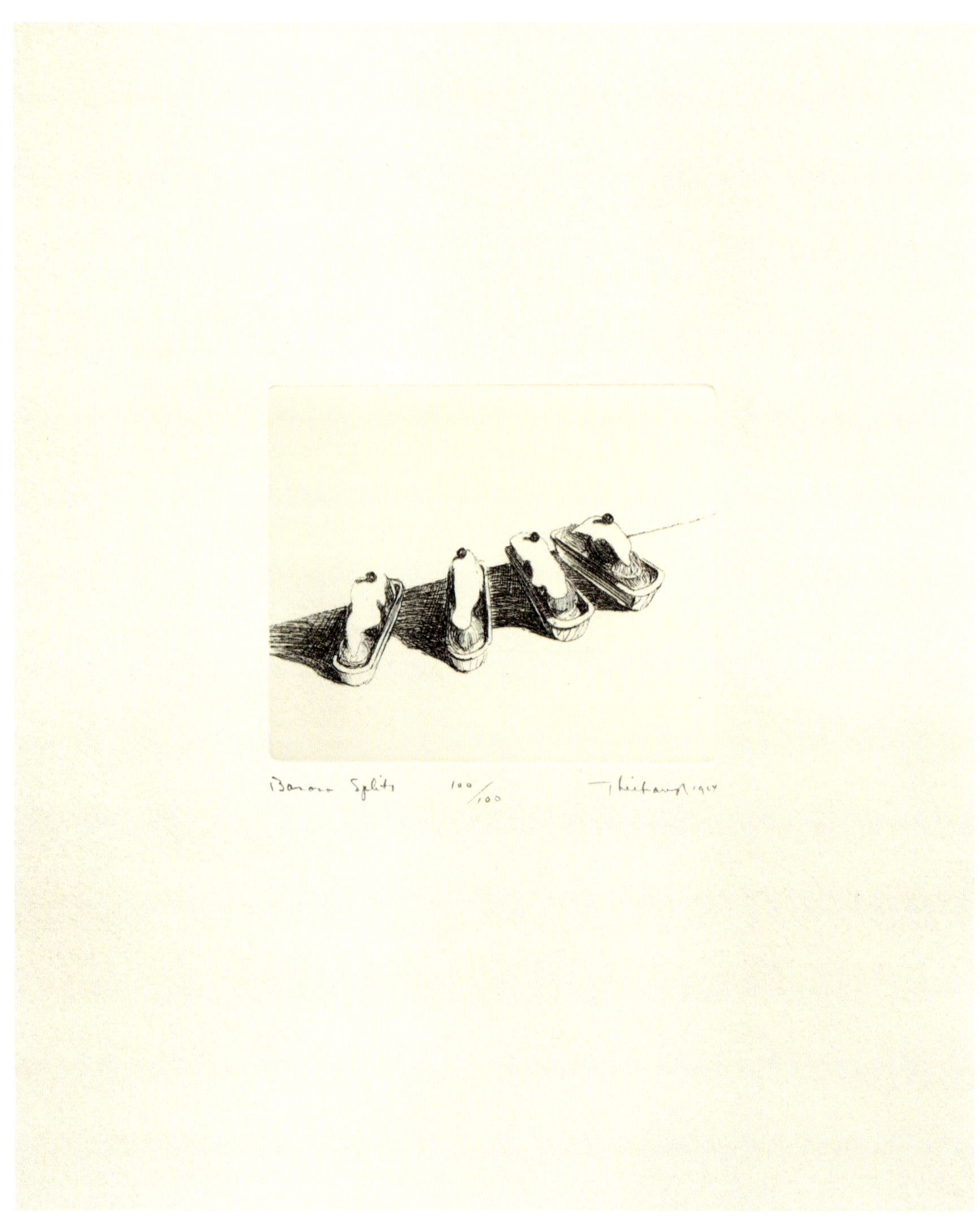

33
Banana Splits

Third plate
Etching
Plate size: 10 x 12.5 cm

146

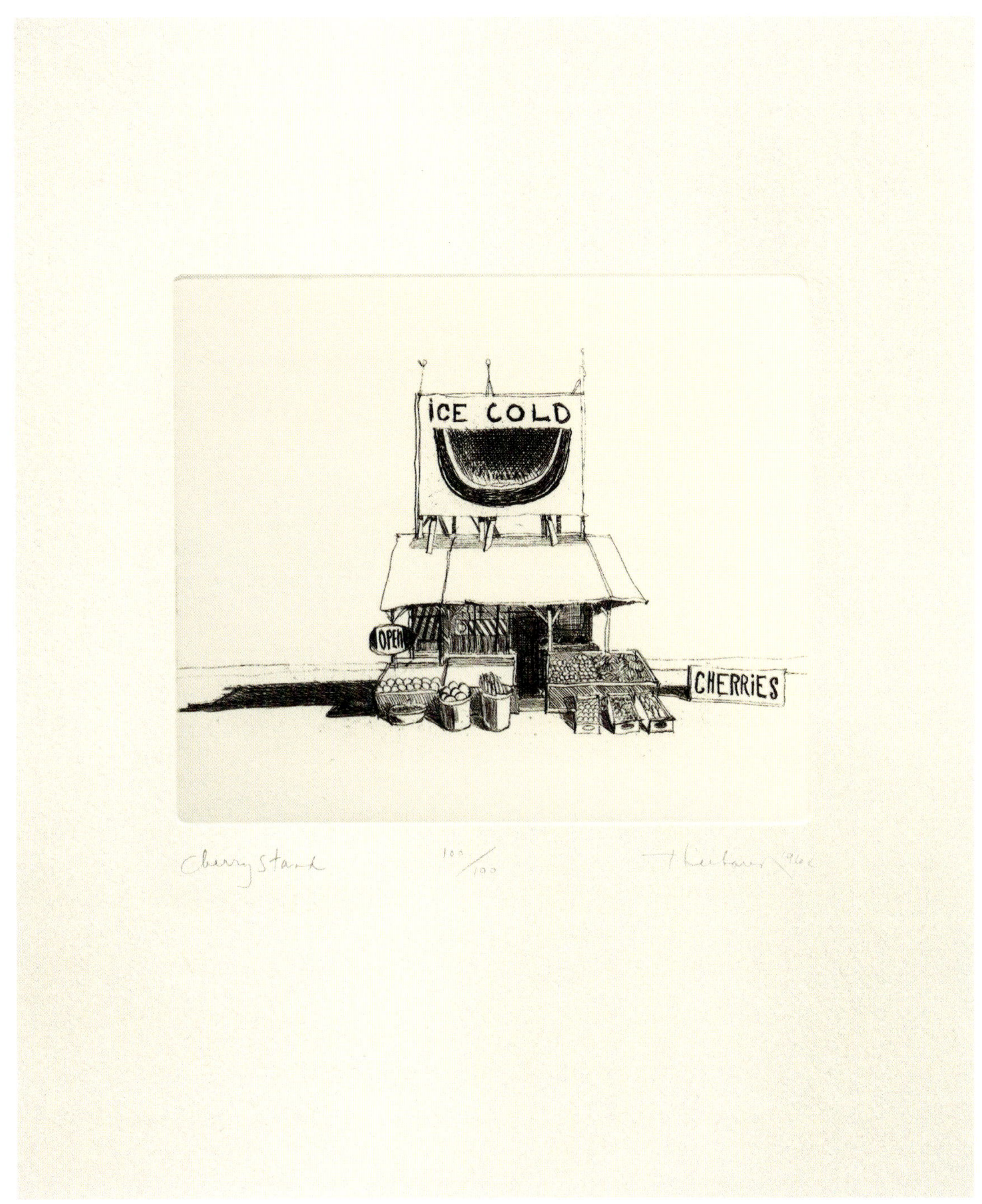

34
Cherry Stand

Fourth plate
Etching
Plate size: 14.5 x 17.4 cm

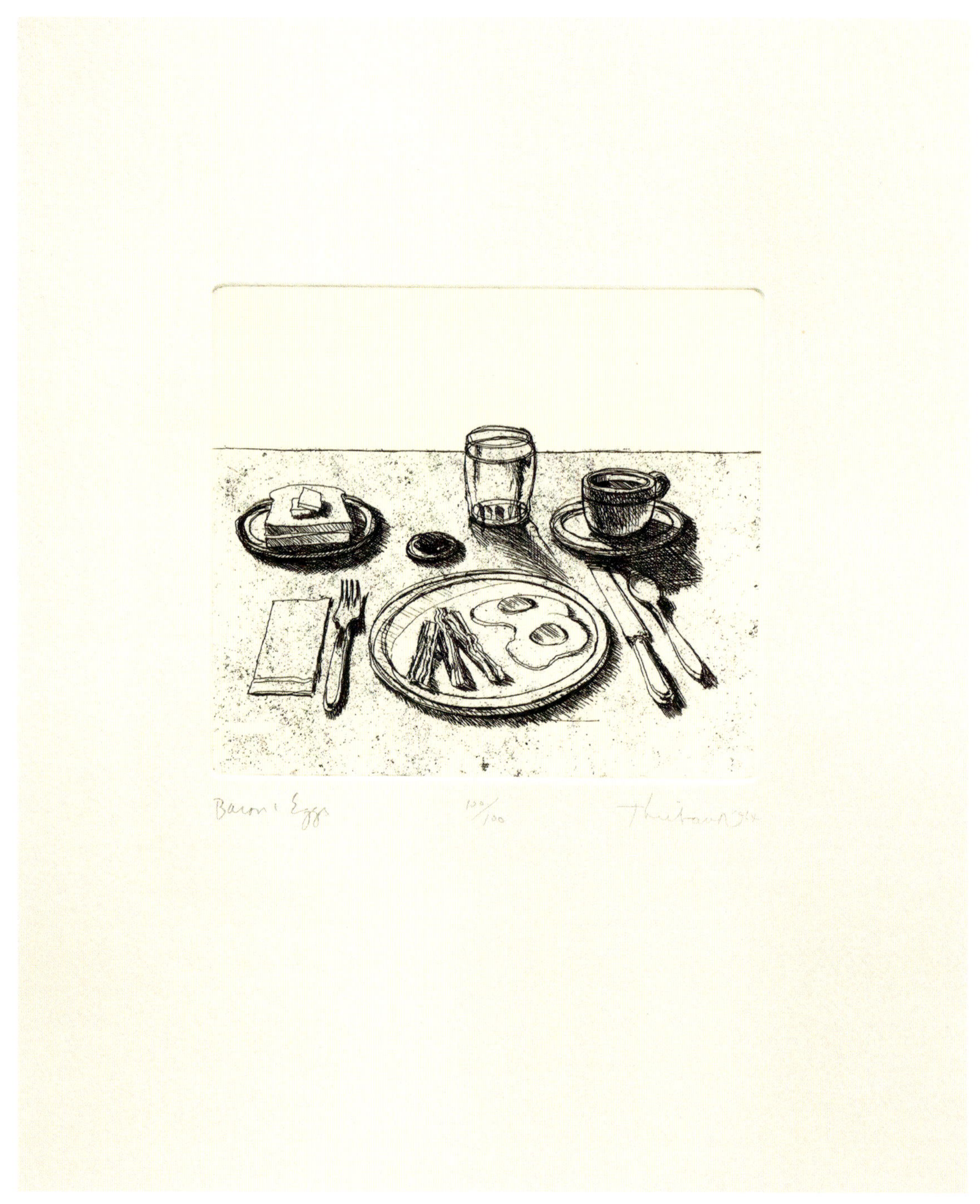

35

Bacon and Eggs

Fifth plate
Etching
Plate size: 13 x 15 cm

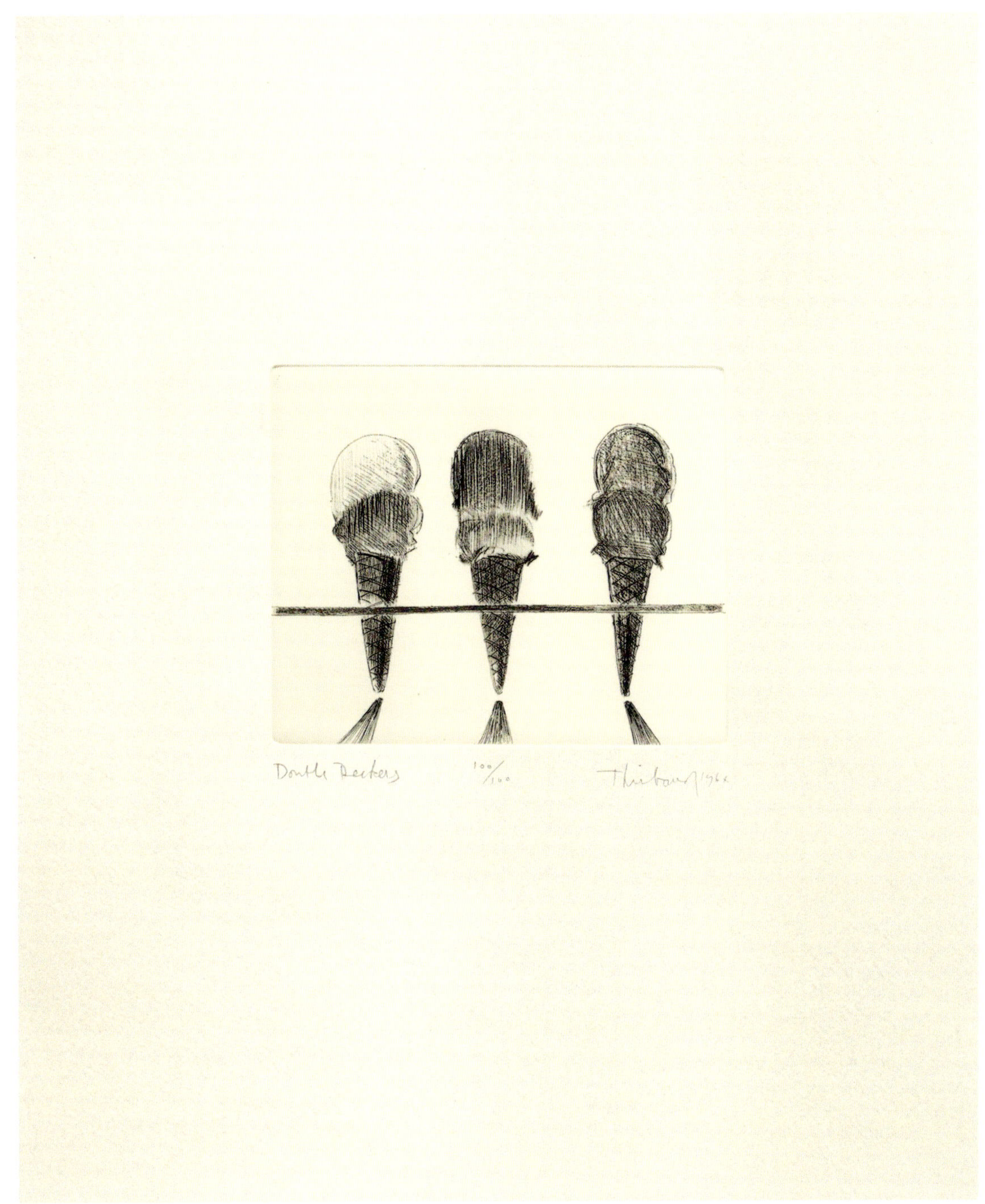

36
Double Deckers

Sixth plate
Drypoint
Plate size: 10 x 12.5 cm

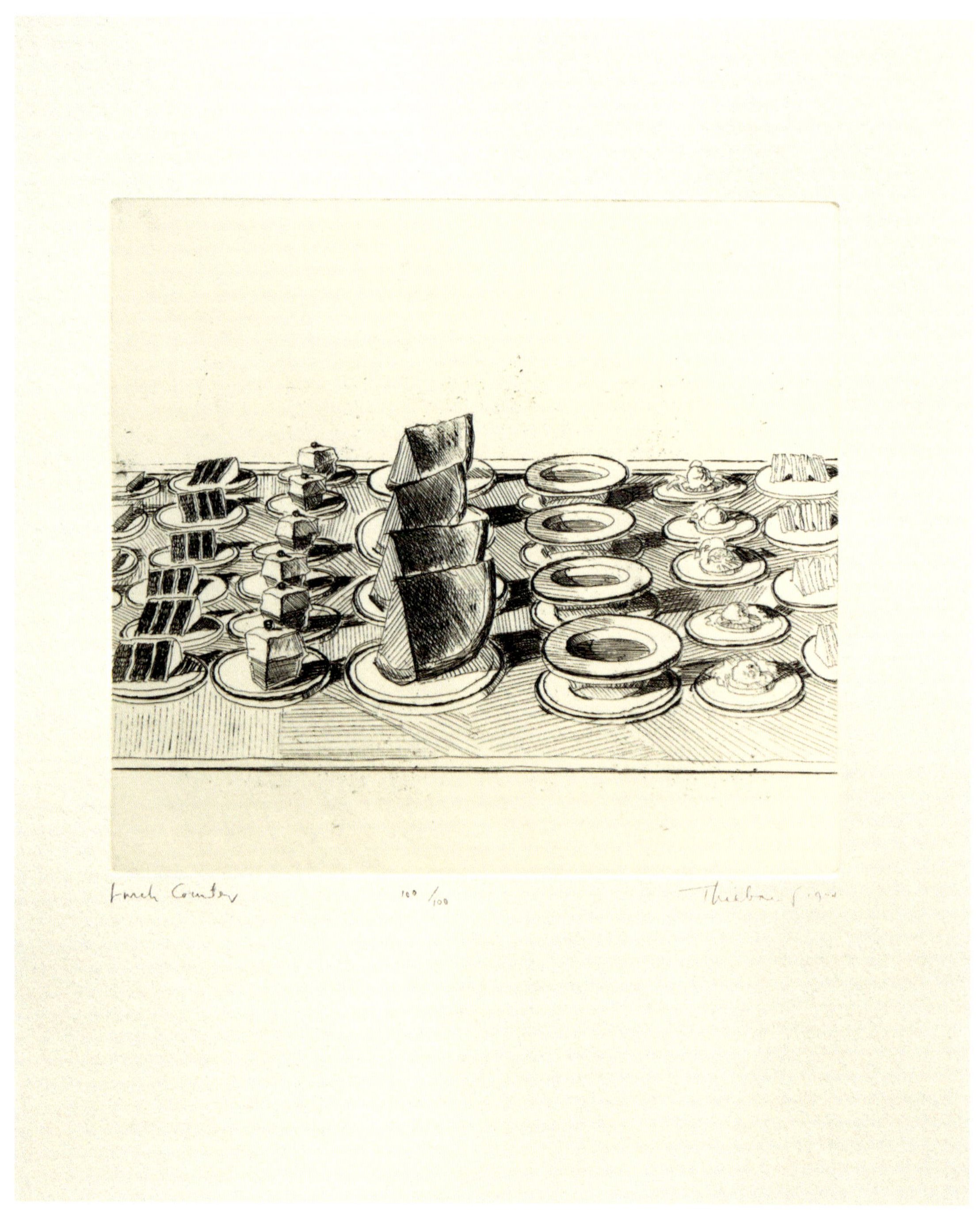

37

Lunch Counter

Seventh plate
Etching
Plate size: 17.5 x 19.5 cm

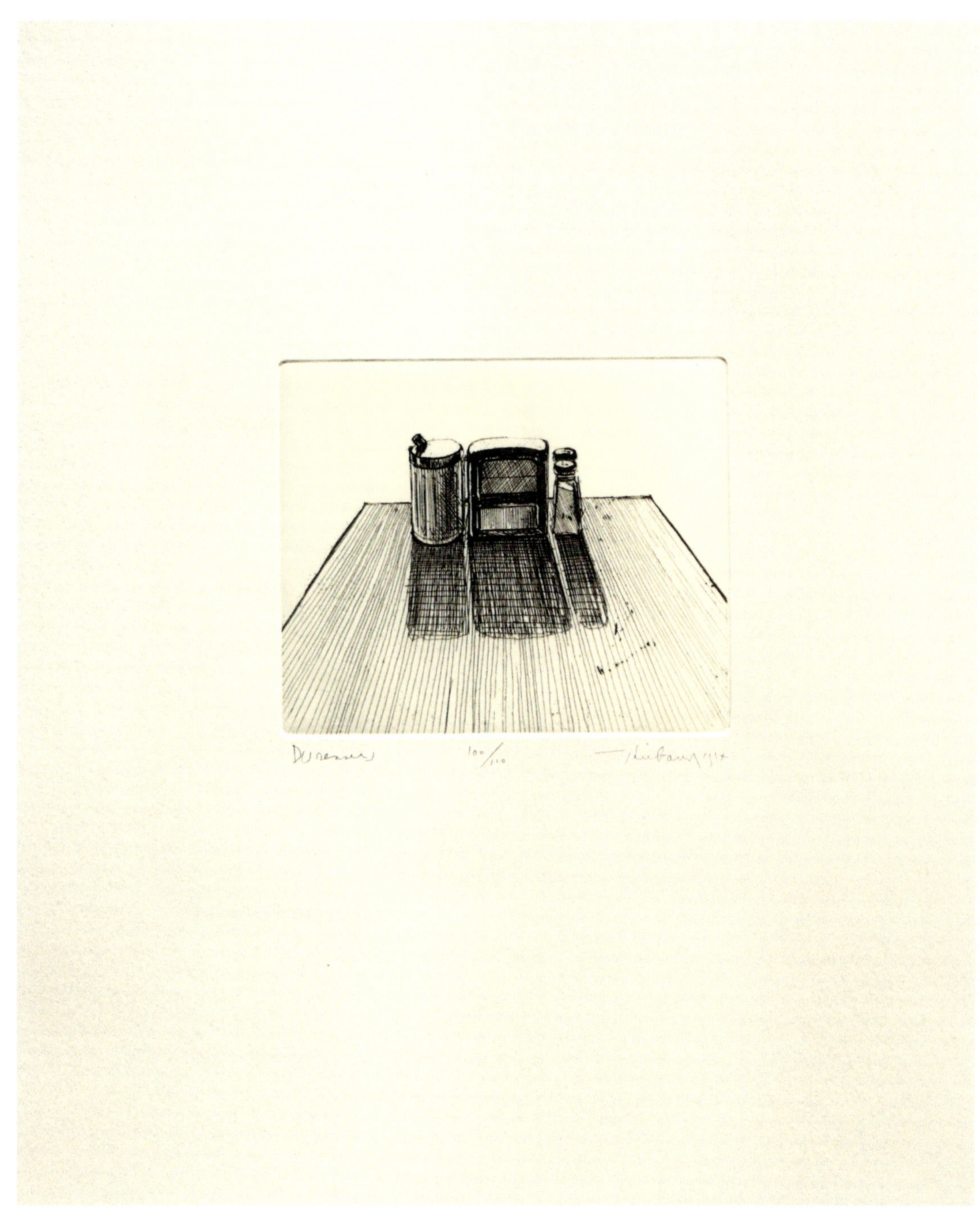

38
Dispensers

Eighth plate
Etching
10 x 12.5 cm

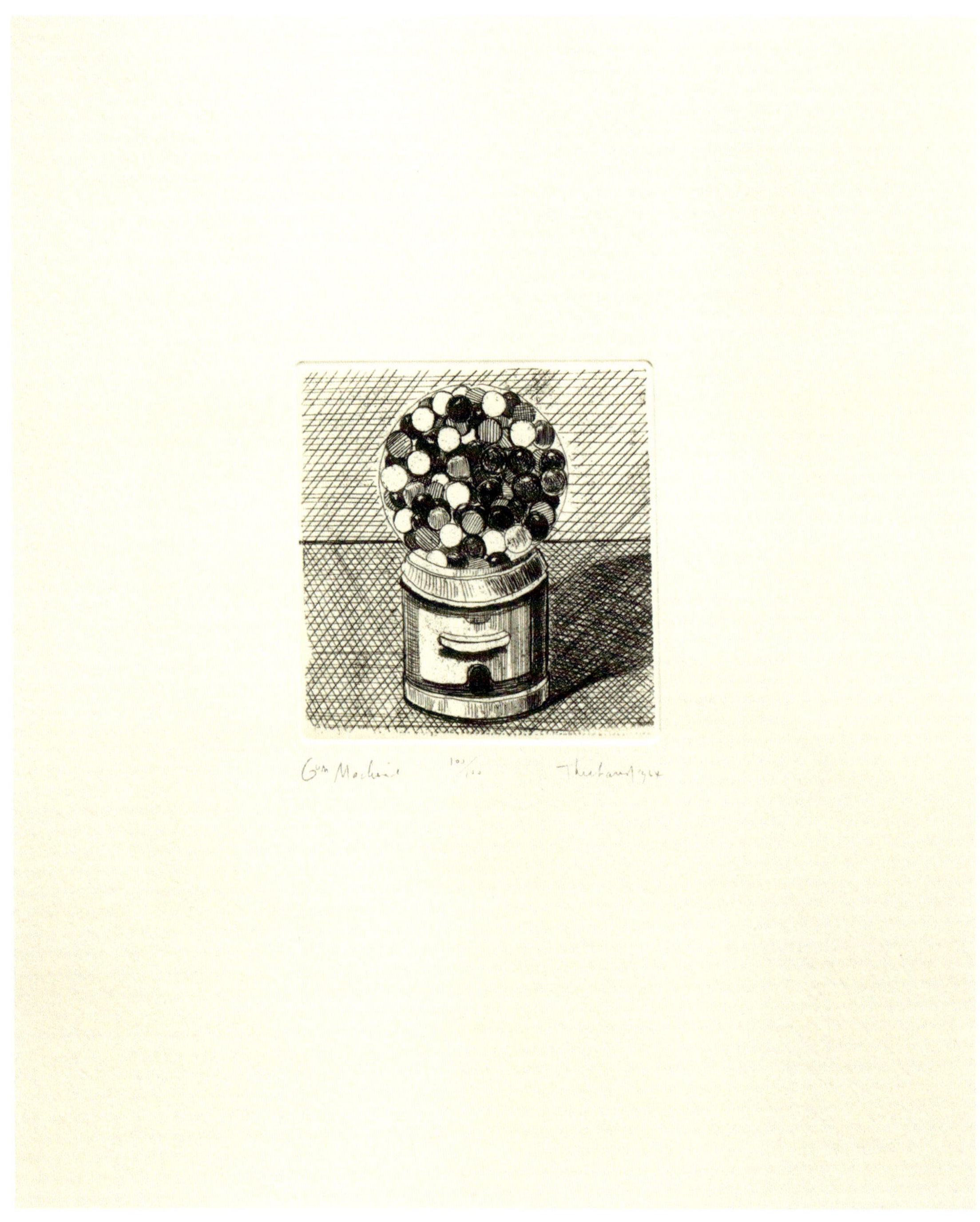

39

Gum Machine

Ninth plate
Etching
Plate size: 10 x 9.7 cm

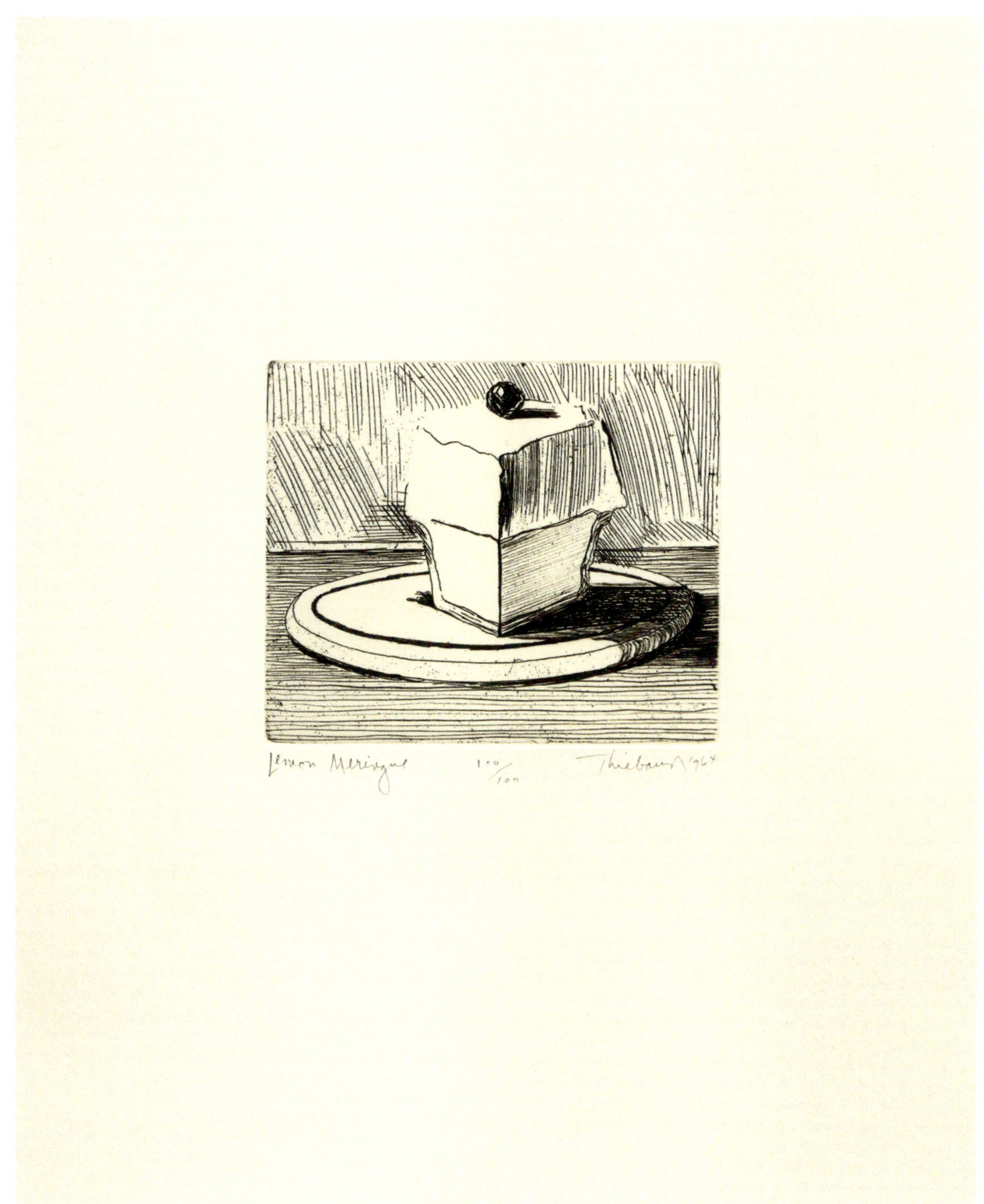

40
Lemon Meringue

Tenth plate
Etching
Plate size: 10 x 12.4 cm

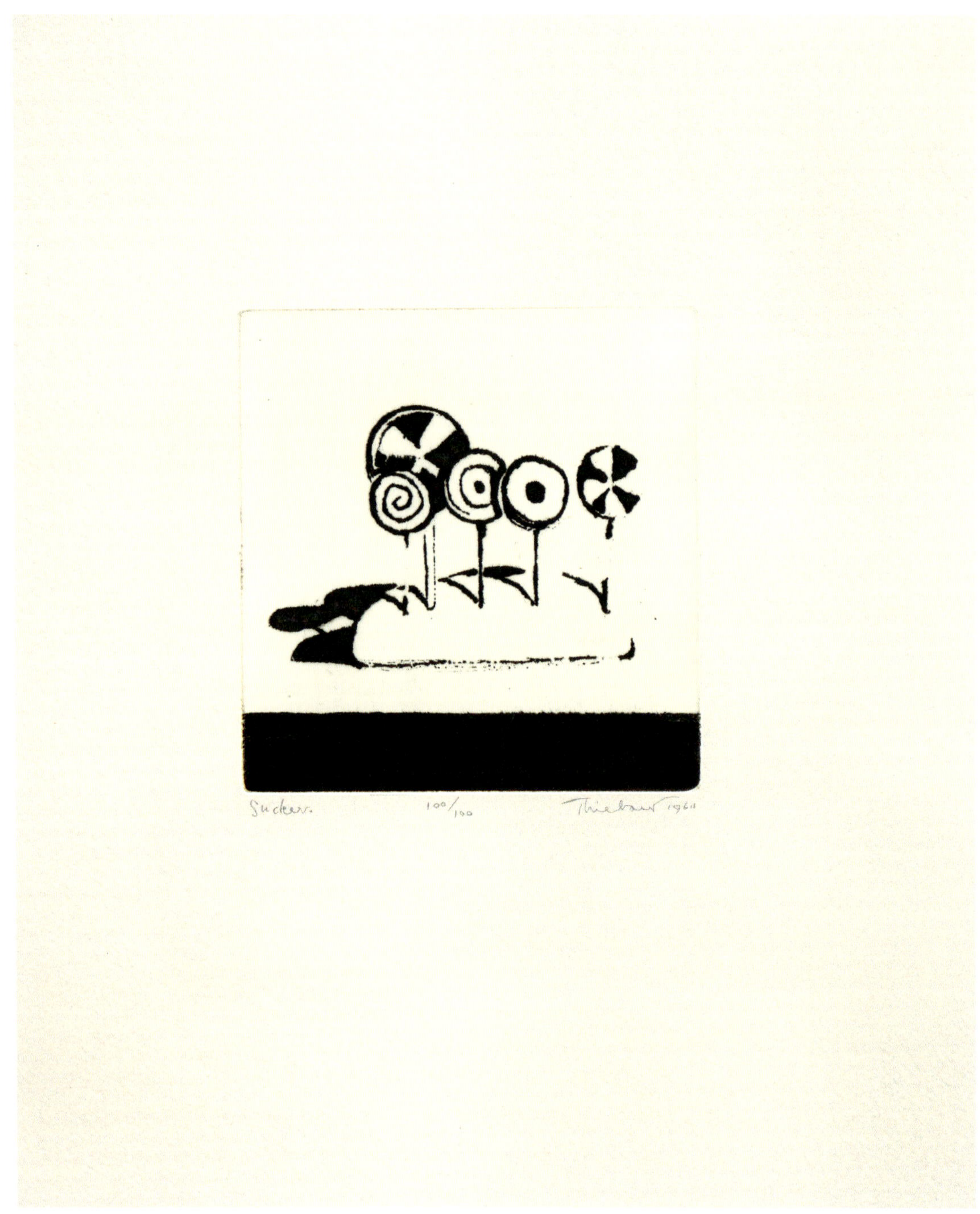

41
Suckers

Eleventh plate
Aquatint
Plate size: 12.5 x 12.5 cm

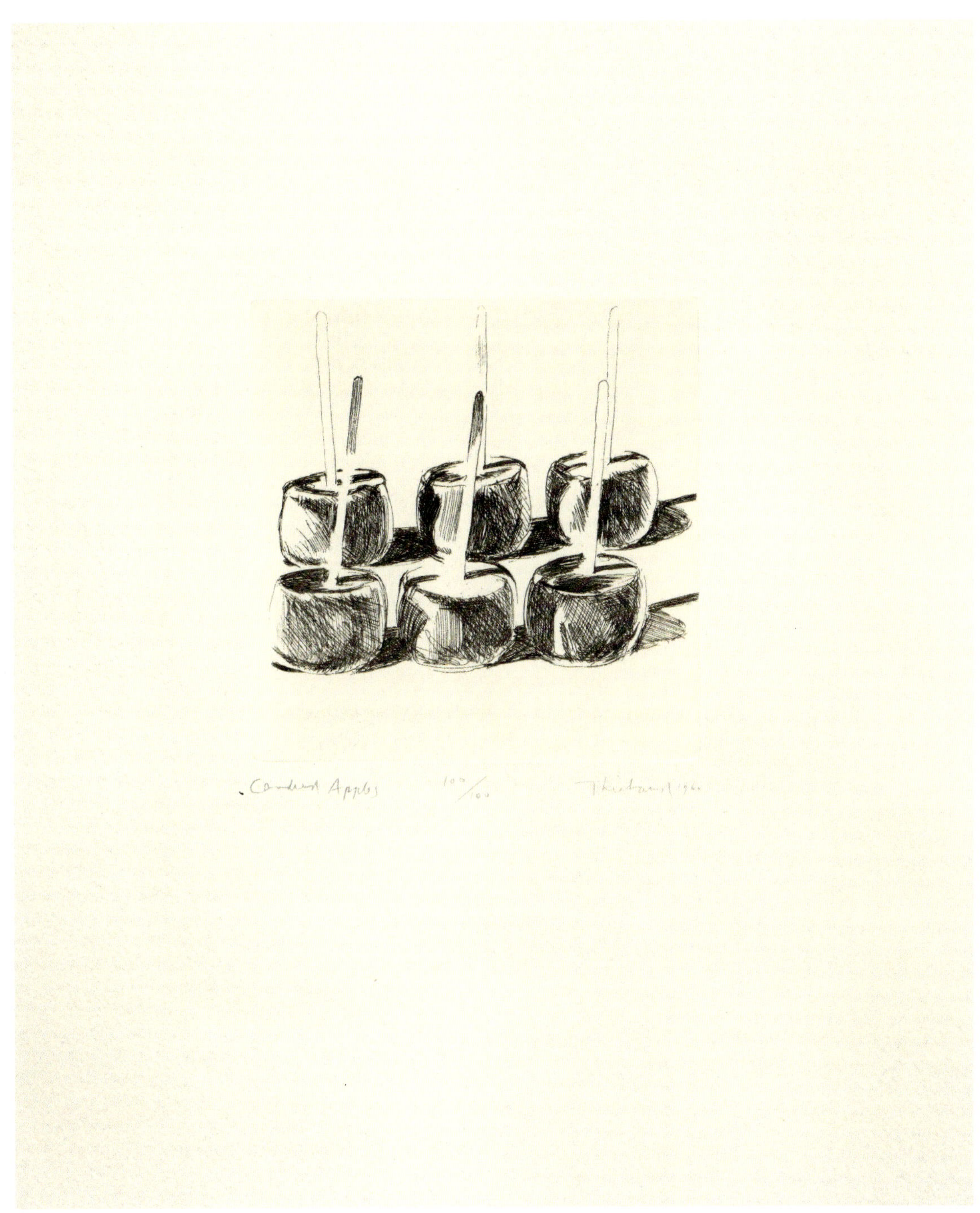

42
Candied Apples

Twelfth plate
Etching
Plate size: 12.5 x 12.5 cm

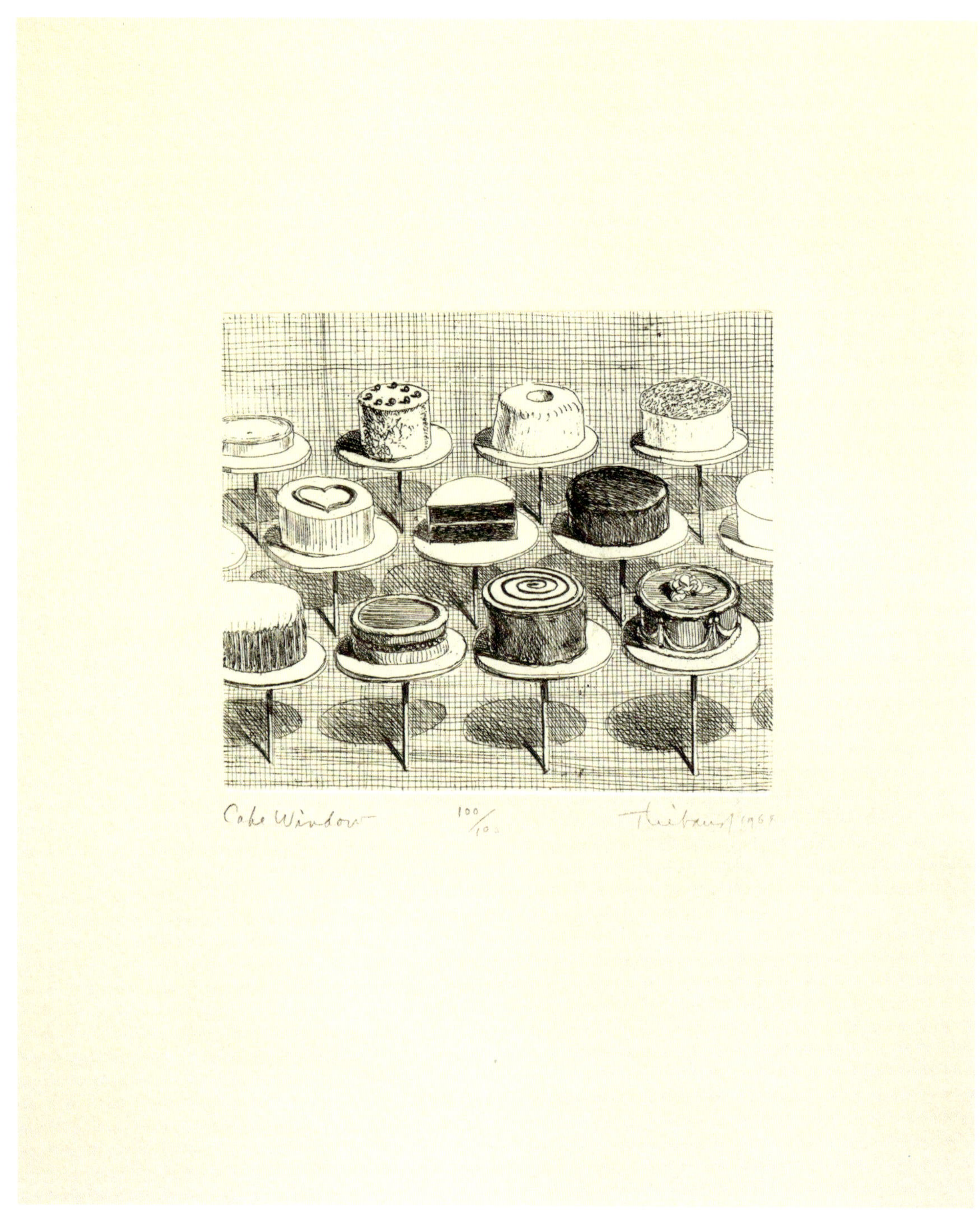

43
Cake Window

Thirteenth plate
Etching
Plate size: 12.5 x 15 cm

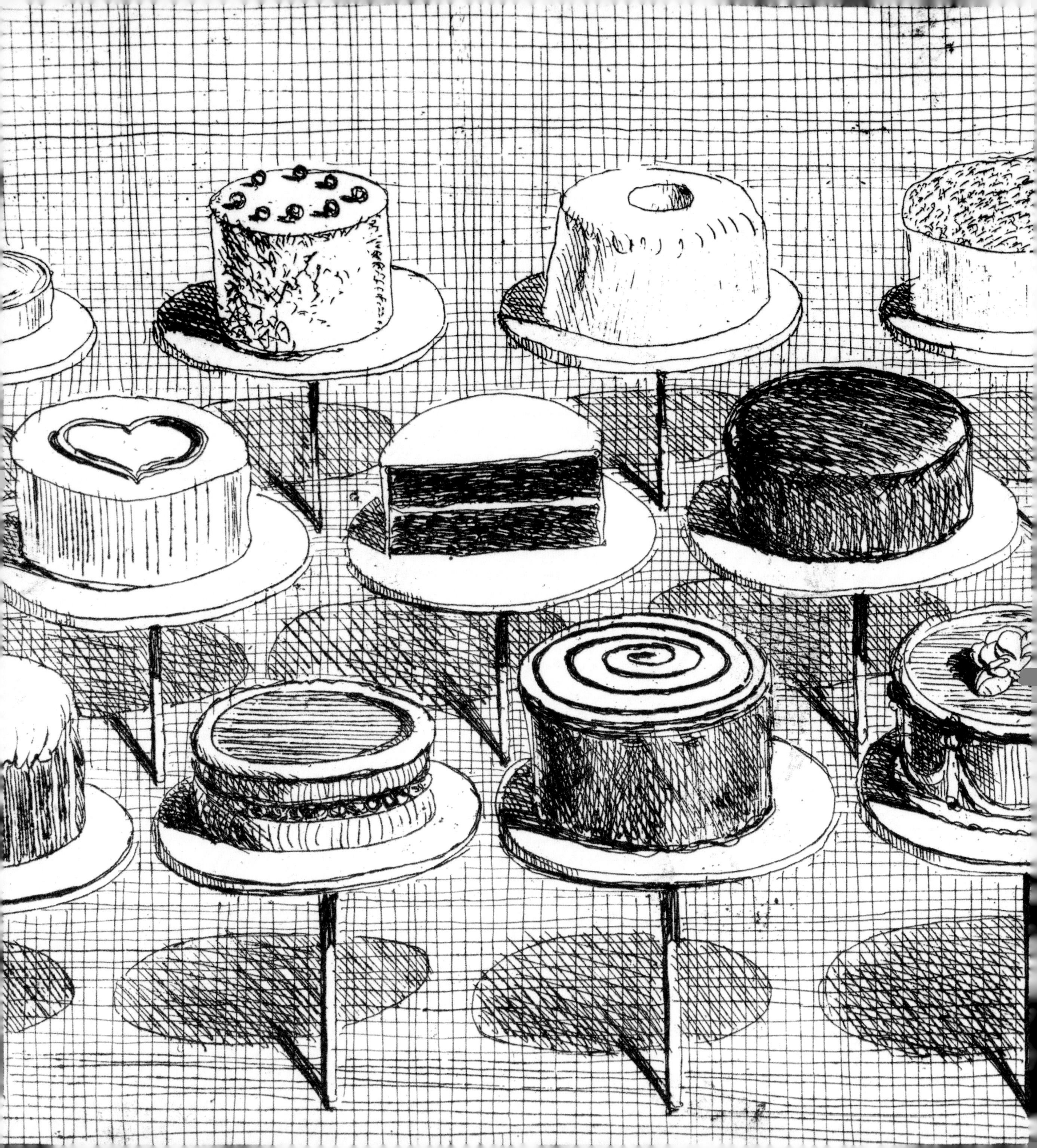

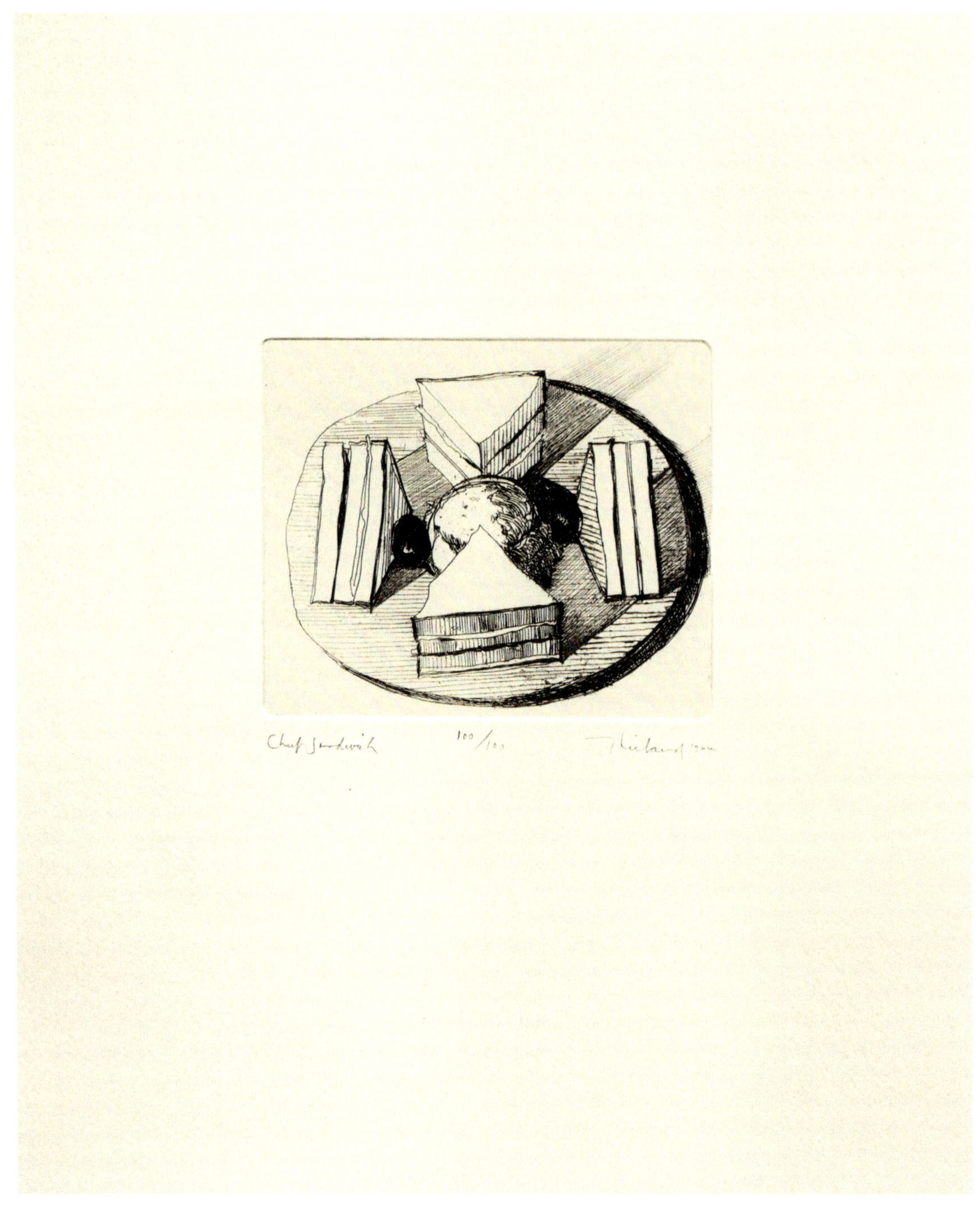

44
Club Sandwich

Fourteenth plate
Etching
Plate size: 10 x 12.5 cm

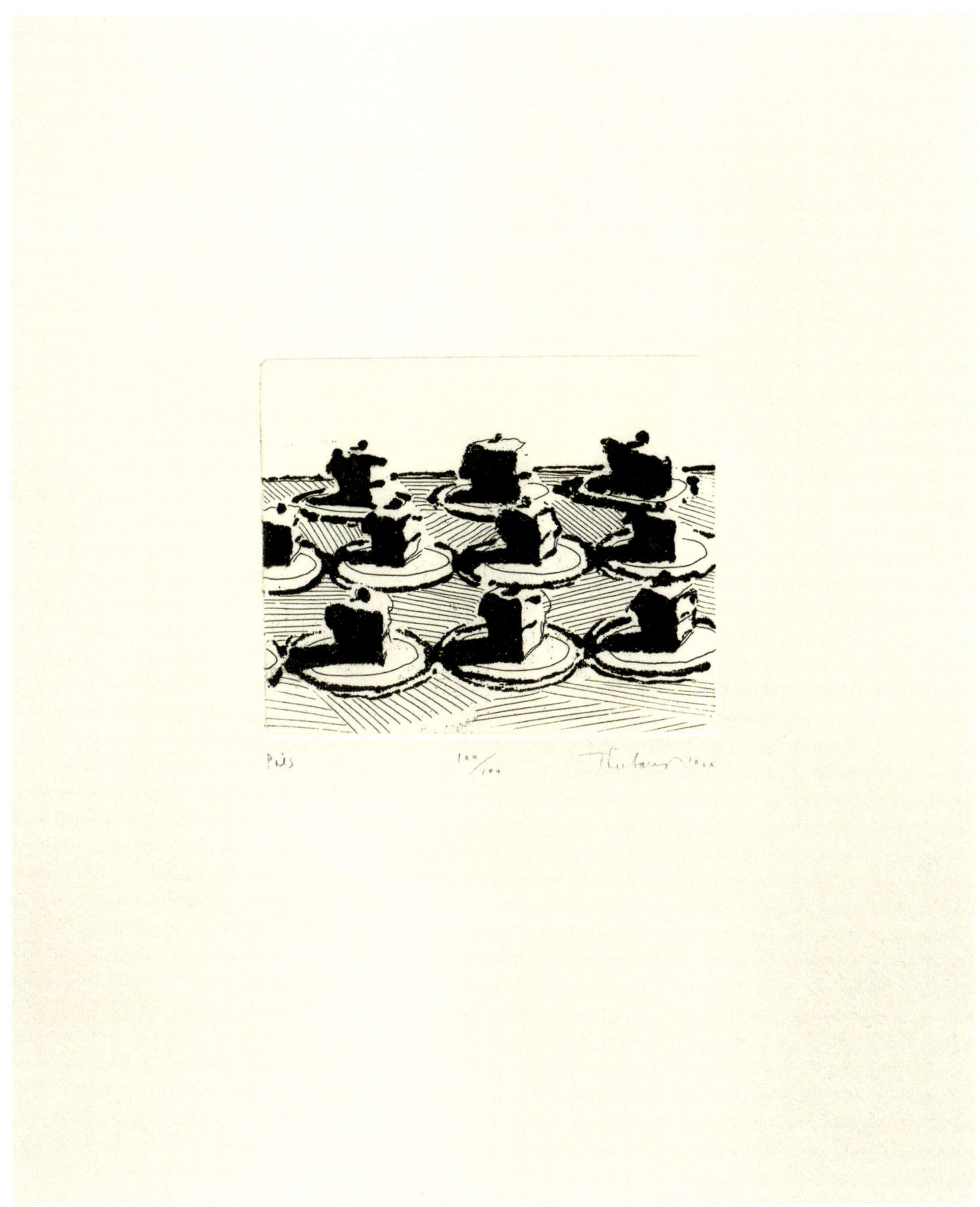

45
Pies

Fifteenth plate
Etching with aquatint
Plate size: 10 x 12.5 cm

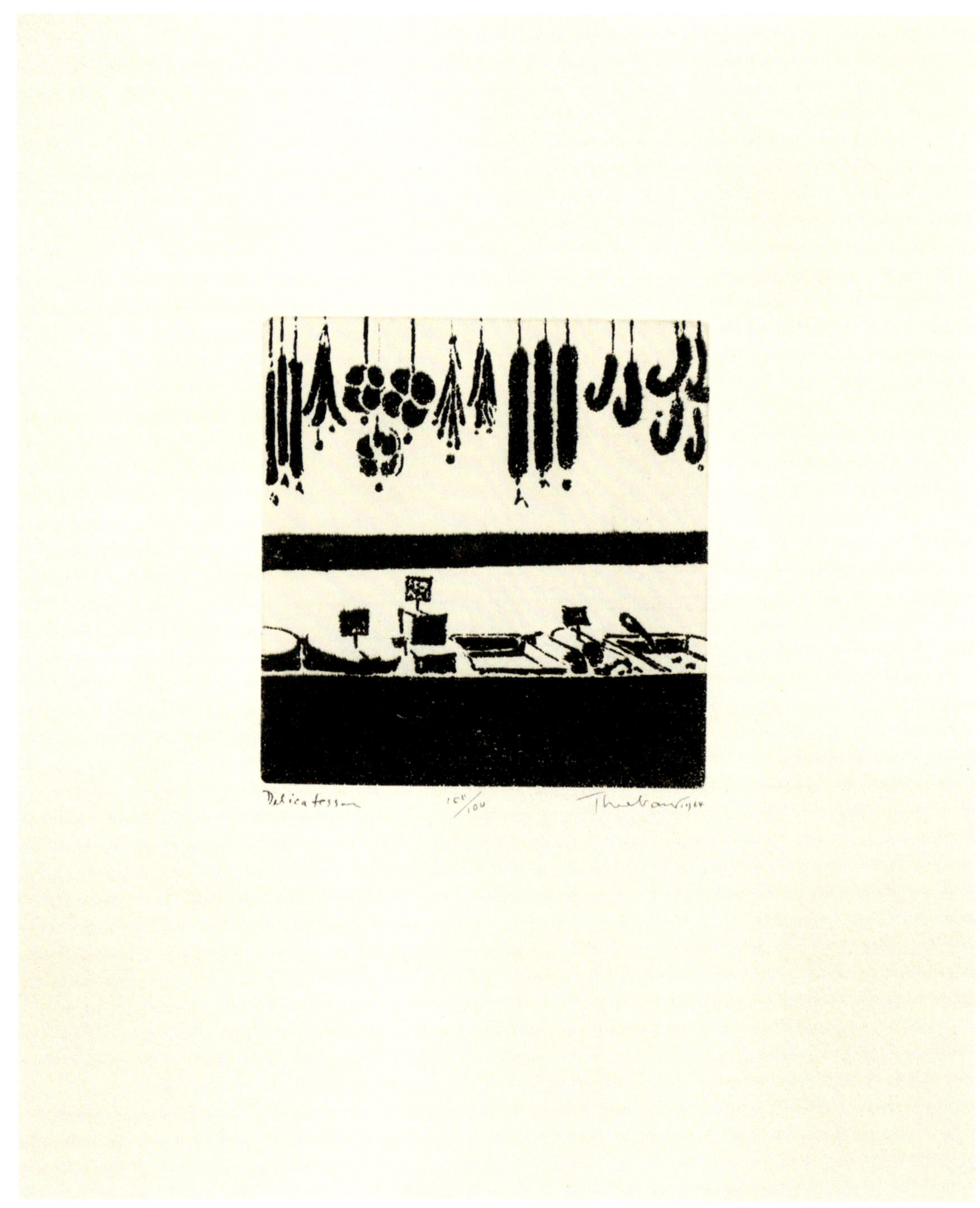

46
Delicatessen

Sixteenth plate
Aquatint
Plate size: 12.5 x 12.5 cm

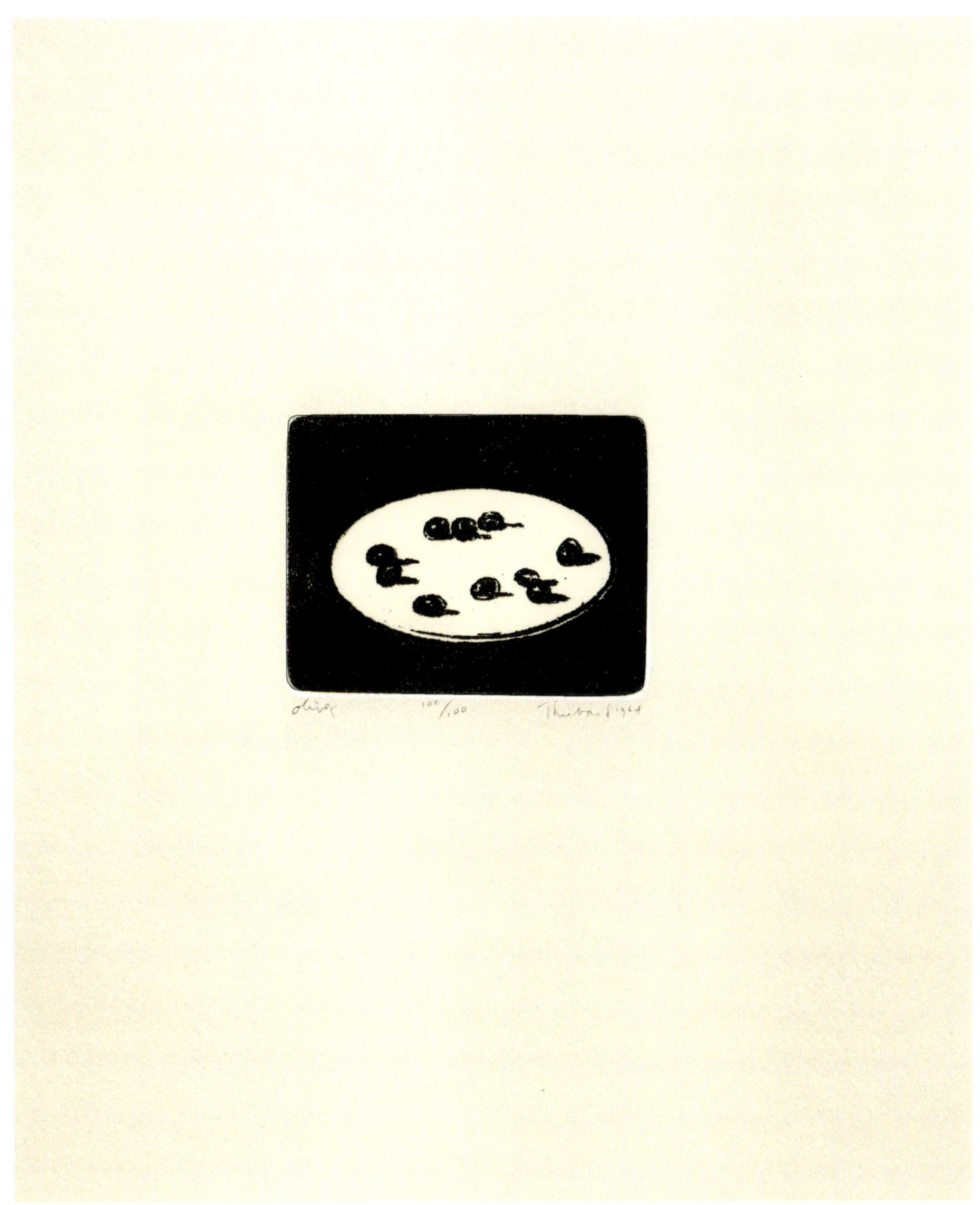

47
Olives

Seventeenth plate
Aquatint
Plate size: 7.5 x 10 cm

Hand-coloured etchings

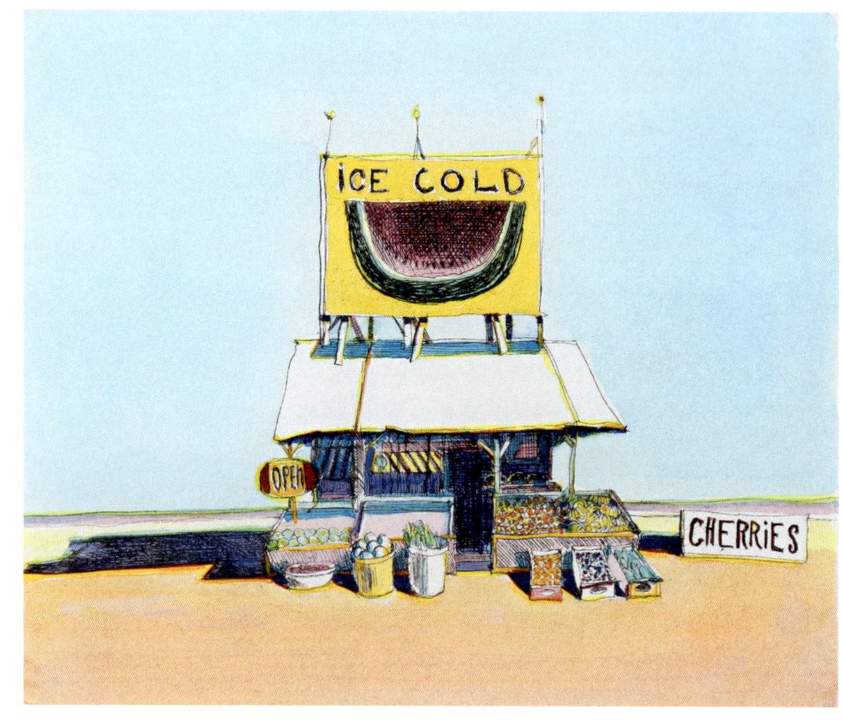

48

Cherry Stand

(from the *Delights* series)
1964 (date of hand colouring not recorded)
Etching and watercolour on paper
Plate size: 14.5 x 17.4 cm
Collection of John Berggruen

49

Cafeteria Counter

(from the *Delights* series where titled
'Lunch Counter')
1964, hand coloured 1990
Etching and watercolour on paper
Plate size: 17.5 x 19.5 cm
Collection of the Wayne Thiebaud Foundation

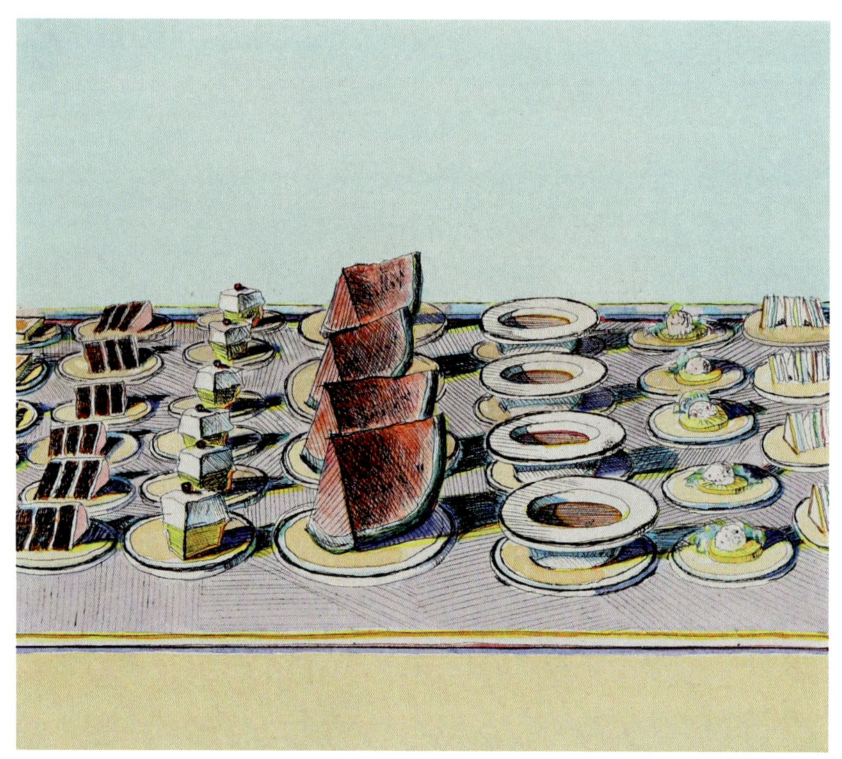

50
Nickel Machine

1964, hand coloured 2005
Etching and watercolour on paper
Plate size: 20.3 x 12.7 cm
Collection of John Berggruen

51
Untitled [Cake Slices]

1964, hand coloured 2014
Etching, watercolour and pastel on paper
Plate size: 10 x 15 cm
Inscribed at the bottom of the sheet:
*A unique trial proof hand-colored with watercolor and
pastel. April 2014*
Collection of the Wayne Thiebaud Foundation

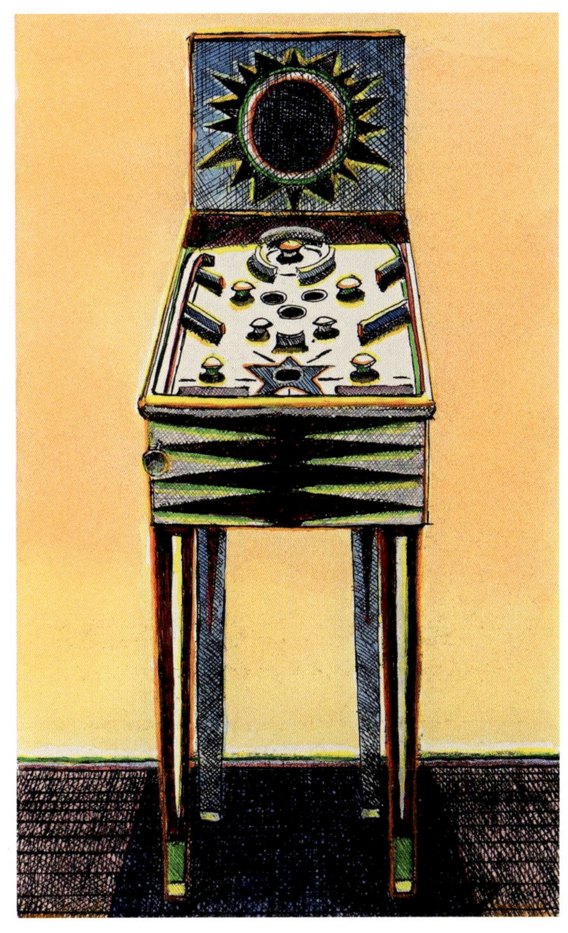

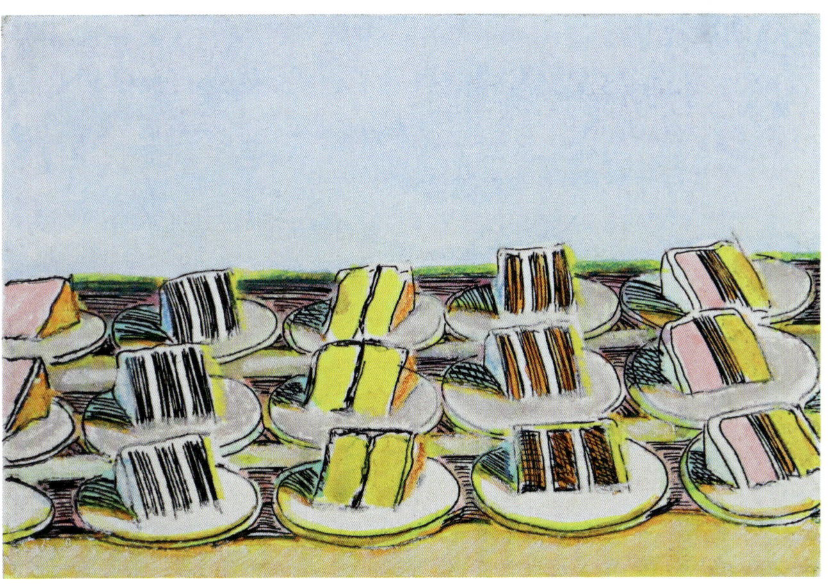

Notes

1 Dervaux 2018a, p. 356.

2 Ibid.

3 Tooker 1974, p. 22.

4 Artist's statement, 1962, reproduced in Teagle 2018, p. 150.

5 https://www.coca-colacompany.com/about-us/history/the-history-of-the-coca-cola-contour-bottle.

6 Arthur 1983, p. 120.

7 'Art: The Slice-of-Cake School', *Time*, 11 May 1962, p. 52.

8 John Coplans, 'Wayne Thiebaud: An Interview', in Coplans 1968, pp. 23–36, at p. 23.

9 Artist's statement, 1962, reproduced in Teagle 2018, p. 150.

10 Aschheim and Daubert 2014, p. 7: Thiebaud's education in the graphic arts influenced many of the approaches and techniques that he applied to what he termed, in contrast to this training, his 'research painting'.

11 Joy Santlofer, 'Vending Machines', in Smith 2007, pp. 609–10, at p. 609: the first such vending machine sold Tutti-Frutti chewing gum and was introduced on a platform of New York's elevated train in 1888.

12 Strand 1983, p. 188.

13 Benson with Shearer 1969, p. 66.

14 Artist's statement, 1962, reproduced in Teagle 2018, p. 150.

15 Strand 1983, p. 189.

16 John Wilmerding, 'Wayne Thiebaud: The Emperor of Ice Cream', in *Wayne Thiebaud*, exh. cat. Acquavella Galleries, New York (New York: Rizzoli), 2012, pp. 9–31, at p. 30.

17 Joy Santlofer, 'Cold Cereal', in Smith 2007, pp. 101–03, at p. 102.

18 Alessia Masi, 'Interview to Wayne Thiebaud', in Masi 2011, p. 37.

19 Arthur 1983, p. 120.

20 Tooker 1974, p. 22.

21 Letter from Wayne Thiebaud to Allan Stone, c. October 1962, Allan Stone Gallery records, 1960–2019, box 88, folder 58, Archives of American Art, Smithsonian Institution.

22 Aschheim and Daubert 2014, p. 52.

23 Gene Cooper, 'Thiebaud, Theatre, and Extremism', in *Wayne Thiebaud Survey 1947–1976*, exh. cat. Phoenix Art Museum, 1976, pp. 11–29, at p. 13.

24 Dervaux 2018a, p. 356.

25 Kaufman 2023, p. 140.

26 Ian Parker, 'Oldies but Goodies', *The New Yorker*, 10 November 2014, pp. 25–26, at p. 25.

27 The introduction to Allan Stone came via his friend and mentor, the sculptor Robert Mallary. As Thiebaud recalled, 'I showed them [his paintings] around the galleries – not very many – and no one liked the new work, so I was preparing to leave, and a friend of mine, Robert Mallary, a sculptor, had talked to his dealer, who was Allan Stone …. So, I went over and showed him the work': Tooker 1974, p. 25.

28 Tooker 1974, p. 25.

29 Thiebaud's first solo exhibition with Allan Stone was preceded by the inclusion of one work in a group show at the gallery in December 1961.

30 Letters from Allan Stone to Wayne Thiebaud, 25 March and 4 April 1962, Allan Stone Gallery records, 1960–2019, box 88, folder 58, Archives of American Art, Smithsonian Institution.

31 Tooker 1974, p. 25.

32 Brian O'Doherty, 'Art: America Seen Through the Stomach; Catalogue of Food by Wayne Thiebaud', *The New York Times*, 28 April 1962, p. 22.

33 Donald Judd, 'In the Galleries: Wayne Thiebaud' (September 1962), in Judd 2005, p. 60.

34 'Art: The Slice-of-Cake School', *Time*, 11 May 1962, p. 52.

35 Hess 1962.

36 Artist's statement, 1962, reproduced in Teagle 2018, p. 150.

37 Stowens 1980, p. 48.

38 Lewallen 1990, p. 7.

39 Donald Judd, 'In the Galleries: Wayne Thiebaud' (September 1962), in Judd 2005, p. 60.

40 Artist's statement, 1962, reproduced in Teagle 2018, p. 150.

41 Ibid.

42 Arthur 1983, p. 116.

43 Bruce Kraig, 'Hot Dogs', in Smith 2007, pp. 303–04, at p. 303.

44 Dervaux 2018b, p. 150.

45 Aschheim and Daubert 2014, p. 12.

46 Jules Langsner, 'Los Angeles Letter, September 1962', *Art International*, vol. 9, issue 1, 25 November 1962, pp. 49–52, at p. 49.

47 Gene Cooper, 'Wayne Thiebaud: Beach Memories', in Gene Cooper ed., *Wayne Thiebaud: Seventy Years of Painting*, exh. cat. Laguna Art Museum, Laguna Beach (Laguna Art Museum & Palm Springs Art Museum), 2007, p. 14.

48 These included *Six More* at the Los Angeles County Museum of Art and *Pop Art U.S.A.* at the Oakland Art Museum (both 1963), and *The Popular Image* at the Institute of Contemporary Art, London in 1964.

49 Benson with Shearer 1969, p. 70.

50 Ibid, p. 68.

51 Professor Paul Beckmann taught Thiebaud at Sacramento State College (now California State University, Sacramento), where he obtained his bachelor's degree in 1951 and master's degree in 1952.

52 Unpublished interview with Jacquelyn D. Serwer, 10 April 1995, typescript in the archives of the Smithsonian American Art Museum, Washington, D.C.

53 Ibid.

54 Ibid.

55 Jonathan P. Binstock, 'Wayne Thiebaud's *Jackpot Machine*', *American Art*, vol. 10, no. 2, summer 1996, pp. 78–82.

56 A photograph of this work in progress shows the right-hand panel clearly painted with the jackpot prizes – $7.50 and $15 – which he later obscured: see Allan Stone Gallery records, 1960–2019, box 175, Archives of American Art, Smithsonian Institution.

57 *Four Pinball Machines* might have also been exhibited at the Allan Stone Gallery in 1962, but this is not clear from the exhibition lists in the Allan Stone Gallery records, 1960–2019, box 90, Archives of American Art, Smithsonian Institution.

58 This study was also shown in the M.H. de Young Memorial Museum exhibition in 1962.

59 The ball release lever-handle to the bottom right of Thiebaud's machines are a feature on some models from the 1930s.

60 For a fuller discussion of these references, see Timothy Anglin Burgard, 'Wayne Thiebaud, Art History and "The Bureau of Standards"', in Burgard 2025, pp. 11–31, at pp. 27–29.

61 John Coplans, 'Wayne Thiebaud: An Interview', in Coplans 1968, pp. 23–36, at p. 30.

62 Although Thiebaud titled the work *Boston Cremes*, these cherry-topped cream cakes do not bear a resemblance to the chocolate ganache-covered dessert that is more typically associated with this name.

63 Robert Hughes, 'The Poet of Pastry: Wayne Thiebaud offers deep pleasures in the everyday, from pies and cakes to slices of landscape', *Time*, 17 September 2001: https://time.com/archive/6953373/the-poet-of-pastry-wayne-thiebaud-offers-deep-pleasures-in-the-everyday-from-pies-and-cakes-to-slices-of-landscape/.

64 Tsujimoto 1985, p. 36. Allan Stone would write to Thiebaud ahead of his first exhibition: 'it's the painter in me that your work appeals to… they're so lush and painterly…wow!!!!': letter from Allan Stone to Wayne Thiebaud, 25 January 1962, Allan Stone Gallery records, 1960–2019, box 88, folder 58, Archives of American Art, Smithsonian Institution.

65 John Coplans, 'Wayne Thiebaud: An Interview', in Coplans 1968, pp. 23–36, at p. 30.

66 Kozloff 1962, p. 407.

67 Arthur 1983, p. 120.

68 The exhibition was titled *Influences on a Young Painter* and included 60 works.

69 Letter from Allan Stone to Wayne Thiebaud,

c. March 1964, Allan Stone Gallery records, 1960–2019, box 88, folder 59, Archives of American Art, Smithsonian Institution.

70 Arthur 1983, p. 120.

71 Rachel Teagle, 'Presence from Absence: Wayne Thiebaud and the Future of Painting', in Teagle 2018, pp. 12-48, at p. 15.

72 Adam Gopnik, 'An American Painter', in Nash with Gopnik 2008, pp. 39–67, at p. 55.

73 Abraham Stein [Allan Stone], in *Wayne Thiebaud*, exh. cat. Galleria Schwarz, Milan, 1963, n.p.

74 Artist's statement, 1962, reproduced in Teagle 2018, p. 150.

75 Ibid, p. 149 (original ellipsis).

76 John Coplans, 'Wayne Thiebaud: An Interview", in Coplans 1968, pp. 23–36, at p. 36.

77 Seymour Howard, 'Wayne Thiebaud, *Salad, Sandwiches, and Dessert*, 1962: The Persistence of Academic Norms and Bittersweet Visions of Popular Nostalgia', in Seymour Howard ed., *The Counterpoint to Likeness. Essays on Imitation and Imagination in Western Painting*, University of California at Davis, 1977, pp. 54–56 at p. 56. I am grateful to Timothy Burgard for sharing this essay with me.

78 The additive Thiebaud used was a product called ZEC, manufactured by Grumbacher. He was introduced to it by a colleague, Roland Peterson, soon after he started at University of California, Davis, in 1960. See the catalogue entry for this painting by Francesca Wilmott in Teagle 2018, p. 112.

79 Artist's statement, 1962, reproduced in Teagle 2018, p. 150.

80 Aschheim and Daubert 2014, p. 61.

81 Artist's statement, 1962, reproduced in Teagle 2018, p. 150.

82 Alloway 1963.

83 Artist's statement, 1962, reproduced in Teagle 2018, p. 150.

84 Bult 2012.

85 Benson with Shearer 1969, p. 71.

86 Ibid, p. 68.

87 Strand 1983, p. 192.

88 Benson with Shearer 1969, p. 66.

89 John Coplans, 'Wayne Thiebaud: An Interview", in Coplans 1968, pp. 23–36, at pp. 23–24.

90 Artist's statement, 1962, reproduced in Teagle 2018, p. 150 (original ellipsis).

91 Conversation with the artist recorded in 'Examination and Treatment Proposal, Wayne Thiebaud, *Cakes*, 31 January 1991', Conservation files, National Gallery of Art, Washington, D.C., p. 2. I am grateful to Elizabeth Walmsley for allowing me access to these archives.

92 Albright 1978, p. 84.

93 John Coplans, 'Wayne Thiebaud: An Interview", in Coplans 1968, pp. 23–36, at p. 26.

94 Ibid, p. 34.

95 Bult 2012.

96 Timothy Anglin Burgard, 'Wayne Thiebaud, Art History, and "The Bureau of Standards"', in Burgard 2025, pp. 11–31, at p. 26.

97 Thiebaud film 1971, 8'11"–8'15".

98 Benson with Shearer 1969, p. 66.

99 Ibid.

100 Timothy Anglin Burgard, 'Wayne Thiebaud, *Three Machines*: The Real Ideal', in Timothy Anglin Burgard ed., *Masterworks of American Painting at the De Young*, Fine Arts Museums of San Francisco, 2005, pp. 432–35, at p. 435.

101 Benson with Shearer 1969, p. 66.

102 John Coplans, 'Wayne Thiebaud: An Interview', in Coplans 1968, pp. 23–36, at p. 34.

103 Ibid. p. 30.

104 Thiebaud film 1971, 9'30"–9'38".

105 Jonn Coplans, 'Wayne Thiebaud: An Interview', in Coplans 1968, pp. 23–36, at p. 26.

106 'Line', With Wayne Thiebaud, part of the television series *Behind the Scenes*, season 1, episode 4, 1992, PBS (US), running time: 30 minutes, at 22'54" (accessed 19 August 2024). I would like to thank Chloe Nahum for sharing this reference.

107 Artist's statement, 1962, reproduced in Teagle 2018, p. 150.

108 Stowens 1980, p. 102.

109 John Coplans, 'Wayne Thiebaud: An Interview", in Coplans 1968, pp. 23–36, at p. 32.

110 Dervaux 2018b, p. 15.

111 Steven A. Nash, 'Unbalancing Acts: Wayne Thiebaud Reconsidered', in Nash with Gopnik 2008, p. 22.

112 Benson with Shearer 1969, p. 68.

113 Dervaux 2018a, p. 364.

114 Constance Glenn, 'Introduction', in *Wayne Thiebaud: Private Drawings. The Artist's Sketchbook*, New York: Harry N. Abrams, 1987, pp. 1–7, at p. 6.

115 Dervaux 2018b, p. 113.

116 Strand 1983, p. 192.

117 Aschheim and Daubert 2014, pp. 64–65.

118 Dervaux 2018b, pp. 30–31: the copying of Old Master drawings had long been central to artistic training, before notions of artistic originality lessened their bearing in the latter part of the nineteenth century. For a fuller description and analysis of Thiebaud's teaching methods and style, see Rachel Teagle, 'To teach is to paint. To paint is to teach', pp. 33–39, and Eve Aschheim, 'Relentless Inventing: Notes from Wayne Thiebaud's Classroom', pp. 41–59, both in Burgard 2025.

119 Dervaux 2018b, p. 150.

120 Aschheim and Daubert 2014, p. 32.

121 *Thiebaud via Morandi* 2011.

122 Wayne Thiebaud interviewed by Carol Mancusi-Ungaro, 27 June 2001, Artists Documentation Program, Video Interview Transcript, p. 19: https://adp.menil.org/sites/default/files/2025-04/adp2001a_20110831_002m_transcript.pdf

123 Aschheim and Daubert 2014, p. 39.

124 Larsen 2001.

125 Arthur 1983, p. 128.

126 Dervaux 2018a, p. 359.

127 In relation to this development in Thiebaud's practice, Dervaux notes that, during the mid 1960s, the food dyes used in America expanded rapidly due in part to the influence of colour television and the need for 'visually appealing food in advertising': Dervaux 2018b, p. 26.

128 Kathan Brown, *Ink, Paper, Metal, Wood: Painters and Sculptors at Crown Point Press*, San Francisco: Chronicle Books, 1996, p. 34.

129 Kathan Brown, *Know that You Are Lucky: A Memoir*, San Francisco: Crown Point Press, 2012, p. 46.

130 Quoted in Ruth E. Fine, 'Kathan Brown and Crown Point Press', in Breuer, Fine and Nash 1997, p. 7.

131 Lewallen 1990, p. 17.

132 Quoted in Steven A. Nash, 'From Paper to Canvas: Prints and the Creative Process', in Breuer, Fine and Nash 1997, p. 64.

133 This practice was not limited to his 1964 prints. Thiebaud would revisit and rework various of his printed proofs; see *Vision and Revision: Hand Colored Prints by Wayne Thiebaud*, exh. cat. Fine Arts Museums of San Francisco (San Francisco: Chronicle Books), 1991.

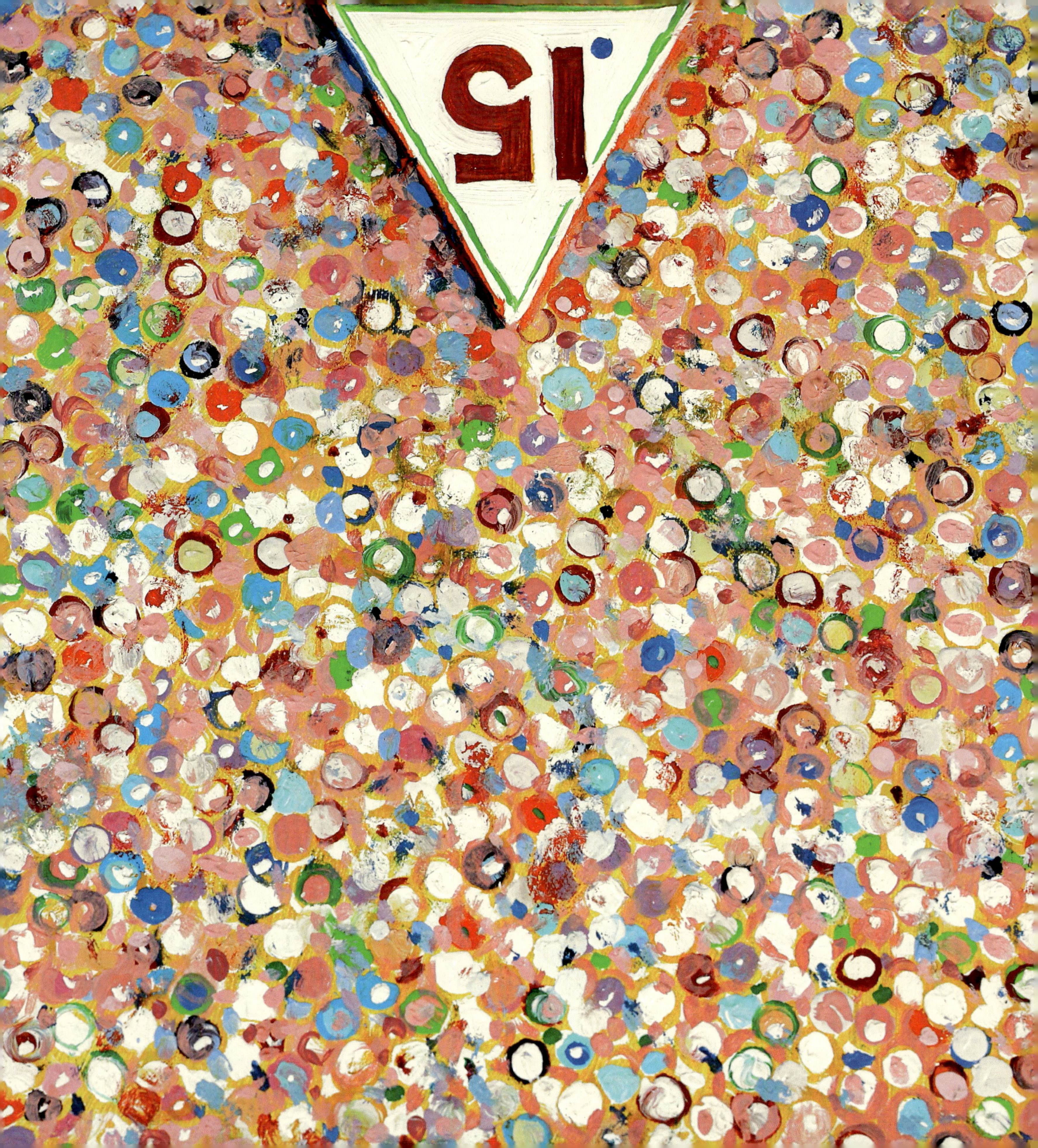
.15

Sources and Publications Cited

Albright, Thomas, 'Wayne Thiebaud: Scrambling Around with Ordinary Problems', *Art News*, vol. 77, no. 2, February 1978, pp. 82–86

Alloway, Lawrence, Introduction to the exhibition *Six More*, exh. cat. Los Angeles County Museum of Art, 1963, n.p.

Arthur, John, *Realists at Work*, New York: Watson-Guptill Publications, 1983

Aschheim, Eve and Chris Daubert, *Episodes with Wayne Thiebaud: Four Interviews 2009–2011*, New York: Black Square Editions, 2014

Benson, A. LeGrace G. with David H. R. Shearer, 'An Interview with Wayne Thiebaud', *Leonardo*, vol. 2, no. 1, January 1969, pp. 65–72

Brauer, **David E. ed.**, *Pop Art: U.S./U.K. Connections, 1956–1966*, exh. cat. The Menil Collection, Houston (Berlin: Hatje Cantz), 2001

Breuer, Karin, Ruth E. Fine and Steven A. Nash eds, *Thirty-Five Years at Crown Point Press: Making Prints, Doing Art*, exh. cat. National Gallery of Art, Washington, D.C., and Fine Arts Museums of San Francisco (Berkeley, Los Angeles and London: University of California Press), 1997

Bult, Matt, Edited interview with Wayne Thiebaud on 'Still-Lifes', 21 September 2012, n.p., Archives of the Wayne Thiebaud Foundation

Burgard, Timothy Anglin ed., *Wayne Thiebaud: Art Comes from Art*, exh. cat. Fine Art Museums of San Francisco (Oakland: University of California Press), 2025

Coplans, John, 'The New Paintings of Common Objects', *Artforum*, vol. 1, no. 6, November 1962, pp. 26–29

Coplans, John, *Wayne Thiebaud*, exh. cat. Pasadena Art Museum and touring, 1968

Dervaux, Isabelle (Dervaux 2018a), 'Wayne Thiebaud Talks about Drawing', *Master Drawings*, vol. 56, no. 3, autumn 2018, pp. 355–68

Dervaux, Isabelle (Dervaux 2018b), *Wayne Thiebaud: Draftsman*, exh. cat The Morgan Library & Museum, New York (London and New York: Thames & Hudson), 2018

Factor, Don, '"Six Painters and the Object" and "Six More"', *Artforum*, vol. 2, no. 3, September 1963, pp. 13–14

Hess, Thomas B., 'Wayne Thiebaud', *Art News*, May 1962, p. 17

Judd, Donald, *Donald Judd: Complete Writings 1959–1975*, Halifax: The Press of the Nova Scotia College of Art and Design, 2005 (originally published 1975)

Kaufman, Jason Edward, 'Wayne Thiebaud: The Last Interview', in Ulf Küster ed., *Wayne Thiebaud*, exh. cat. Fondation Beyeler, Basel (Berlin: Hatje Cantz), 2023, pp. 139–48

Kozloff, Max, 'Art', *The Nation*, vol. 194, no. 18, 5 May 1962, pp. 406–07

Larsen, Susan, oral history interview with Wayne Thiebaud, 17–18 May 2001, Archives of American Art, Smithsonian Institution

Lewallen, Constance, 'Interview with Wayne Thiebaud at Crown Point Press, San Francisco, California, August, 1989', *VIEW*, vol. VI, no. 6, winter 1990, pp. 2–22

Lippard, Lucy R. ed., *Pop Art*, London: Thames & Hudson, 1966

Masi, Alessia ed., *Wayne Thiebaud at Museo Morandi*, exh. cat. Museo Morandi, Bologna (Mantua: Corraini Edizione), 2011

Nash, Steven A. with Adam Gopnik, *Wayne Thiebaud. A Paintings Retrospective*, exh. cat. Fine Arts Museums of San Francisco and touring (Fine Arts Museums of San Francisco and New York: Thames & Hudson), 2008 (originally published 2000)

O'Brian, John ed., *Clement Greenberg: the Collected Essays and Criticism*, 4 vols, Chicago: University of Chicago Press, 1986–93

Pardee, Hearne, 'Wayne Thiebaud with Hearne Pardee', *Brooklyn Rail*, March 2019: https://brooklynrail.org/2019/03/art/WAYNE-THIEBAUD-with-Hearne-Pardee/ (accessed 7 March 2025)

Smith, Andrew F. ed., *The Oxford Companion to American Food and Drink*, Oxford: Oxford University Press, 2007

Stowens, Susan, 'Wayne Thiebaud: Beyond Pop Art', *American Artist*, vol. 44, no. 458, September 1980, pp. 46–51 and 102–04

Strand, Mark ed., *Art of the Real: Nine American Figurative Painters*, New York: Clarkson N. Potter, 1983

Teagle, Rachel ed., *Wayne Thiebaud 1958–1968*, exh. cat. Jan Shrem and Maria Manetti Shrem Museum of Art, University of California, Davis (Oakland: University of California Press), 2018

Thiebaud, Betty Jean dir., *Wayne Thiebaud*, film, running time: 20 minutes 16 seconds, 1971, Archives of the Wayne Thiebaud Foundation

Thiebaud via Morandi, video by Victor Loh and Germano Maccioni, 2011: https://paintingperceptions.com/wayne-thiebaud-at-the-morandi-museum/ (accessed 7 March 2025)

Tooker, Dan, 'Wayne Thiebaud', *Art International*, vol. 18, no. 9, November 1974, pp. 22–25

Tsujimoto, Karen ed., *Wayne Thiebaud*, exh. cat. San Francisco Museum of Modern Art (Seattle: University of Washington Press), 1985

Wollheim, Richard, 'On Thiebaud and Diebenkorn: Richard Wollheim Talks to Wayne Thiebaud', *Modern Painters*, vol. 4, no. 3, autumn 1991, pp. 64–68

All works by Wayne Thiebaud: © Wayne Thiebaud/VAGA at ARS, NY and DACS, London 2025

Other credits

Image courtesy the Wayne Thiebaud Foundation: figs. 1, 3, 4, 5, 6, 10, 11, 27, 39, 40, cat. 1, 4, 5, 15, 22, 24, 25, 27, 28, 29, 30, 31, 32, 33, 34, 35, 36, 37, 38, 39, 40, 41, 42, 43, 44, 45, 46, 47, 49, 51; California Art Gallery and Museum Ephemera Collection, courtesy of the California Historical Society (ART EPH_001): fig. 2; © Ed Ruscha. Courtesy of the artist and Gagosian: fig . 7, 13; © 2025 Estate of Roy Lichtenstein. All Rights Reserved, DACS Images: fig. 8; Courtauld Gallery Archive: fig. 9; Image courtesy Sheldon Museum of Art, University of Nebraska–Lincoln: fig. 12; Image © 1989 Christie's: fig. 14; Image: Bonhams: fig. 15; © Richard Diebenkorn Foundation / DACS 2025: fig. 16; © Courtesy of the estate of Joe Goode. Image courtesy Michael Kohn Gallery, Los Angeles: fig. 17; © Vija Celmins, Courtesy Matthew Marks Gallery. Image courtesy Museum of Contemporary Art San Diego Museum. Photo:

Pablo Mason: fig. 18; Photo Paul Mutino: fig. 19; © 2025 The Andy Warhol Foundation for the Visual Arts, Inc. / Licensed by DACS, London. Digital image, The Museum of Modern Art, New York/Scala, Florence: fig. 20; Photo: Albert Mozell. Science History Images / Alamy Stock Photo: fig. 21; Digital image, The Museum of Modern Art, New York/Scala, Florence: fig. 22; Image courtesy Detroit Institute of Art: fig. 23; Photo © The Courtauld: figs. 24, 28, 32, cat. 23; Bridgeman Images: fig. 25; Courtesy of The Fine Arts Collection, Jan Shrem and Maria Manetti Shrem Museum of Art, University of California, Davis: fig. 26; Image: Allan Stone Projects, New York: fig. 29; Image Courtesy Spencer Museum of Art, University of Kansas, 1982.0144: fig. 30; Image Allen Phillips / Wadsworth Atheneum: fig. 31; Image courtesy of Paul Thiebaud Gallery, San Francisco, CA: fig. 33; © The Claes Oldenburg Estate. Image courtesy The Warehouse Dallas. Photo: Kevin Todora: fig. 34; © The Claes Oldenburg Estate. Art Gallery of Ontario / Bridgeman Images: fig. 35; Image courtesy of Paul Thiebaud Gallery, San Francisco, CA. Photo: Matthew Miller: fig. 36; Image courtesy

of Sotheby's: cat. 2; Image courtesy of Berggruen Gallery: cat. 3, 26, 48, 50; Photo © 2011 Sotheby's: figs. 37, 38; Photo John Janca: cat. 6; Courtesy of The Fine Arts Collection, Jan Shrem and Maria Manetti Shrem Museum of Art, University of California, Davis. Photo M. Lee Fatherree: cat. 7; Image: Smithsonian American Art Museum, Washington D.C.: cat. 8; Image courtesy of Acquavella Galleries: cat. 9, 20, 21; Image courtesy Crocker Art Museum: cat. 10; The San Diego Museum of Art, Museum purchase through the Earle W. Grant Acquisition Fund. 1977.109: cat. 11; Image courtesy the Anderson Collection at Standford University. Photo M. Lee Fatherree: cat. 12; Photo Hickey-Robertson: cat. 13; Image: Julia Featheringill Photo: cat. 14; Digital image Whitney Museum of American Art / Licensed by Scala: cat. 16; Image courtesy of the National Gallery of Art, Washington, D. C.: cat. 17; San Francisco Museum of Modern Art / Bridgeman Images: fig. 41; Photograph by Randy Dodson, courtesy of the Fine Arts Museums of San Francisco: cat. 18; Photo Tom Loonan, Buffalo AKG Art Museum: cat. 19; Image courtesy of Crown Point Press. Photo Patrick Dullanty: fig. 42.